Getting to Ellen

3/1/13
Andell -
I so value
knowing you - your
spirit, your essence,
your way. Thank you,
for teaching me!
ellie ♡

Getting to Ellen

a memoir about

love, honesty

and gender change

BY ELLEN KRUG

STEPLADDER PRESS   MINNEAPOLIS, MINNESOTA

ISBN: 978-0-9886989-0-1
Library of Congress Control Number: 2012955013

Stepladder Press
Minneapolis, Minnesota
www.stepladderpress.com
www.gettingtoellen.com

Printed in the United States of America

For the girls of Knollwood,
with love.

Contents

Getting to Ellen

AUTHOR'S NOTE

As with any human, my life is intertwined with the lives of others. Out of respect, some names have been changed and characters combined. To a very limited extent, the chronology of some events has been altered.

ONE: *Glimpse*

I was barely eight years old—a human *tabula rasa*—when I first saw what made girls different from boys.

It happened in the side yard of our house behind the carport next to a tall fence, a ten-foot patch of dirt and weed, not far from a couple of banged-up tin garbage cans.

We lived in Jersey then, in Parlin, an ink spot thirty miles south of Newark. Home was a three-bedroom, one-bathroom ranch with a crab-grass lawn at the bottom of the big Kendall Drive hill—the main drag in a subdivision where houses repeated in Levittown fashion, inhabited by swarms of kids named Kislowski, DeAngelo, and Needham.

By 1965 the neighborhood was already into its first wave of remodels, one-stories turned into two, carports morphed into garages, and chain-link fences erected to keep out the swarms.

Two other kids, the Dolan brothers from up on Kendall, had corralled the girl who lived next door. Christine Trovatelli was a long-legged Brillo-haired and olive-skinned fourth grader.

Mikey Dolan, freckled and crew cut, was two weeks older than me. He centered a shiny quarter in his palm. His big brother Jimmy, a sixth grader who liked to push me around, did the talking. Their offer: if Christine would pull down her shorts, the quarter would be hers.

I was simply present, an unindicted co-conspirator, in awe of the process.

"It's a fucking quarter, Christine, enough to buy an ice cream cone," Jimmy cajoled.

As if on cue, from five blocks away, bells jingled, a signal that the Good Humor truck would soon crest the other side of the Kendall Drive hill.

3

"No, I'm not doing that," Christine answered. Her eyes—fixed on the gleaming head of Mr. Washington—conveyed something else.

"Come on, Christine, it can be yours. Just show us," Jimmy pressed. He looked at Mikey and grinned.

I hoped a hope.

We waited.

Christine stood with crossed arms. She could have turned around and walked away. She didn't.

Soon, the Pavlovian beat of the Good Humor bells—*jing, jing, jing-a-ling*—was a mere half dozen houses away.

Christine tilted her head and sighed. Catlike, her hand shot out and grabbed the quarter.

My pulse went into overdrive. I swallowed big as I fought a Catholic urge to run from something so wrong. My agnostic legs held firm.

The deal sealed, Christine bent forward and effortlessly slid plaid shorts and pink underwear down to her knees. Hesitantly, she straightened up and flashed a nervous smile. Her arms were cocked at each side.

I froze. I locked onto wonderful nothingness: a smooth, hairless valley between sweet puffy foothills of skin that disappeared at the fleshy apex of Christine's mile-long legs. So unexpected, it was a glorious combination of clean lines that met at one magnificent place, the center of Christine's feminine universe.

How wonderful!

Kodak-like, my retinas flashed a thousand times. They soaked up the unobstructed lines that were so different from the small but very visible glob of penis and scrotum I owned. Instantly, I understood that this secret place on Christine's body was special, even magical.

How could I have not known?

I felt a confused gut pang of something—jealousy, desire, wanting, or maybe all three—for the freedom that Christine breathed merely by being a *she* instead of a *he*. There was no hindering skin, no ugly little-boy penis, no protruding unnatural body part holding her back.

In ten seconds, the Dolans and I were gone, panting hard in a gallop to the woods behind my house. I glanced back and saw Christine fumbling with shorts and underwear.

She never told on us.

After that, fragments began to form in my brain, nothing solid. For years, decades actually, I couldn't get the image of Christine's magical clean lines out of my head.

TWO: *Tom Terrific*

3:47 p.m. on January 31, 1990.
BANG!

———————

It's noon now, two days later. I'm in Aisle 7 of a Kroger's Super in Dallas, standing next to Mark, my kid brother.

We're trying to decide on a cleanser from fifty different choices. I'll admit it: even though I'm thirty-three years old, I know nothing about cleaning up blood—my father's blood. Tom Terrific's blood, to be precise. Blood that's caked and dried in a bathtub for nearly forty-eight agonizing hours since my mother found him. I'm just guessing at the magnitude of the mess, too, since I haven't had the guts to actually look in the bathroom myself.

Mark bends down to examine the options. "Ed, what do you think we should use?"

"I've got no idea."

On top of everything else, I can't begin to register the word "suicide." My mind is too slow, and the word too laborious. It's part of some foreign language that I've suddenly been called upon to speak fluently.

I want nothing to do with it.

Focus, Krug.

I scan the neatly faced shelves with their symmetry of colors and shapes. I wonder. Mr. Clean?

Sure, that bald guy's pretty tough looking, but I'm guessing not tough enough for ten thousand gallons of clotted blood.

I move on to Spic and Span. I visualize a smiling housewife wearing pearls and an apron living a Beaver Cleaver life. I'm sure Mrs. Cleaver never had to deal with the mess we're facing. Hell, no one in a Spic and Span household would even bleed from a .38-caliber shot in the mouth.

Mark shifts to the bleaches. It reminds me of the day my father used bleach to wipe out a colony of ants that had taken up residence in our garage. There was my old man on a hot August afternoon twenty years ago, sweat beads on his forehead, hunched over a million ants as they went at a half-eaten donut that had missed the garbage can.

"Bleach is an acid," he whispered, as if the damn ants could hear him. He poured a whole gallon of Clorox on those suckers. Pools of ants floated down the driveway, struggling into stillness.

Lesson learned.

"Yeah, go with the Clorox," I say.

Mark gets up, but loses his grip and the Clorox jug thuds on the floor. He recovers and we head toward the check-out, cleaning crew comrades-in-arms. Before we get there, I think about how bleach has a way of splashing back. If you don't watch it, you can ruin something, like your sweater or your skin or maybe even an eye if you're really unlucky.

I imagine little white bleach dots on my body, one more memento of this unexpected trip to Dallas.

"Let's use garbage bags as smocks," I blurt, a brilliant idea even if I say so myself. I figure we can cut holes for our heads and arms. We'll look like plastic-covered space creatures, but hey, it'll work and it's practical, my modus. We find big green bags—two dozen, since I'm sure this is going to be a long, drawn-out operation.

On the way to the check-out, I grab a twelve-pack of Heineken for fortitude.

———————

I learned that my father liked the nickname "Tom Terrific" when I was in college. We met at his favorite bar, the Sirloin and Brew, one of the fancier places in Cedar Rapids—where we moved after Jersey. The bar sat at the end of a strip mall with faded yellow parking lines, next to the only Target in town. Outside, it looked like one of those Western forts, the kind where the Cavalry hid when they weren't killing Indians. Just inside the entrance, patrons walked beneath a pair of steer horns. The wait staff dressed as cowboys and cowgirls, but that's as far as the Western theme went. You never heard even a "howdy" or "pardner" once you committed to staying.

I always thought of it as a kind of bait and switch. I mean, really, if you're going to the trouble, why not go all the way?

I walked into the bar from a sunny afternoon and adjusted to the dark. My father was seated at the bar, smiling. He held an oversized ceramic mug with both hands above his head, like how someone would raise a trophy after a big race. On the outside of the mug was "Tom Terrific," written in big, textured red letters, as if from dried lipstick.

I plopped onto a bar stool and looked up. There were other mugs hanging above the bar, all with their own nicknames. Only one spot was empty. That's where Tom Terrific (the mug) hung when Tom Terrific (the dad) was doing something other than drinking. It was like I was visiting his second home, this bar. It made me think.

So this is where you hid out when we waited on dinner for you.

Dad motioned to the bartender, a slender brunette named Sandy.

"This is my son, Ed," he said. "He's going to be a lawyer."

The words stuck in the air for a moment, as if clipped together with a clothespin. Something registered with Sandy and she smiled. It was one of those I-don't-know-what-to-think-or-say smiles.

Finally, Sandy answered. "A lawyer. Every family should have one."

I laughed and nodded as if I agreed.

My father had a way with people generally, but bartenders in particular. He was a big tipper and congenial, always good for a joke or two. The more he drank, the more congenial he got. My mother used to say the only time my father ever talked, ever allowed her in, was when he reached the fine line between happy drunk and obnoxious lush. In those moments—they could speed by—he would lean in and whisper, "You're my Star." He'd say he loved me, too, but it was always too late by then. His slurred words, colored by Scotch or Bud or both, didn't sound genuine.

If you really loved me, and Mom and Mark, and my baby sister Jacki, I thought, *you'd stop drinking.* I knew he could do it. Sometimes, he'd go sober for weeks or a month, or once, for nearly half a year. The abstinence was usually precipitated by a legal problem brought on by his drinking, like the time he drunkenly broke into another green-colored house up the street thinking that he'd lost his house key.

I warmed up during his sober stints. "Way to go, Dad!" I once wrote in a card. He always went back to the booze. By the time I sat with him at the Sirloin and Brew, I had stopped caring.

Or so I thought.

In the end, I became the lawyer my father advertised to his bartending friend. I got further than either he or I had expected: honors at Coe College, Boston College Law School, five years with a Boston civil trial firm, and then partner at a Cedar Rapids law office.

The partnership came just a month before I found myself reluctantly shopping at Kroger's. Dad never actually congratulated me on it. In fact, he never said anything about my partnership, as if by then, my success was a reminder of how things could have been different for him.

For me, it always went back to a memory burn. I was maybe seven years old when my father didn't come home one Friday night. I didn't know to be afraid until early Saturday morning when I saw Mom pacing between living room and kitchen. Soon, she was bawling.

"He's dead in a gutter somewhere," she choked.

I pictured my father's lifeless body next to a curb. A frayed *Daily News* page blew past him. Fat gray pigeons scurried nearby.

It was easy to spot Mom worrying. If she didn't cry, she chain-smoked Virginia Slims. She'd go quiet, near paralysis, and then she'd yell—at us kids, the dog, or anything in her way.

She taught me well. Soon, I was worrying on my own.

Call it maternal osmosis.

My father eventually made his way home that Saturday afternoon. Forever thereafter, I understood the Krug family had a big Parent Missing In Action problem.

The Kendall Drive living room window extended from floor to ceiling. The window was always covered by a large heavy-layered curtain, the kind that required two hands and real strength to pull aside if you wanted to let daylight in. On Friday nights after my father's first PMIA incident, I would stand between that curtain and the living room window. Hidden from anyone in the house, I waited for Dad's car to appear at the top of

Kendall Drive. I stood there for an hour, or two, or sometimes three, my gaze fixed. I counted every car that came down the hill and assigned Dad's Pontiac a number, like twenty-five. When car number twenty-six blew by, I reset to give Dad another chance. Most of the time, he eventually pulled into the driveway, a cause for "Daddy, Daddy!"

Sometimes, though, he didn't make it.

Later, when we moved to Cedar Rapids, the missing got worse. A couple times a week, we played a one-sided game called "Six O'Clock Roulette." With spaghetti sauce simmering, Corelle plates set, four Krugs waited for the esteemed Tom Terrific.

"I don't know when your father will be home," Mom would say.

At night I lay in bed, unable to sleep, riveted with sweat and worry. I prayed for a garage door moan and the rumble of eight cylinders, announcements that my father had finally made his way home, who knew from where.

The hours of waiting, the years of uncertainty, and a decade of randomness chipped away at me. At the end, all that remained were ice-cold resentment and an appalling lack of self-confidence in just about everything.

By the time I was a teenager, I had plotted my escape. I would leave someday and be entirely self-sufficient. The fear would end, and I'd owe my parents, the people who were supposed to love and protect me, *nothing*. I paid for college, and then law school, so that my parents could never say, "We did this for you."

I wanted no hint of a family contract where, some decade later, I'd need to make repayment.

Of course, I wondered why my poor mother put up with Dad's alcoholism. If only she had done something other than run from it, maybe things would have been different. Aunt Rita, Mom's half-sister, eventually confided, "I told your mother she had a big yellow streak running up her back. She didn't deny it but said, 'Rita, what can I do?'"

I'll tell you what she *did* do: she went bowling. It was an excuse to be gone three or four nights a week, leaving us kids with my father and his booze, or with a sitter if we were lucky. With three kids in a 1960s and '70s society that hadn't yet accepted that some marriages were better undone, Mom hung on to my father. She believed that if she kept him in debt, he wouldn't leave. If only she hadn't done that—god, they had racked up $45K in credit card bills and were behind on their mortgage—maybe Dad wouldn't have been so desperate or depressed.

If only they had thought of what they were doing to Mark and Jacki and me. If only someone had been brave, had made the hard choices, maybe I wouldn't have needed to buy a gallon of Clorox at some shiny Dallas supermarket.

Traffic in Dallas.

The Kroger's supplies are bagged and perched on the back seat of my father's small white Nissan. Mark is driving. The car reeks of cigarette smoke from Dad's two-pack-a-day Camel habit. My fingers smudge gray and grainy against ashes that overflow the ashtray. I hate this car.

I wonder why we didn't buy a bottle opener at Kroger's so that I could have a starter Heineken for the trip between store and destination.

I distract myself and ask for the hundredth time, "How much blood do you think there'll be?"

Mark sighs. In a pained voice, he answers, "Too much, whatever amount."

Impulsively, I grab Mark's hand and put it over my heart.

"I love you," I say. I haven't said that to him in years. Mark nods numbly and pulls his hand away. The Nissan crawls forward.

My little brother—barely two years younger—is leaner than me, a product of his long-distance-running compulsion and recent dalliance with eating vegetarian. He was always considered the smartest of us three, with Jacki a close second. He earned near straight A's, and along with them, my parents' hope that he'd be the big success story. It didn't matter that Dad called me "Star:" Mark was *the one*.

I'm sure it had something to do with Mark's good, generous heart. In our family, generosity meant helping a boozed Tom Terrific navigate the treacherous journey from living room to master bedroom.

That wasn't me. I'd leave my old man passed out on the couch.

I was the pushy, vocal, underachieving firstborn who always threw a punch—at Mark, who had a half dozen stitches before he turned ten—or anyone else. I channeled toughness into karate and football. When I was barely a teenager, I sparred in karate with someone twenty years older. I ran up the points and didn't give it a second thought. Afterward, Dad said, "You didn't need to do that. It was obvious in the first minute that you had him beat."

I didn't care.

In my high school freshman year, Dad drove me home from football practice. He unexpectedly smiled.

"Guess what Coach Larry told me," he said.

I sniffed for the scent of Bud or Scotch, but only came up with stale coffee breath. I relaxed.

"I don't know, Dad. Tell me, what did Coach Larry say?"

My father's grin widened. "He said you were the toughest player on the team. He told me you hit guys twice your size and knock them on their asses."

It was true. At 135 pounds, I was quick and tenacious. Football and anger complemented each other well.

I feel the Nissan lurch as Mark shifts from first to second gear.

In reality, this trip to Dallas isn't about me. Mark's got the real emotional stake. I can only imagine his pain as we crawl from one Dallas stoplight to the next.

Mark's lost his father, a man with whom he has had many private conversations and who undoubtedly gave Mark counsel in moments of sobriety and drunkenness.

My little brother doesn't resent Tom Terrific like I do.

He misses him.

Everyone said I looked like my father. We shared similar faces, hair color, and body frames: angular, dark, and small. When I was a kid, Dad carried a pocket comb to slick back his Brylcreem-coated hair; he'd then hand it to me. "There you go, Eddie."

Later, when puberty set in, I grew a mustache, just like his.

I told myself, *It's so I look older.*

Mom was a Lucille Ball look-alike. She was tall and slender, with glowing eyes—luckily, I got those, too—that illuminated any room she entered. She had a booming voice and bellowing laugh; you could hear her from across a restaurant or bar, more of what I inherited.

Neither of my parents made it to college, but that didn't stop them from grabbing a good chunk of the American Dream. Dad leveraged Navy electronics training into a tech writing job in Manhattan, and then to manager of a start-up satellite office in Cedar Rapids. The promotion, when he was barely thirty, took us to a brand-new house in the most exclusive subdivision in Cedar Rapids. My father legitimately earned bragging rights about jumping a socioeconomic hurdle overnight.

Mom was a numbers whiz. She held bookkeeping positions, starting with her first at sixteen, when a business recruited her. She, too, was personable and could sit with girlfriends for hours over coffee and cigarettes, forming forever friendships.

"Your mother is the kindest person I know," a friend once told me. Yes, Mom had a good heart, even if, Oz Lion-like, it was devoid of courage.

Eventually, I understood my parents never had a chance. They grew up blocks apart from each other in the tenements of Newark. My father's mother died an alcoholic death when he was in high school. His father abandoned Dad's much younger sister Margaret and baby brother Bud. Both ended up at an orphanage, where Bud was adopted out. Margaret left the orphanage when she was sixteen and became our live-in babysitter.

By then, my grandfather was long gone, the first Krug to permanently go PMIA. The man became a ghost named "Peter Davenport," without a forwarding address.

Sometimes, my boozed-up father searched for his father. On cold, austere nights, from the next bedroom over, I heard the long, crisp reports of a rotary telephone as Dad dialed White Page listings and directory assistance guesses. "Is this Peter Davenport from Rutledge Street in Newark?"

He desperately wanted one last conversation with his father, a let's-tie-this-all-up-in-a-neat-package kind of talk.

Mom didn't have it much better. My grandmother, Nan, divorced Mom's father—a cheat caught in bed with the other woman—in the early 1940s, when divorce was *really* a stigma. Mom never heard from her father again. When she was just seven, Nan sent her to a boarding school for a year. It killed every bit of Mom's self-confidence. You could see it in the way she needed my father's approval on everything.

"The United States has more cars than any other nation in the world, isn't that right, Tom?"

"Right, Satch," my father would say, using her pet name.

"We have more college-educated people, too, isn't that right, Tom?"

"Yes, that's true too."

"New Jersey produces more tomatoes than any other state, isn't that right, Tom?"

"You're correct."

You get the idea. Even with her smarts, Mom couldn't ever get comfortable relying on the one key person in her life: herself.

It's not like Mom didn't understand the deck was stacked going into the marriage. A couple years after my father died, and in a moment of rare self-honesty, she confessed that Nan had warned, "Don't marry Tommy. His parents are drunks, and he'll be a drunk too."

In a near whisper, Mom added, "I didn't listen to her."

Even with all of that, my parents couldn't stop believing something better always lay around the corner. By the time reckoning day—January 31, 1990—came along, my parents had job-hopped from Cedar Rapids to Dallas to Long Island and then back to Dallas. Hop Number 2, Long Island, was precipitated by my father quitting his office manager position without lining up another job beforehand.

"Your father will find a position in no time, isn't that right, Tom?" Mom proclaimed-asked a week into his unemployment.

"You're right on that, Satch."

One year, and a forced house sale later, my father located a non-management job.

A couple years before the end, they thought they'd found the answer to their financial and marital problems. "Soon, I'll have more money than I'll know what to do with, and all of us will walk the beaches of the world," my father slurred on a late-night telephone call.

Yep, they'd found the answer all right: Amway.

On that last afternoon of his life, after he parked the Nissan in the garage of their townhouse for the final time, Dad walked past a dozen dust-coated cases of Amway stuff.

I wonder if he even gave it a thought.

———————

Life had been normal. Everything changed with a five o'clock phone call from Lydia, my wife. I was in the firm's law library researching a brief.

"Ed, I just got home from work. There's a message from your father on the answering machine. You need to listen to this."

Lydia held the phone up to the answering machine and hit a button. My father's booze-tinged voice, labored with pauses, had just enough clarity:

Ah, Ed, this is Dad...You are my most brilliant...About two summers ago, while I was visiting you and Lydia, you complained that Mark got special treatment. Well, yeah, he did...Jacki had Mom and you had Uncle Ed and Nan. It didn't start out that way, but I zeroed in on Mark...You are my most brilliant... Thank you for letting me be your father.

The message ended with an irritating answering machine *beeeeep.*

My mind raced. It was as if my father was taking inventory. Mark, my sister, Mom. Uncle Ed was my mother's uncle, thus my great-uncle, and a teetotaler. Nan was another non-drinker. I don't know if my father ever made that connection, but I didn't analyze the call that way.

It just didn't sound good.

I quickly did some mental math and realized my father should have been at work when he called. It was way too early for him to be stumbling over words. His tone suggested the past tense, as if something was over, ended. It made me think of that special radio frequency, the kind used only for emergencies.

Wait a minute.

Oh shit.

My heart pounded. A thousand-degree heat flash went up my back into my brain.

Lydia pulled the phone away from the message machine. She tilted from confusion to fear.

"What's this about?"

"I don't know."

There had to be a dozen innocent reasons why my father would make that kind of telephone call at 3:36 in the afternoon, but I couldn't think of any. I asked Lydia if she had talked with Jacki, who lived in Cedar Rapids, too, or Mark, who was in Minneapolis.

She hadn't.

"Okay," I instructed, "I'll call my mother and then call you back. Let me know if you hear from anyone."

My take-charge attorney instincts kicked in. I tried my mother at the townhouse. The line was busy. I used the redial number on my office phone. Still busy. I tried at least twenty times. My panic grew with each failed attempt. When I finally got through, I didn't waste a second.

"Mom, what the hell's going on?"

By then, I didn't need for her to actually answer.

I knew.

"Oh, Eddie, please don't blame me! I beg you, don't hold this against me!" She was bawling, her voice hijacked by fear.

"What's happened? Tell me what's happened!"

I heard a sound reserved only for the absolute worst moments of one's existence, a wailing wrapped around a bet-your-life plea for supreme dispensation. In between sobs and gasps for breath, she explained that she had come home from her bank job and saw the Nissan in the garage. When Dad didn't answer her usual "Hello," she went looking. In the master bathroom, the door was closed, light off. She opened the door and flicked on the light to find him in the tub, still dressed but bloody. She ran out of the house screaming to a neighbor, who called 9-1-1.

My brain became numb, Novocain-like.

I pushed on. "What's happening now?"

The sobbing ramped back up. "They're with him upstairs, the ambulance people and the police," she reported in word bursts.

For a second, I wondered whether there was hope. Maybe he was wounded but alive. I asked how long they'd been there.

"About forty-five minutes."

That confirmed it. They wouldn't leave him half-alive in a bathtub for almost an hour.

I heard more of my mother's desperation, her pleading-sobs, a soul choking on harsh reality. She had no close friends in Dallas, and part of me wanted to be there to hold her, as the good son. Another part, the one chiseled by a cold inability to forgive, and who had to blame *someone* for a tainted start, wanted to hang up the phone.

"I'll catch a flight and be down there tonight," I said, now trapped by the situation. "I'll call Jerry and Mary Tharp and ask them to come over." The Tharps, my best friend's parents, had moved to Dallas from Cedar Rapids a few years before.

I called Lydia, who picked up before the first ring was complete.

"He's dead! He killed himself," I screamed. "They haven't taken his body out of the condo yet. My mother's beside herself."

Lydia began to cry.

"I can't believe he'd do this," she said. I imagined her body shaking. "I want to be with you, let me come to you."

"No, don't do that," I barked. "Keep trying Mark and Jacki. I'll get a flight to Dallas. You'll need to meet me at the airport. Pack my suitcase . . ."

I waited for Lydia and Jacki at the American Airlines counter. With not even a minute to spare, Jacki and I sprinted to the gate. Ten minutes later, we were on a plane to Dallas, holding hands.

As the youngest, Jacki had gotten the absolute worst of my parents' dysfunctional marriage. By her high school senior year, Tom Terrific and Satch were tired: tired of their marriage, tired of attending kids' sporting events, and tired of fighting the drinking and out-of-control spending. Jacki endured a year of solitary without a Mark to pick Tom Terrific up off the floor. It was horrible, and it scarred her for life.

Years later, Jacki went the other way, a contra-Mom. She obsessed over her kids ahead of everything else, even herself. Once, when we recounted our childhoods, she offered, "At least I'm not like Mom."

Jacki was sure right about that; she wasn't anything even remotely close to our mother. Instead, like Mark with his running, and me, a budding workaholic/alcoholic, Jacki was compulsive.

Alcoholic families create compulsive children. It's that simple.

On the other hand, maybe I (and who knows, maybe Mark and Jacki too) have more in common with my parents than I'd ever be willing to admit. Just like Tom Terrific and Satch, I'm tainted by my childhood. Like them, I don't know how to deal with that pedigree.

I know it's toxic, but yet, I don't have much to go on in terms of the *right* alternative. As a result, I've done the only thing I know: sprint away from my parents as fast as possible. The problem is that I've done it with my eyes closed. Even worse, I have only one speed—fifty miles an hour.

It's damn near inevitable I'll crash into something like a tree, or a house, or my shadow.

And, it wasn't like I welcomed having a cold heart. I *wanted* to love my parents and honor everything they did for me, for giving me a boot-strapped life that allowed me to go further than they did. I *wanted* good memories of growing up, of being a family.

But what I *wanted* wasn't reality. Instead, I reached for what I *needed:* some sense of control and a rock-solid vow that I wouldn't repeat their mistakes.

In the end, it was blind sprinting at its very finest.

Twenty minutes after our cleaning-supply run, Mark and I and the Nissan make it to my parents' townhouse. The place is empty; Mom and Jacki flew back to Cedar Rapids this morning.

I open the front door and feel the heavy sensation of death, like oxygen drained from a closed space. Mark puts the shopping bags on the kitchen counter. I can't wait for a Heineken and locate an opener while Mark snips holes in the garbage bags. I chug the beer, and without having had anything to eat all day, the first glint of relief comes quickly.

I still can't believe what we're about to do.

I point at the yellow film on the kitchen windows and joke, "Well, this may be the first tub cleaning in the two years they've lived here."

Mark barely reacts.

He finishes scissoring our innovative smocks, and we slip them over our heads. The garbage bags stick to our bodies. We look like cartoon characters with terminal static cling.

Mark opens a Heineken. I'm already on my second. We've got the bleach, a bucket from the kitchen closet, and a big pink sponge. I find a toilet bowl brush, figuring it will give us crucial added distance from the blood.

"Your blood-cleaning skills will make some woman proud," I say.

This time, I get a laugh.

I shake my head, and frown. "Goddamned cleaning services. You'd think one of them would've taken the job for the extra money I offered." But this is 1990, and human blood is AIDS scary.

The second beer gone, I reach for another. I feel the alcohol now, but I'll need more to be completely gone, away from here, away from everything.

We linger in the kitchen, mum.

I drift.

I imagine my father in the tub, fully clothed, the gun on his lap. The bathroom is pitch black. He's smoking one of those fucking Camels, the fiery end glowing redder with each drag. His Scotch is there, too, in one of those squat glasses, the kind that might lose the ice if you toss it too hard. I picture Dad processing his life and ticking off each memory with his signature "aw shit" sigh—another thing embedded in my DNA.

He sluggishly brings the revolver to his lips. He flinches and hesitates against the cold register of the barrel. He's near the point of no return, with the nothingness he seeks waiting for him, like some beckoning mistress. She's giving him the "Come fuck me" look and Tom Terrific smiles. His lips part and the gun barrel enters.

He's ready.

Years later when I would allow it, the scene plays out completely. I want to think that even with the raw steel of a Smith & Wesson pressing against his tongue, his parting thought of us kids was something good rather than a pain he endured. Still, I can't convince myself of this.

Dad—my genetic father, the man who created me—holds the cocked gun with both hands. He closes his eyes for the final time, needed relief. There's one last sigh, and then a neuron, a squeeze, and an echoless explosion of glistening warm wetness in the tub.

Mark finishes his beer. We look at each other. No more trying to joke the situation away. It's time to go upstairs, time for our work.

I lead, oldest first. We step silently, riser to riser, weighted as if forty pounds are strapped to each ankle. Sweat presses against my dark green plastic smock; for Christ's sake, my heart's pounding a hundred beats a minute; my imagination's running wild.

Am I really doing this?

We make it to the top of the stairs. The bedroom door, straight ahead, looms.

God. They took his body away, right?

I push the door open to a stale-cigarette smell. Mark is right behind me. We swish into the room, our cleaning arsenal and beers in hand.

I scan. The bathroom is to the right; their bed, nicely made, is room center. A couple of quart-sized Ziploc storage bags are on the multicolored bedspread. I recognize my father's wallet inside one of the bags. The other bag has his gold chain, watch, and wedding band.

"Hell, Mark, look at this stuff, organized to the end," I say. We stand next to the bed, like junior archeologists caught in the surreal.

I tip back for a long drink of Heineken and put the half-empty bottle on the nightstand. I grin and shoot Mark a look.

"Aw shit. Let's do it."

We enter the bathroom single file. Some crumpled blue latex medical gloves lie on the floor near the toilet. A faded gold plastic shower curtain is pulled back. Next to the tub is one of my father's cocktail glasses with a fake newspaper headline, "Tom Krug Declares Drinks on Him!" There's still Scotch in the glass, as if the paramedics intended for someone to find an accomplice at the scene of the crime.

It's only a few feet from the door to the tub. I hold my breath and take a couple steps. I force a look downward. I expect a Lake Superior of blood but instead see only a puddle. It's more stain than anything else — crimson with yellow and green mixed in, a death rainbow, the residue of an incredibly bad decision.

My gut starts to hurt and I yell, "I need more beer!" I nod toward the bedroom. Mark looks pissed. "I'll be right back," I say as I head for the rest of my Heineken.

I see the bathroom door swing shut just as I feel liquid against my lips. I gulp and yell, "What the fuck are you doing?"

Nothing.

I rush to the door and try it. Locked.

"Come on Mark, open the door."

Nothing.

I bang, pound, and kick at the door.

Nothing.

"You little prick, let me in! You're not doing this alone! Goddamn it, Mark! Let me in, you fucking idiot!"

Nothing.

"Let me in!" I yell it with fast-growing ambivalence.

I hear a tap turn on full bore, followed by the sound of churning water and the *gug gug gug* of the tipped Clorox bottle. A life-killing smell reaches my side of the door. Toilet brush bristles scratch against fiberglass tub.

"Mark, please open up."

Nothing.

It's no use.

I'm relieved, of course. My little brother has made yet another rescue: mine. He's getting Tom Terrific settled once more, this time for good.

Without my help.

Thank god.

I drop to the edge of my parents' bed among artifacts from a sad life, where my father spent endless nights fighting the demons that eventually got him. I think about how my life will never be the same ever again; that his suicide will always be a reference point, and that Tom Terrific will forever be something, someone, standing in the back of every room I enter.

THREE: *Beezer*

My father was right: I had Great-Uncle Ed.

And his carnival lights.

Ed Graney was a six-foot-two former WWII tech sergeant who didn't talk about the war, or for that matter, about much of anything else. He had a red-tinged exterior that erroneously suggested a difficult, even angry disposition.

Not that my uncle was beyond holding grudges. Once, when the man next door failed to wave hello, Uncle Ed gave him the cold shoulder for months. That ended the day the neighbor's wife banged on the front door, pleading.

"Help me, Ivan won't wake up!"

My uncle leapt out of his easy chair; sheets of the *Star Ledger* flew in his wake. He rushed a revived but disoriented Ivan to the hospital. After that, Ed Graney checked in almost daily to see if Ivan needed anything.

That was my uncle: loyal and committed, as long as he got the chance.

He was also a builder.

"Hey Beezer, hand me that box of nine-penny nails over there, will you?"

I looked up from a battalion of green plastic soldiers and artillery pieces laid out in perfect formation on a crisp stack of plywood. My uncle pointed to a cardboard box from Palmer's, the hardware store. It was filled with silver caulk cartridges and sky blue boxes of nails.

We were at Uncle Ed's spot in the Jersey woods, seventy miles north of and an entire universe away from Newark. It was a place everyone simply called "The Country." I was nine.

I scurried twenty feet to the Palmer's box and grabbed the nails. In no time flat, I handed them to my uncle.

"Thank you, sir," he said with a grin. Sweat dripped from his chin; he pushed his glasses back to the bridge of his nose, making them fog.

After the war, Uncle Ed forsook the hills of western Maryland—home—for Newark, to be with his big sister (and my grandmother), Nan. By then, Nan had married a gentle hard-of-hearing man nicknamed "Poppy."

That was a lot better than his real name—Bill Blow.

Later, there was a failed engagement. Nan liked to remember: "Then Eddie came home and slammed a big diamond ring down on the kitchen table. 'You were right about her,' he said."

That was it. Uncle Ed was done with women, a bachelor for life. From then on, he was stuck in Newark, living with Nan and Poppy and their daughter Rita, and my mother until she married Dad. The proximity to Western Electric, where he worked as a welder, was the only thing that made living in Newark worth it.

The Country was my uncle's answer, his escape. When he plunked down money on two lots a couple years after I was born, it was a naked spot in an ocean of oaks, with a gleaming lake beyond the next hill. He quickly erected a tar-paper shack, barely large enough for a cot. From there, cinder block by cinder block, he built a box—part garage, part sleeping space—with a sink and toilet in the back. Later, he doggedly started on a house in the lot behind the garage.

I was his "helper," something I took damn seriously, toy soldiering notwithstanding. I shoveled sand and gravel and powdery white cement into a mixer for sidewalks and two patios. I carved my initials, "EJK," along with the year—"1966"—before the cement dried.

I fished out tools and learned the difference between a level and a square. I steadfastly held tight as Uncle Ed pounded plywood to joist, and sheetrock to stud.

"That'll do, Beezer," he'd say, followed by *bam! bam! bam!*

By then, we were close to inseparable, at least on the weekends. Later, it was entire summers.

I'm sure it helped that we shared complete names: he was Edward Joseph William Graney. Switch "Krug" for "Graney," and you had me. When it wasn't "Beezer," I answered to "Little Ed."

My uncle laid claim to his namesake early on. I wasn't even five when we took our first road trip down the Jersey Turnpike, then west into "Pennsy" and finally south into western Maryland, landing in a town named Lona Coning.

"I've got to make sure the graves are being tended to," he said.

We visited distant family and a cemetery outside St. Mary's. We stayed in a '50s-style motel where side-by-side rooms faced a parking lot, what I called "rooms-in-a-string." We ate Howard Johnson's scrambled eggs with sides of peas.

On the way back to Jersey, there was a pilgrimage to Gettysburg.

"Take a good look, Beezer. You'd never know that a lot of fine men died here," Uncle Ed said on a golden day in May as he scanned the greenness of Seminary Ridge, now a lush park. His voice cracked, one soldier familiar with death talking about other soldiers who had sacrificed their all.

It was another graveyard, another place to honor.

My parents never resisted letting me spend time with Uncle Ed. Maybe it was the respect accorded a family patriarch; then again, maybe it was because there was one less kid around.

The thing about Ed Graney: you'd never find a twelve-pack of Bud in his refrigerator or a bottle of Scotch in the living room cabinet. The strongest thing the man drank was skim milk for a chronic case of indigestion. I could count on him showing up on time doing what he promised. Most of all, it meant that, on those rare occasions when he talked, it'd be something I understood, not some foreign booze language.

On a menthol-cool summer evening, with us satisfied over adding a dozen new plywood squares to the rising skeleton of a house, Uncle Ed and I sat outside the garage, perched on red steel lawn chairs with backs shaped like clam shells. Above the next hill over, at the top of the oaks, I saw the sliver of an orange sun. Shadows crept, giving rise to a cicada chorus. Off to the right, a fire snapped and cracked in a rusty and holey fifty-gallon drum, a combination garbage incinerator/marshmallow roaster.

There wasn't much left of our Swanson's fried chicken TV dinners, the real kind with aluminum trays and pockets for always-too-hot vegetable soup. In front of us, mimosa leaves, fragile but firm on baby trees that Uncle Ed had planted the previous year, were clasped together in homage to the passing daylight.

"Uncle Ed, how old are you?" The question had shot into my head.

My uncle put down his iced tea and processed.

"Forty-nine," he said. "Why?"

"Oh, I don't know. Just curious," I answered with a smile.

Actually, I knew *why.* I had counted time, a habit I picked up from waiting at the Kendall Drive living room window. I needed to know how many years Uncle Ed and I had left together. I did the math: maybe we'd have another thirty years, or even forty if I was really lucky.

I'd be all grown up by then, surely able to handle anything.

I shuddered.

Please, God, I said to myself, doing what Sister Mary-Margaret had taught at catechism. *Don't take him before I'm ready. I'll never be able to survive.*

"Beezer, do you want a sweater?"

"No, I'm okay, Uncle Ed."

The cicadas ramped up for another chorus.

A few minutes later, my uncle fed the fire one last time and flicked a switch for a couple strings of lights he had hung from garage to tree to tree and then back to garage. These weren't just any ordinary lights, either. They were 100-watt bulbs, juicy with color—reds, yellows, greens, even purples—the kind that any half-legitimate carnival would make sure to have strung from cotton candy booth to ring-toss pit.

There we were, out in the wilderness as far as I was concerned, lit up like Times Square.

I imagined a plane flying above us and the pilot reporting back.

Ah, Control, this is Pan Am Flight 938. We're over northwest New Jersey at the moment, and in the middle of all the blackness we see these brilliant lights. It looks like a carnival down there.

Come again, Pan Am, you say you see a carnival?

Roger, that. A carnival.

Of course, not a real carnival—there wasn't a Ferris wheel for fifty miles—but it didn't matter. It was just Uncle Ed and me.

That was enough.

We sat for a while, no words needed, my uncle's way. I heard the fire crack as it worked its way up some house-building scrap.

25

"It's getting late. I'll put a blanket on your cot in case you get cold," Uncle Ed said.

"Okay."

My uncle got up from his clamshell seat and headed for the garage. I heard the screen door creak and then slam. I stayed for a few dozen extra seconds, watching flames lick at the barrel's lip.

I love this place, I thought. *I love you.*

Still living in Jersey, Sunday mornings after Mass were spent watching New York City television. One day in early 1968, I saw big-toothed, wavy-haired Bobby Kennedy. He talked about Appalachia—instantly, I thought of Lona Coning—and "the plight of the poor and the Negro."

We were barely four years past the sadness of President Kennedy's assassination. It wasn't so long since *Life Magazine,* which came every week like clockwork, chronicled the Freedom Riders. Television images of the Tet Offensive were still fresh; even as an eleven-year-old plastic soldier commander, I understood the value of surprising your enemy. My brain kept repeating a specific loop: the South Vietnamese colonel putting a pistol to the head of a VC infiltrator named Ben Ken. *Pop!* The poor VC grimaced and then plopped to the ground with gushing blood and brains.

More television images. Martin Luther King's death and people pointing from the Lorraine Motel balcony. A drawing of some man named Ray.

The news bulletin about King's murder interrupted *Batman* on Channel 7. I had been enamored with King and I didn't need an adult to tell me the significance of his murder. I was in my pajamas, fifteen minutes from bedtime, watching as someone—Cronkite or Brinkley or Huntley—said the word, "killed."

I knew this was bad. A year before, Uncle Ed had finished the house in The Country and moved everyone out of Newark, just in time to miss the '67 riots. Now, with King dead, who knew what would happen.

Later that night—my parents let me stay up—there was another news bulletin. This time, Bobby Kennedy stood on the back of a flatbed truck in Indianapolis, surrounded by Negroes. He had planned to speak at a campaign event. Instead, he went to the worst part of Indianapolis, its poorest ghetto. Mindful of Watts burning in '65 and Detroit and Newark two years later, he knew the situation could be volatile.

I heard Bobby talk about President Kennedy's death, and about how great a man King had been. He quoted a poem by the Greek philosopher Aeschylus, someone I'd never heard of, which was full of words that tugged at my emotional heart:

> *Even in our sleep,*
> *pain which cannot forget*
> *falls drop by drop upon the heart*
> *until, in our own despair,*
> *against our will,*
> *comes wisdom through*
> *the awful grace of God.*

He closed with words that I'd never forget: "What we need in the United States is not division; what we need in the United States is not hatred...but love and wisdom, and compassion toward one another, and a feeling of justice towards those who still suffer... whether they be white or whether they be black."

Mesmerized in the tomb of the Kendall Drive living room, I cried.

Two months after that, we began to pack up the house for a move to Iowa. Everyone would go but me; I'd spend the summer in The Country, putting off the inevitable for eight weeks.

In the last week of school, the entire fifth grade visited the science museum in Philadelphia. The night before the class trip, Sirhan Sirhan got to Bobby. Still, hours later, Bobby was alive, if barely. The bus driver left the radio on for news reports.

By the time we got to Philadelphia, Bobby, just like King, was gone.

I found a corner in the noisy museum, not far from the dinosaur bones, and let go with more tears.

A couple years later, the lime green walls of my bedroom in Cedar Rapids hosted three icons. One was a realtor's placard with the cutout figure of a man holding a "Sold" sign, which I ripped off from some neighbor's lawn when carousing with the guys. Another was a black-light poster of bombs falling from a B-52 with the tag line, "Chicken Little Was Right."

Most prized was a crookedly clipped picture of Bobby Kennedy taken during the 1968 campaign, torn from an *Esquire Magazine*. It showed Bobby on yet another flatbed truck reaching toward a thousand outstretched hands, a crowd also in love with him. Rosey Grier's arms, wrapped around Bobby's waist, kept my Bobby upright from the surging humanity.

Idealism. The power of well-chosen words. Emotion. Longing for something better. Believing that a single person could make a difference.

After a few hundred looks at Bobby on that truck—the picture was next to my bed—I knew what I would do with my life.

I'd be a lawyer. Just like Bobby.

———————

Nan and Poppy, along with Rita, also mattered. My grandparents spoiled me with food—rice pudding dessert from one, and soft-boiled-egg-and-Thomas' English muffin breakfasts from the other.

Nan was a gin rummy player who meticulously kept track.

"You're beating me by ten points, Mister."

My grandmother sentimentalized her Lona Coning childhood and growing up at the Hotel Brady, a family enterprise and eventual Depression casualty. She had lost one kidney as a young woman, and fretted about losing the other.

Then there were the Jews.

"They weren't the only ones the Nazis killed, you know," she'd start. "There were plenty of others: Gypsies, the Poles, a lot of different kinds. I don't know why the Jews get all the attention."

I let the words slide by. Bobby would have wanted it that way.

If you shouted loud enough, Poppy might be able to hear you, but it was always hit or miss. "How are you doing, Pop?" might evoke, "Yes, I think it feels like rain too." In the summers, he'd be in his bedroom planted on a plastic lawn chair in front of the TV watching the Yanks or, if he didn't have a choice, the Mets. He had survived growing up in Hell's Kitchen and a Navy career on a minesweeper that spanned three wars. He carried a scar on his upper arm.

"Shrapnel. Lucky hit," he told me.

He'd done all that without becoming a drunk.

Rita lived with them in The Country for a while. She'd drive me to the lake, where I'd work on swimming to the raft, a white wood and steel drum target fifty yards from shore. Mom had ordered me to wait until I was twelve to swim it alone, but Rita let me do it solo long before that.

Her fiancé, Rich, liked cars, both talking about and owning. He put up with my grandmother's opinions and ground rules; Rita had to be home by 11:00 p.m. regardless of how close they were to the wedding date.

Once, I was at the lake with Rita and Rich. I was lanky then, a bean in a tight red bathing suit. Something—who knows what for an eleven-year-old boy—had triggered an erection. Without any degree of modesty, I walked from the concession stand to our blanket, thinking no one on a beach checkered with bathers would notice my bulging hard-on.

Twenty minutes later, Rich asked me to take a walk. I had no clue why.

"Eddie, you need to tuck it under," he whispered with half a cough. His voice was so soft, I didn't understand.

"What did you say?"

I had a flowered towel—roses, I think—wrapped around my shoulders. The yellow-white sand was foot-hopping hot.

Another half cough.

"I said, 'you need to tuck it under.'"

I stopped hopping when I realized what he was talking about.

"Oh," I answered. Nothing else seemed appropriate.

After that, I always made sure my penis and scrotum glob were in their proper place—tucked down, away from the world, as if in their own special orbit.

I thought, *None of this feels right.*

In two weeks, the summer of '68 would be over and Nan would take me to Cedar Rapids. It would be by train; she was certain we'd die if we went by plane.

Uncle Ed had dug a ditch for a sump pump line from the basement to a cistern. He hadn't yet laid the pipe. Next to this ditch was one of my favorite dirt piles, a natural landscape for my Matchbox cars.

"Remember, you're going to help me with that pipe on Saturday. Until then, stay away from the dirt pile," he said, pointing. "Promise that you will."

I looked up from the comics. "Okay, I promise."

Uncle Ed held his thermos and flashlight. He was about to head out the door for second shift at Western Electric. He bent down and kissed my cheek, and he was gone.

From the kitchen, I heard Nan—another worrier—yell, "Drive safely, Eddie."

By then, my uncle's boots had reached the bottom stair of the stoop. The pitch changed as he turned the corner to get past the garage. A second later, there was the roar of his Chrysler Newport coming alive. I heard gravel crack as the car headed down the driveway aimed at Newark.

It shouldn't have been a hard promise to keep; I had plenty of other places to play around that house and garage. Still, by late afternoon I was on hands and knees, building imaginary streets for Matchbox cars— exactly where Uncle Ed had forbade.

I didn't think he'd notice how dirt had collected in the ditch.

That night, the beam of Uncle Ed's flashlight revealed that his name- sake had broken a promise.

The next morning, I walked into the kitchen and found an Uncle Ed I didn't know. At breakfast, where we always sat together, he didn't even look up from the newspaper.

After a few glacial minutes, I became afraid. I wondered if he'd send me to Iowa early. "What's wrong, Uncle Ed?"

I knew it was the dirt pile. He asked if there was something I should tell him. I confessed to the obvious.

"I'm disappointed in you, Beezer. You had given your word," he said.

The deafening tone of his words made my heart hurt.

I pleaded. "I'm sorry, Uncle Ed, I knew I shouldn't play there. Please forgive me." I wanted to curl up in his lap and grab at his Saint Christopher medal, like I did when I was a baby.

My uncle looked up from his shredded wheat. He held his spoon upright, pointing.

"Giving your word to someone is the most important thing you can do. Don't let it ever happen again."

I had never seen him so mad or disappointed in anyone, and he was talking to *me*.

Decades after that, as Ed Graney's body lay in a flag-draped casket, I eulogized my uncle and talked about the dirt-in-the-ditch incident. I related how something so small—silly, really—held such power for me: it epitomized the value of keeping your word and fulfilling responsibilities undertaken.

For the rest of my life, when I promised something, I became bound by God and all things decent. Nothing good would ever come from a broken promise.

It was a simple formula for living life in two colors: black and white. Gray wasn't an option.

"Marion is coming up! Marion's the next station."

The nameplate on the conductor's square black cap read, "Milwaukee Road."

Nan and I were on the last leg of a cross-country trip speeding through the near-midnight Iowa countryside on the Arrow, with the *clickety-clack, clickety-clack* report of steel wheels on steel rail.

I'd never before heard the word, "Marion." It sounded lyrical. *How beautiful!*

We had left Newark the evening before. Uncle Ed, Poppy, and Rita saw us off. I grabbed at my uncle's shoulder, and held tight.

"I don't want to leave you," I whispered in between tears.

"It's all right, Beezer," he said as he hugged back. "Your mom's promised a phone call every Sunday."

My grandmother tugged at me. "We need to get on the train or we'll miss it."

Twenty-eight hours later, Nan clasped her purse and said, "Gather your things, Eddie. This is our stop. Your mother and father will be at the station."

I felt the train slow. Once more, the conductor walked past.

"Marion's next. All for Marion, please."

Nan and I got off on the station side of the train. The night air was heavy with humidity, like I'd never felt in my life. The depot was unkempt and dirty. Schedules with grainy footprints littered the floor.

Quickly, Nan and I scanned. My parents weren't there.

Where are they?

A solitary phone booth stood outside the depot. Nan fumbled with her purse and squeezed a thick green plastic coin carrier. Worried, she put a dime in the pay phone; a *ching* answered back. She looked at a half-torn sheet of paper with numbers as she dialed. Her forehead, already moist, became wet as she held the phone to her ear. Her eyes got bigger with each ring.

"They said they'd be here," she blurted, as she hung up. I saw panic now.

It made my heart skip beats.

They've left me. I defaulted: *I want my uncle.*

Nan piled quarters and dimes on a steel ledge below the phone, ammunition for a long-distance call to Jersey. She was still piling when the train whistle sounded and the Arrow began to creak away.

"What's happened to them?" Nan asked. "They should be here."

I watched the caboose roll by, gently rocking back and forth. On the other side of the tracks, now visible, were four silhouettes of varying heights, backlit by a car's high beams. The silhouettes were moving, as if waving.

Mom, Dad, Mark, and Jacki came into focus.

"Welcome to Cedar Rapids!" my mother's voice boomed.

Nan scooped the coins into her purse. "You had us worried sick," she yelled. "I thought there was a car accident."

"No accident," my father answered. "Just late. The train got in before we could get to the station."

My mother reached for a hug. She embraced a rock.

We piled into a new Pontiac station wagon. I sat in the wagon part of the car and looked backwards. Brake lights illuminated a huge dust trail from the gravel road—it was impossible to see anything behind me.

In the morning, I scanned the countryside from my new bedroom on Kent Drive. On the next street over, there were a dozen half-built houses. Beyond that, I saw field after field of gold-topped corn.

There wasn't a single tree in sight.

You could say the same thing about carnival lights.

FOUR: *Finding Lydia*

Soul mate.

As in, "I think I've met my soul mate."

It's a platinum-level phrase reserved for that once-in-a-lifetime love. One can't use the words too casually or too soon; most listeners will certainly give a disapproving look.

The thing about soul mates: you never know when they'll show up. For some, it's a first grade romance that never ends. Others find their soul mate on the hundred-and-tenth blind date. Some meet their soul mate while living as widows or widowers.

And me? I found my soul mate when I was barely fifteen.

Lydia King was my soul mate-in-waiting.

We began easy enough; a match-up through her friends. A quick-witted cute blonde with a Mona Lisa smile, Lydia had a girl-next-door persona. She was always willing to touch—a hand, a sleeve, a shoulder—when she spoke, which made her impossible to resist. She smelled wonderful too; every morning she spritzed a tiny shot of *Heaven Scent* on her neck. Most of all, she had a generous giving heart one size larger than Alaska.

On the other hand, it shouldn't have worked. Lydia was Missouri Synod Lutheran in a family of before-dinner grace prayers. Unbelievably, her parents didn't even drink. Barbara and Samuel King also weren't crazy about Lydia dating anyone outside their religion. Catholics in particular, especially Catholic boys with booming voices like mine, were off-limits. Lydia was a year older, too—tenth grade to my ninth—at a time when dating younger boys was borderline heretical.

"You were hard up," I always kidded her.

33

Lydia thought I was nice, and she liked my sense of humor. She bucked her parents.

"You're so sensitive," she said one night as we sat in her car, trying to French kiss for the first time. "You're not like other boys; you aren't afraid to tell me what's in your heart."

Certainly I was willing to talk about many things that most fifteen-year-old boys wouldn't even consider. Like her interest in fashion design. I actually asked questions as she described dress patterns or explained how to make the perfect dart. It didn't scare me to say that I liked her, or more importantly, to show it.

Before long, I had written a couple dozen notes and cards telling Lydia how special she was.

My best friend, Dennis Tharp, whom I nicknamed Thap, understood that Lydia was a keeper.

"Krugger, what the hell is a girl like Lydia King doing with you? She's a sweetheart, and way too good for you," he said with a wink. "She should be dating me instead."

I thought he might be a little serious.

"Leave me alone, Thap. Get your own girlfriend from the dozens standing in line."

"Seriously, Krug, she's such a nice person. If you have any sense at all, you'll hang on to her."

Thap definitely had enough experience to spot an exceptional girl. We had been friends since the first day of eighth grade, when he walked up the aisle of our loud school bus. He had a fresh crew cut to jet black hair and wore brand-new blue jeans topped by a white button-down shirt. I saw a smile and an offered hand.

"Hi, I'm Dennis."

In retrospect, it's a wonder Thap was so friendly; with shaggy hair nearly to my shoulders, striped multicolored bell bottoms, and a Nehru jacket, I was my own special mix of Iowa hippie and weirdo. A four-inch silver medallion hung around my neck. Mom thought it made me look cool.

I smiled at this new kid, flashed the peace sign, and replied, "Peace, man."

It was 1970, after all.

Thap and I fell in as friends. Soon, we were nightly telephone junkies, sharing about girls, music, and whatever else teenage boys talk about. Eventually, we both made the football team, with Thap as quarterback and me as front line guard. I was tasked with keeping Thap safe from rushing linemen hell-bent on taking him down.

"Krug, do your job and don't let that son of a bitch get to me!"

Because of Thap's drop-dead gorgeous features—the hair, the tight jaw, and the everlasting cocky spirit—he quickly faced the dilemma of choosing among multiple girls. Yet, for some inexplicable reason, he always wanted my opinion.

"What do you think, Krugger?" he risked during one lunch period. "Should I spend my energy on Carmen, who's happy to make out, or should I go for Michelle, the smart one, who I really like but will need convincing? I'm sure she'll never let me get to second base, either."

The poor guy. He had no clue that I was clueless.

I listened to Thap's pronouncement about Lydia. No doubt, Lydia oozed genuine goodness. Maybe a sheltered life had preserved her innocence and values. Maybe it was that we seemed to just *click*. Regardless of why, I was going to hang on to her.

I needed to.

Sometimes, my father stopped cold—drop-dead drunk—after too many Scotches. Mark learned this the hard way one evening when he couldn't open the front door. Tom Terrific had passed out the moment he got in the house.

Mark didn't tell me about this until we were adults. As kids, the code was to never talk about Dad's boozing.

A year into dating, I brought Lydia back to Kent Drive after a Friday night basketball game. She bolted ahead into the kitchen. I was halfway up the split-level's stairs when I saw her back out of the kitchen. She turned around, looking puzzled and alarmed.

"What's your father doing asleep on the floor?" she whispered, pointing behind her.

My heart stopped. I looked beyond her into the kitchen and saw my old man's crumpled legs.

"We're outta here!" I yelled.

I retreated to the landing. "Come on, let's go," I ordered as I held the front door open.

35

We got back in the family Corolla parked in the driveway. Lydia demanded, "Tell me what's going on!"

The car didn't move. I couldn't concentrate on driving, but I also didn't know what to say. I had never talked to anyone about my father—not even Thap—and I didn't have a rehearsed script.

I went for honesty.

"He drinks too much," I said, deflating fast. "He always drinks too much. Then he passes out, but I've never seen him like this, in the middle of the goddamned floor."

Lydia frowned. "Really? When I've been here, he's never seemed to drink very much. I've never even heard him slur his words."

"Yes, *really*," I answered defensively. "He holds it well until a certain point, but once he gets there, forget about it, he's gone." Still stumbling, I added, "I hate it. I so want to leave this house and him and my mother."

I felt tears welling. I tightened. The last thing I wanted was to cry.

Lydia grabbed my hand. "What does your mom do about your dad?"

"She puts up with it," I said. "She doesn't know what to do, and she's afraid. Sometimes she joins him, and then both of them get bombed."

Lydia gently squeezed. "Oh, Ed, why didn't you tell me?"

I stared straight ahead; I couldn't look at Lydia without breaking down. Finally, I answered. "I'm so ashamed of him. I'm worried the guys will think I'm a loser."

I heard her tears, and from my eye's corner, saw her reach for a tissue. A second later, she leaned over and grabbed at my letter jacket, searching for body mass. I fell toward her, over the stick shift, onto her seat.

That was enough to loosen the grip on my tears. Lydia held on like a human sponge, absorbing my pain as I cried.

"I don't care," she said above my bawling. "I'm sorry you didn't think you could talk about this but, Ed, I don't care. It's you, not your family, that matters to me."

Her words melted something inside me, like a red-hot flame burning through ice-cold wax.

If I had to pick the moment when I fell in love with Lydia—real love, not that puppy stuff—this was it. I never expected someone, especially this sweet untarnished girl, to know and still want *me*.

As we each held on tight, I told myself that I'd never let her go, not now, not after she knew about my father and didn't run away. Finally, I had someone who would love me regardless of my history, someone who was willing to stick with me and my fears.

We coined a pet name for each other after that. Both of us had taken Spanish and learned that "bobo" meant "crazy." After wearing out the fun of calling each other "Señor Bobo" and "Señorita Bobo," we settled on *our* special name for each other: "Bo."

"You're my Bo, and I'm your Bo," I told Lydia after the moniker was ingrained. "I'm so lucky to have you."

"No," Lydia answered. "I'm the lucky one."

Hearing that made me feel so incredibly good.

Everything changed after that night in the driveway. Lydia and I went from talking about my dream (lawyer) or her dream (fashion designer-buyer) to our dream of a life together. We dreamed a plan, a *Grand Plan*: college, law school, our respective careers, children, and a big house where we'd live happily ever after.

I surprised Lydia with a promise ring. "I'm yours forever," I wrote in the card.

"Oh Bo! I'm yours too. I love you so very much."

Love. What an incredibly powerful word.

Almost as powerful as *soul mate.*

I had another secret, far worse than my father's drinking, that I kept from Lydia and everyone else in the world.

I was in sixth grade and alone in the house on Kent Drive.

Something that's as impossible to explain as breathing pulled me into Jacki's pink-walled bedroom.

At the bedroom threshold, I was greeted by two Daves—posters of the Monkees' Davy Jones and David Cassidy, of *Partridge Family* fame.

Ignoring the masculinity, I crept into the room.

I stopped in front of a white wooden dresser. A pang, a need, an urge, call it what you will, beckoned me to reach.

Breathing deeply, I slowly pulled at the top drawer. The wood squeaked and reluctantly gave up the drawer, revealing patches of pinks and blues amid a sea of whites, delicate flowers in a well-tended garden. I picked through camisoles and underwear until a pair of nylon panties with small yellow daisies surfaced. I pulled the panties from their sanctuary and held them by the waistband with both hands, and stretched gently to create an air mannequin. Starstruck, I watched the daisies sway. The fabric spoke, inviting me.

I'm for you, the pretty panties urged.

The contours of fitted crotch and narrow leg openings were enticing reminders of Christine's unforgettable clean lines.

The nylon fabric, oh so soft, felt like woven baby powder.

My heart thumped, just as my penis awoke. I trembled. I was on forbidden ground at razor's edge between boy and girl, male and female.

Quickly, I slipped out of my corduroy pants, revealing bulky, unwanted white Fruit of the Looms. A second later, they came off too.

Another deep breath.

Hesitation.

What am I doing?

Before my brain could process, I bent down and slipped my feet into the panties. I tugged upward, inch by inviting inch, until the daisies were firmly around my thin waist, the elastic gripping, but not pinching, my inner thighs.

I vibrated, as if an invisible switch had been flicked. A million watts of electric current flooded my veins.

My...oh my....

More breaths.

A full-length mirror occupied the corner of Jacki's room. I took a couple steps and looked at the image.

Oh god!

Reflected back was something far closer to Christine than I could have ever imagined. In an instant, years of segmented thoughts and images connected.

I pulsed.

Beautiful. Absolutely beautiful!

The view wasn't complete. I returned to the underwear drawer and retrieved a matching camisole. Fumbling, I unbuttoned my plaid shirt and tossed it off. In a flash, I shimmied the camisole over my bony shoulders until it pressed against my chest.

Once again, the mirror.

A shaking, terrified, excited, smiling *girl* looked back.

Turn around.

I twirled for the view from behind without any penis bulge to ruin the scene. The panties and camisole fit like they were made for me.

How glorious! You'd never know I was a boy!

A minute later, fear outpaced excitement; my parents and siblings would be home any minute.

I stripped off my sister's top and bottom and returned them to the dresser drawer, trying to recall exactly how everything had been arranged before my secret intrusion.

I ran to my room with my clothes in hand, where I dressed, boy resumed, forever changed.

After that, whenever I was alone in the house, the mirrored images became a second skin. They were Teflon-like, and allowed me to slip past anything that made me afraid—my father's drinking and PMIA, being without friends in this new place, even my ingrained fear of UFOs and space aliens.

By the time Lydia King came along, I thought of clean lines on my body almost every day. I had perfected the art of "grab and stroll" at the local Kresge's, with its bins of delightful striped and polka-dot bikini underwear. Sometimes, I'd leave the house with something pretty on underneath my jeans, a hint of *what it might be like.*

It all made no sense, I know, and I did my best to not think about the dichotomy—Ed Krug the jock versus the stranger who loved to stand in front of a mirror imagining that it reflected back a girl. I thought, too, that it was harmless. I was sure that once I had a girlfriend, my desire for clean lines would evaporate.

Of course, I was a bit wrong about that.

It took almost two years before Lydia and I made our way to real sex. With both parents working and Mark and Jacki in after-school activities, Kent Drive was often empty.

Lydia and I became sex explorers.

That is, until the day my father came home from work early, who knows for what reason. By then, that was exactly opposite of what I expected.

"What was that? Oh no, someone's home!" Lydia caught herself from screaming the words just as she shot to the edge of my bed. We both froze, cocked heads, and listened to the heavier, slightly forceful steps from front door to living room.

My father, I figured.

We stayed frozen and followed Dad's footsteps into my parents' bedroom. We heard the bedroom door close; I presumed he would change out of his suit. In a minute, he'd be back out of the bedroom.

"What the hell are we going to do?" I whispered as Lydia and I both raced to put on clothing.

Lydia looked at me with a panicked face. She had her sweater on and grabbed for her jeans. She didn't fuss with her bra, which she crumpled into her purse.

"Do you think he's going to come in?" she asked, begging for reassurance.

"I don't know. Let's just sit here for a minute and figure this out," I answered.

My father had to know what was up. Lydia's car was in the driveway, and my bedroom door was shut. He couldn't have missed our frantic whispers or the sound of clothing being flung onto frightened bodies.

A couple minute-hours passed. I stiffened when I heard my parents' bedroom door open. Lydia and I sat on the edge of my bed, at attention, and waited for a knock.

It didn't happen.

I heard the refrigerator door, *fump.* Dad had bypassed us and instead headed for his first drink, a beer. I heard the *phish* of a beer pull-tab. A few seconds later there was a distant familiar groan, a signal that he had settled into his favorite living room chair, which by coincidence was situated near the split-level stairs. It was impossible to reach the front door without going past him.

Lydia looked at me, relieved, but only for a second.

"I don't want to go out there," she whispered. "I don't want him thinking I'm some kind of whore."

I paused and then smiled.

"Whore?" I shushed. "What are you talking about? It took me two years to get into your pants."

I couldn't help it. I began to laugh, which spread to Lydia. In an instant, we were whisper-giggling, then cry-giggling. We might have been facing big-time trouble but at least we were going into it with the right attitude.

Eventually I said, "We just need to go out there. When we get to the living room, keep going. I'll handle Dad."

Lydia looked at me like I was crazy but did as I asked. We got to the living room, me leading the way, and Lydia took a quick left down the stairs.

"Have a good afternoon, Mr. Krug," she said without waiting for a reply. I watched her haul open the front door and leap through it.

That left me alone to face the consequences.

I looked over at my father. He sat with crossed legs, the newspaper folded halfway on his lap. Wearing reading glasses, he hunched while holding pen to crossword. He never looked up from the paper, nor did he say a word.

Not wanting to miss a perfect chance to escape, I went back to my room, where I stayed until my mother and siblings came home. I emerged at dinner time and acted as if nothing had happened.

Dad never said a word to me. I'm sure he didn't tell my mother, either. She wouldn't have let it pass had she known.

I never thanked him for cutting me the slack.

Yes, I loved sex with Lydia. But instead of evaporating thoughts of clean lines—*now this crap in my head will go away*—sex created even more duality, a sort of gender bipolarity. On one side, I was a normal boy caught up in love and a physical relationship with my first real girlfriend. On the other, there was a deep fuzziness that centered around evolving fantasies about clean lines on my body.

If anything, eyeing Lydia's clean lines fueled my fantasies even more.

Hey Lydia, what's it like to have such freedom? Could I borrow your body for an hour? Or a day? Would you be willing to trade vagina for penis and scrotum glob?

I developed a plan. I felt that talking—speaking the actual words, *these thoughts keep coming into my brain*—would be enough to exorcise the fuzziness. Sure, I understood it might freak out Lydia, too, but then again, she hadn't run away when she learned about my father.

Besides, I reasoned, if you really love someone, it's important that they know you completely, including even your deepest secrets.

It was also the right thing to do. I wanted to learn from my parents' obvious mistakes.

I got up the guts during an evening phone call. I used the teen line in my bedroom and looked at Bobby's picture as I started a rehearsed speech.

"I need to tell you something about me that you'll think is weird," I said, laying the groundwork. "I'm afraid that you'll not want to be with me anymore."

I hoped that I might get some sympathy bonus points if things sounded worse than what they actually were, forgetting that really, this stuff about me was pretty damn bad.

"What kind of weird thing?"

"Well, it's pretty weird."

At that point, Lydia's cheerleading gene kicked in. Her voice sweetly softened.

"Bo, I've known you for two and a half years. I can't imagine anything being so weird that it could affect *us*," she said.

I visualized her holding cheerleader poms. *Rah Rah, Ed Krug, I believe in you!*

Suddenly, I got cold feet.

"Oh, never mind," I said. Maybe this wasn't such a good idea after all.

Lydia wouldn't let it go.

"Come on, Bo. I'm *sure* that whatever you're talking about isn't as bad as you think. You can tell me," she urged.

The line went quiet for a moment. I was scared, but I also trusted Lydia.

"I have this thing about girl's underwear." I paused for a split second as I imagined the words reaching her ears.

"Okay... and..." she said tentatively. I had opened the door. Now I needed to run through it at lightning speed.

"And I like to wear girl's underwear. It makes me feel good."

There, I said it. The secret was out, in the sunlight, exposed to another human being. For an instant, I thought that speaking the truth was the solution to my problem.

The optimism didn't last.

"What do you mean, you wear girl's underwear?" There was real Midwestern Lutheran incredulity in her voice. "You don't really put them on, do you?"

This wasn't going at all how I planned. I thought, *Krug, get out of the hole you are digging for yourself. Quickly!*

"You know what," I said, as my mouth worked overtime, "never mind. No, I don't put on girl's underwear. Just forget that I ever talked about this. It's crazy, I don't even know what I'm saying."

Deftly, I changed the subject to something *normal* for a seventeen-year-old boy. Miraculously, Lydia went with the new topic and let the whole underwear thing drop.

I had gone for broke and it went miserably. I hung up the phone vowing to *NEVER AGAIN* tell anyone about my secret. It was too dangerous, too far out.

The truth would only leave me unloved and alone.

A couple days later, Lydia and I were in my car, driving somewhere. She brought up our telephone conversation, and asked what I meant when I talked about wearing girl's underwear. I cut her off before she could finish the question.

"Bo, I told you, ignore what I said. It's nothing." I used my most convincing voice, a future trial lawyer's tonality.

Lydia answered, "Okay," and it was over. It didn't come up again for another twenty years, and only then because my life depended on it.

I didn't like lying to Lydia. To her credit, I hemmed and stammered so much that it's entirely possible she had no real idea of what I actually meant. Decades later, she reported that all she heard was that *I liked to look at women in lingerie.*

Maybe Lydia didn't want to hear what I said. No one could blame her for ignoring a single, brief, disjointed conversation, if you can even call it that, out of thousands that we'd had by then.

It will just go away, I thought of my love for clean lines. *I'll deal with this by myself.*

The *Grand Plan* began. After a false start at Iowa State, Lydia joined me at Coe College in Cedar Rapids. Never confident about anything, I did what I knew best: I buried myself in work, striving for perfect grades, my ticket to law school. Thus, on Friday and Saturday nights, one could reliably find Ed Krug in the Coe library surrounded by books and legal pads. In the next study carrel over, there would be Lydia, now my study mate.

When the acceptance letter from Boston College Law School arrived in early July, I thought Boston was out of the question. It was too much: too far away, too foreign, and too expensive. Lydia still had another year to go at Coe, meaning we'd be separated by half a country. Even more, I was all set to attend law school in Iowa City; twenty miles away, it was safe and familiar.

I asked Thap about BC. I lived with his family that summer; my parents had started their city and job hopping by then.

"Why would you even hesitate?" he answered. "Sounds like the chance of a lifetime, Krugger."

"Yeah, but I don't want to leave Lydia. We wouldn't see each other for months."

"So what? You're going to marry her someday, anyway. You should go out and explore the world. Who knows, maybe you can find some other girl to pass time with in Boston." He threw me a wink.

"God, Thap. Don't you know me better than that?"

I wasn't surprised Thap would suggest that I two-time Lydia. He had done it once with Lydia's best friend; he slept with Susan while he also chased Roxy. When I told him it was wrong, that both women deserved better, Thap got pissed and barked, "Butt out of my business, Krug."

It was one of the few times Thap and I had ever argued. I learned an important lesson: *You don't mess with a man wanting a woman.*

Thap got back to the subject. "Go to Boston. It would be a huge mistake if you didn't take the opportunity."

I bent sideways and frowned.

Aw shit.

Still, mustering courage I never thought I had, I took Thap's advice.

A month later, it was time to leave for BC. Two hours before my cross-country drive, Lydia and I picnicked on a hillside of yellow and blue wildflowers. The afternoon sun walked its way toward the horizon.

Lydia sighed and put her head on my right shoulder—she always called that her "spot"—and pulled my hand into hers.

"I'm going to miss you so much," she whispered with a squeeze.

"You know we're one," I said. "We'll always be one. My heart is tied to your heart."

"It will be so difficult without you, Bo," she said, now with tears.

"I'll miss you too." I gave my own squeeze, this one vise-like. "Most of the time, I don't know how I'll make it without you standing next to me."

We drove back into town just as the sun disappeared. I packed the car. It was time.

Lydia held something book-sized, gift-wrapped.

"Here, this is for you. A place to write your thoughts."

I tore at the paper and found a brown hardcover journal with virginal white pages.

"You've always said you wanted to write," she said. "Maybe this will give you a chance to pen the *Paper Chase II*."

Outside her apartment on that August night, we hugged tight, kissed, and cried.

I got into my car and started down the street. I looked in the rearview mirror and saw Lydia waving with a cupped hand.

My Bo, the love of my life, left behind while I drove away.

It didn't feel good at all.

Law school became a blur of challenges—a new vocabulary, professorial Socratic call-outs, a writing competition for Law Review, blue books begetting blue hands, moot court exercises, and marathon beer drinking.

I befriended a guy named Hammert, an Irishman who shared that alcoholic father lineage. Only, Hammert revered his father.

We teamed for mock trial. I was certain that back in his day, Bobby Kennedy excelled at mock trial.

On the big afternoon, Hammert was succinct, thorough, and assertive.

In contrast, I sucked. I lacked cohesion, fumbled with exhibits, and spoke in broken sentences.

Afterward, the instructor issued his pronouncements. "Mr. Hammert," he said with glasses propped at the end of his nose, "good job; you've got promise. Keep it up."

The instructor's excitement dropped precipitously when he turned to me. He tossed his glasses aside.

"Mr. Krug, well. You have a long way to go."

I tried to stay stone-faced. It didn't work.

He continued. "Did you say you wanted to be a litigator? Frankly, it requires some natural talent. You'll need to work very hard if you want to try cases."

My ego hit my brand-new wing tips. Thud.

I had come this far—a year of law school and a thousand library hours—only to hear that I just might not have what it took to be a trial attorney.

Bobby never had to put up with such a predicament, I was sure.

Afterwards, Hammert tried to comfort me over beer and gyros.

"Ed, he doesn't know what he's talking about. I know you. You'll be a good litigator, don't worry."

I was a failure.

Lydia, where are you when I need you?

Midway through law school, Lydia moved to Boston. She came just as I was leaving for a summer clerkship at a Cleveland law firm.

"I'll send you a ticket to visit me," I said.

There were three good things about spending a summer in Cleveland. One was the money; in 1981, a gig that paid $2,400 a month was almost unheard of. The second was Thap; he was attending law school in Cleveland.

"Hey, Kruggie, make sure you bring your credit card," Thap reminded me. "You're rich now, and I expect to be treated well."

The last positive about Cleveland? I would be a stranger there. A part of me, the one under the surface, thought I could explore in a new city. By then, my fantasies had expanded to include men adoring me as a woman. A single fantasy in particular dominated: I would prance—that's the right term—in front of a man while I wore nothing but white cotton bikini panties.

You're so beautiful, the man, a nondescript, goateed stranger would exclaim.

Do with me whatever you will, I'd answer.

I barely took note of this cosmic shift in thinking. I still enjoyed sex with Lydia, so there was no way sexual fantasies about men meant anything, right?

Yet, what if I met a goateed stranger in Cleveland? Could I actually let him touch me? I didn't know, but the idea was riveting.

Early on, I discovered a shopping mall not far from my Cleveland Heights apartment. One Saturday afternoon, I walked through a Dayton's and eyed a delectable pair of lavender lace bikini panties. Shoplifting was out of the question; there was too much to lose if I got caught. No, if I really wanted to wear those panties, I would have to buy them.

Just like any woman would.

I paced outside the lingerie department, debating whether to risk running into someone from the Cleveland law firm. I felt a shot of courage and walked over to the lingerie display. I grabbed the lavender panties with shaking hands and racing pulse. Thinking I'd never have the guts ever again, I picked a second pair, this one pink.

A well-dressed woman, sixtyish, with tailored gray hair and pearls, had her back to me at the cash register. As she turned around, I saw smile migrate to frown. I should have expected that—after all, I was a mustached twenty-four-year-old male dressed in a faded tee shirt, baggy shorts, and flip-flops, holding two pairs of panties.

She forced a "Can I help you?"

I pushed the merchandise forward with an unsteady hand. "I'll take these," I said with an equally shaky voice. It sounded more like a question than a statement.

I heard a slight "Hmph" as she took the goods.

The cash register clicked once and then again. "That will be eighteen seventy-three," she said, with no hint of personality whatsoever.

Naively, I wrote a starter check from a Cleveland bank and handed it over.

The clerk glanced at the check and demanded, "Driver's license, please."

That's when it dawned on me. I had an Iowa driver's license; I was 600 miles from home offering check number 002; I looked like a bum; and I had spent the last twenty minutes either pacing outside or walking through the lingerie department.

The situation had "pervert" written all over it.

The clerk's pained face intensified. She picked up a telephone and paged "Miriam," apparently the supervisor. I tried to look as if this was no big deal, like I was fully comfortable hanging out in lingerie departments with unfriendly clerks. By then, a woman, an intended customer, stood behind me with three bras in hand. Her impatient sigh signaled that she, too, wasn't happy with my presence.

Miriam never answered her page. The clerk, now a full-blown sourpuss, returned the phone to its cradle and said, "It will be a minute." She cheerfully apologized to the bra woman behind me and left with my license and check, stranding me like a shipwreck survivor. I rubbed my arm, a lifelong nervous reflex.

I had no choice but to ride it out and wait.

I talked to myself. *God, Krug, what a mistake. Stupid, stupid, stupid. How will you ever get out of this?*

The clerk returned ten minutes later. By then, the bra woman had given up. The clerk pushed my license at me without saying a word. She punched cash register buttons, snapped a bag open, and wadded tissue paper around the pretty panties. She handed over my newly purchased treasures and tersely exclaimed, "Have a nice day, *Sir*."

I ran out of the store, swearing that I would never, ever, under any circumstance, buy lingerie again.

You're done with this, Krug. You really are a pervert.

Still, embarrassment doesn't last. Fantasies and gut tugs, on the other hand, never die.

I never met a goateed man in Cleveland. However, I did know Martin Brown, one of my BC Law classmates.

I always respected Martin because of how he got into BC; like me, he had been wait-listed, but he was never given a slot before the school year began. Undeterred, he showed up on the first day of classes and planted himself in the admissions office. For three days, he smiled, joked, and got to know the staff. Finally, they let him in.

It was a lesson in persistence that I never forgot.

There was something else about Martin. He was blonde, with a delicious smile and sweet disposition. Every time I was near him, I felt a tingle; he was my first male crush. It didn't matter that he was married.

Still, even with that attraction, there was no way that I'd ever act on it. After all, I was a man who enjoyed sex with Lydia.

On a summer night after the Massachusetts Bar exam, Martin and his wife hosted a party at their house in Brighton. It was one of those change-in-life parties—some classmates were starting jobs in Boston, and others were leaving the state. With the Bar exam now over, it was a particularly lively crowd.

Toward the end of the evening, I stood in Martin's kitchen with a plastic cup waiting for my last beer. I watched Martin work the tapper, flexing a ribbon of muscle that stretched from wrist to bicep. We were alone and joked about the very fresh horror of sitting for the Bar.

As my cup filled, Martin drew closer and whispered, "Do you re-member what you said to me at the last party?"

There had been another party in the spring where I had too much to drink. I didn't even remember talking to Martin then.

"Uh, no, I don't recall. Why don't you remind me," I said hesitantly.

Foam breached the rim of my cup. Martin smiled. "Well, Eddie, you said you wanted to *blow me*. You told me I was cute and offered to suck my cock."

His smile turned to a deep laugh, which signaled that at least I hadn't insulted him. He pulled back, still laughing, when someone else came up for a refill.

Goddamn.

Did I really say that? How could I?

At that instant, I remembered Lydia was somewhere nearby. I didn't want her walking into the kitchen and asking, "What are you guys talking about?"

"You know I'm such a kidder," I said, as I grasped for something to explain myself. I quickly followed with, "I've got to go."

I bolted for Lydia and the front door.

I continued to deny the underlying issue. I chastised myself over my drinking—something that wasn't new. *Why do I drink so much and do such stupid things?*

Yes, I loved the idea of actual clean lines on my body and, for sure, I fantasized about sex with men, particularly Martin. But all of that was supposed to be old history.

Now, with law school over, I was ready for a future with Lydia and progression of the *Grand Plan*.

You promised Bo, I reminded myself. *You don't break promises. A promise is forever.*

FIVE: *Killer Krug*

I'd been at Lewis & Bruce barely fifteen minutes when Derrick Bear sat five of us down—all newly minted lawyers—and laid out the rules.

"We bill in quarter-hour increments," Derrick said. He held up a sample billing sheet, which we were to complete daily, as if our professional lives depended on it.

Derrick was short and squat with a calm disposition, an essential quality needed to survive the egos of highly stressed lawyers. He was a crisp office manager when the firm had a half dozen lawyers. Now, in 1982, he was balding with a paunch. I was lawyer No. 42.

Derrick went on. "This means that every fifteen minutes, you put down time. If it takes you two minutes to read a letter in Client A's case, you bill the time as one increment, point two-five of an hour. Then, if you spend three minutes on a letter for Client B's case from the same batch of mail, you bill that as another quarter hour."

One of the other rookies, who was more naive than me, interrupted.

"Isn't that unethical?" she asked. "To use your example, we've only worked five minutes, but billed a half hour. That feels like cheating."

I held my breath as Derrick's eyes bulged. He forced a smile. "No," he said. "That's not cheating. For one, every client agrees to the quarter-hour billing, and they understand that most letters aren't going to take fifteen minutes to read. More importantly, there are things you'll do but can't bill time for, like arranging for files to be retrieved or copied. In the end, it all evens out."

My fellow rookie nodded and smartly shut up.

Derrick looked at me and the others. We were lined up on the other side of a high-end cherry conference-room table, like sitting ducks.

"Another thing to remember is that clients pay for your mind, for the right to occupy your brain," he said. "Some of your best thinking will take place outside the office. So, if you're pondering a summary judgment motion and stumble on some brilliant argument while lathering up in the shower, we want you to bill that time. Got it?"

In unison, the rookie league responded, "Got it."

I quickly found that Derrick was right. In no time, knowing next to nothing, I was handling my own files. I read correspondence, drafted lawsuit papers, and conducted depositions. I was in the office from 7:30 a.m. to 5:30 p.m., with lunch at my desk. At the end of the day, my time sheet showed only five or six hours of billed time. Since Lewis & Bruce required 1,900 billable hours a year, this meant that I had to work even more—either by taking work home or by coming in on the weekends. It didn't matter that I had a whole month of vacation; there was no way I could take all of it. I sure as hell didn't want to lose my big-dollar salary; at $32K a year, I made almost three times what Lydia earned as a department manager at Jordan Marsh.

"I'm chasing time," I said to Denise, my secretary, a barely five-foot-tall cute package of brunette wit and bluster. "I've got to find two more billable hours today to stay on track."

"Well, Killer," she answered, with a Boston roll of the "r" on "Killer," "you better get in that office and sit your butt down. It ain't gonna happen with you standing here."

I trudged back to the small corner office that Derrick let me have when another associate lawyer—a casualty of the billing war—quit after four years of servitude. A couple hours later, I ran out the door for the bus home, still short by three quarters of an hour.

The elevator opened in the building lobby. I spied a sidewalk crammed with stressed-out suits and skirts doing double-time for buses and trains, prisoners on overnight leave.

I thought, *I'll have to make up the missing time tomorrow.*

Married now, Lydia and I rented the bottom of a duplex in West Newton, a working class neighborhood twenty minutes from downtown

Boston on a good traffic day. We spent weekends window shopping in Cambridge or biking along the Charles, witnessing how it changed from tight stream to open river and then on to Boston Harbor and the wonderment of the Atlantic.

Sunday mornings, no longer a day for Mass or Lutheran services, were devoted to bike trips to Faneuil Hall. Once there, we'd grab sloppy ice cream cones or bite-sized chocolate chip cookies—a budget lunch of sweets. Almost always, we ended up on a bench, sharing a Diet Pepsi and watching gawking tourists. Nuzzling, in love and devoted, we whisper-giggled when someone oddly dressed or hair challenged walked by, our shared secret.

Oddly dressed people. If I had thought about the hypocrisy, it might have temporarily—at best—stopped me from dressing in Lydia's clothes.

At first, as a newlywed, I had resolved to be *normal* and stop cross-dressing. When needed, I reminded myself of the night before our wedding, when we had fled the rehearsal dinner for Crystal Lake, not far from BC Law School. It was a beautiful full moon evening. We found two small wooden stools at the water's edge, as if to welcome just us. We sat and leaned into each other, dreaming and loving.

"It's hard to believe that in less than twelve hours, we'll be man and wife," I said.

"You mean husband and wife," Lydia gently corrected.

"Right. We'll be married," I rebounded.

"It'll be so good, Bo," she cooed. "What makes it great is that I'm marrying my best friend."

I put my arm around her. "I so love you," I whispered.

I truly believed that marrying Lydia would be the end-all for any problem I'd ever face. Almost daily, I projected forward and counted time, where I pictured us in our fifties, in the next century, living the high life, happy and still in love. I so wanted to clear my slate that, a few nights earlier, I had thrown away every piece of lingerie—some recently bought, some left over from years before—that I had hidden in my apartment closet.

I told myself, *You need to be totally committed to Lydia. This little problem needs to end.*

I was certain I could do it.

But a year into our marriage, I wore myself out trying to stay sober. I had put up a good fight against fantasies and gut tugs for clean lines, only to give in on a day that Lydia was out shopping. Lydia had wonderful lingerie, along with the most delightful pink sundress; simple but flowing, it was a lush waterfall of soft cotton. With the help of athletic socks in Lydia's bra and some tucking away in her panties, there *she* was, me as a woman, at least from the neck down.

Certainly, my mustache, the masculine marker that I'd retained since high school, destroyed the image.

I always did well with ignoring the obvious and even better at imagining the impossible.

The telephone rang at nine on a Sunday morning. Rita started talking before I could even say hello.

"Uncle Ed's had a stroke. You need to get here. Now."

By then, Nan and Poppy were gone, and the house in The Country had been sold. Uncle Ed, along with his mutt Stubby, had moved to a mobile home in Connecticut near Rita and Rich.

Lydia and I sped to a Connecticut hospital where we found Uncle Ed on oxygen but awake. Even stroked-out, my uncle brightened when he saw me.

"Hey, big guy," I said as I leaned in and kissed his forehead. "What kind of trouble did you get yourself into now?"

Uncle Ed tried to speak but nothing came out. He struggled to move his head, and then I saw the tears.

My heart broke.

The stroke had paralyzed much of his left side, including his tongue. He'd be in the hospital for weeks, and then in rehab for months more. No one knew whether he'd ever be able to live alone again.

Later that day, we met Rita and Rich at Uncle Ed's mobile home to retrieve Stubby for safekeeping. Maybe my aunt didn't notice the *Playboy Magazine* on the stand next to the Barcalounger. It was open to a centerfolded buxom, long-legged redhead. I had never fathomed that my seventy-year-old uncle would be interested in *Playboy*.

Every Saturday for three months, I drove 200 miles roundtrip to visit Uncle Ed at the rehab hospital. I usually brought along some treat: a donut, fast food takeout, all tasty but unhealthy. Week by week, he inched along the rehab hallway, first with walker, then with cane.

His words came out distorted, another foreign language, but not the self-inflicted kind. He persevered to get home to Stubby and regain self-reliance and respect.

He succeeded.

I was barely thirty, and not yet to the point where I'd be able to survive life without him. Both of us had missed a bullet.

"I'm proud of you," I said on my last visit before his release from rehab hell. "Once again, you've taught me the value of hard work."

My uncle smiled and nodded. "Thank you, Beeter." The "z" got caught up in his tongue.

I knew what he meant.

"We're trial lawyers, not litigators," Brendan Lewis said one day. "Litigators push paper and never set foot in a courtroom. Trial lawyers prepare for trial and actually try cases. And win."

Lewis never smiled. It wasn't in his constitution; most of the time he just growled. He sported horn-rimmed glasses and a cherry red complexion, as if constantly fueled by the toxicity of high blood pressure and ego. I was still learning the ropes, but at least I understood this part of Lewis's mentality: if you're a trial lawyer, you're always on the attack, always looking for the needed angle to defeat whoever was after your client—or you.

The process at Lewis & Bruce was almost mechanical. Brendan Lewis would receive new lawsuits from insurance companies, which he'd send to associates like me with a curt memorandum: "Do the necessary to get this ready for trial."

It was up to me to figure out what "the necessary" was. Lewis wouldn't look at the file again until the case was ready for trial—two or three years down the road. God forbid if you missed something that he felt should have been done. Once, Lewis called me an "idiot" when I forgot to ask for a certain medical record.

"I was commanding a ship in the Pacific when I was your age," he said with a head shake.

Luckily, I had two other mentors. Richard Finch exuded teddy bear. Stocky with a mustache and glasses, he was soft and gentle, someone who nudged more than pushed.

My other mentor, Max English, was stunningly gorgeous with long, flowing blonde hair and a walrus-style mustache. He was a brilliant trial lawyer with a quick mind.

Within weeks of Derrick Bear's lecture about billing time, I was in a courtroom as Max's second chair. The plaintiff, a middle-aged commercial painter named Johnson, had suffered a fractured hip. He had fallen at a job site and sued our client, the property owner.

On direct examination by his attorney, Johnson testified that the property owner should have provided scaffolding for Johnson to do his work.

When it was our turn for questions, Max stood in front of Johnson and asked when he first believed the job site needed scaffolding.

"Right from day one," Johnson answered confidently.

Max pressed, "Are you telling the jury that not having scaffolding is the guts of your case?"

Johnson glared. "That's right."

"That you've always thought the lack of scaffolding was the one essential reason why my client is at fault for your injury?"

"Yes."

Max strolled to our courtroom table and asked me to hand him a thick black notebook. It contained questions and answers called "interrogatories," which Johnson had completed months before the trial.

Max returned to the witness stand with the notebook opened to "Interrogatory No. 5." He had Johnson read the interrogatory question out loud: "State in full and complete detail every essential fact on which you base your claim that the defendant is at fault for your injuries."

Max pulled the notebook away and asked, "Do you recall answering that question?"

"I do," Johnson replied.

"You signed these answers under oath, didn't you?"

"That is true," Johnson dutifully answered, sensing now that maybe all was not good.

"An oath is a promise you make, right? A promise to be honest, correct?"

Hesitantly, Johnson said, "I'll agree with that." He looked over to his attorney, whose face was fixed downward on a legal pad with pen in hand.

The courtroom was dead silent. The jury smelled that something was up. I had no idea where Max was going.

Once again, Max leaned into the witness stand. He pointed at Johnson's answer to Interrogatory No. 5.

"Take a good look at the sworn answer you gave to this interrogatory, which asks about the essential facts of your case."

Johnson slowly hunched forward and looked at his answer.

"Isn't it true you made absolutely no reference to scaffolding? In fact, the word 'scaffolding' doesn't appear anywhere in your answer."

Barely audible, Johnson answered, "That's right, I didn't say anything about a scaffold."

Max went for the kill.

"So, let me see if I have this correct. You're here in this courtroom claiming that your case absolutely depends on my client's failure to provide scaffolding, and yet today is the very first time you ever said a word about scaffolding. Do I have that right?"

Max looked at the jury. A couple women jurors smiled back.

Johnson had the Hobson's choice of arguing with Max or conceding the obvious. He chose the latter course.

"Yeah, I never talked about scaffolding before today." He said it with a shrug and glance to his lawyer.

Twenty minutes later, the trial recessed for lunch. Before the lunch hour was over, Johnson's attorney agreed to settle for much less than what he had demanded prior to the trial beginning.

"It's called boxing-in the witness," Max explained later. "You go around him on all four sides so that he can't squirm out of an answer."

Wow, I thought. *They sure don't teach you this in law school.*

I received a memorandum from Theo Forsythe, one of the power partners at Lewis & Bruce, assigning a pro bono lawsuit filed by a heroin addict named Eugene Smith. He had been arrested for violating parole due to continuing drug use. Once in custody, Smith went into heroin withdrawal. Despite getting sick, Smith was denied medical treatment.

What no one knew was that Eugene Smith had the distinction of suing every attorney who had ever represented him. I learned this only after Smith became my client.

Forsythe's memorandum directed that I wasn't to spend much billable time on the case without Forsythe's prior consent. Smith was still in prison and had no money to pay for our services.

Forsythe was fastidious and dressed in imported suits. He had a taut jawline, and wore his hair slicked back, which lent to a falcon-like appearance. This matched his aggressiveness; he had earned partner status earlier than anyone else in firm history. He was quick to anger, and he never hesitated to call people incompetent, an opinion he had of most other lawyers, or for that matter, humans.

Immediately, the U.S. Attorney's office filed a motion seeking to dismiss Smith's lawsuit. I dutifully researched and drafted a brief opposing the dismissal motion. I recorded my time for all of that work, just as Derrick Bear had instructed on day one. I defeated the government's motion, meaning that Smith's case would eventually proceed to trial.

Not long after this, Forsythe showed up at my office doorway holding my time records.

"What were you doing putting so much time into that case?" he asked, hungry and perched. He caught me off guard.

"Uh, well, it took that much time to do a good job," I said.

With a cold stare, he pressed. "I thought I told you not to put a lot of work into the case."

I felt the heat. "I'm sorry, Theo. I did what I felt was necessary."

Surprisingly, Forsythe backed off. I still don't know why.

"All right, but don't let it happen again. I want to know if anything else occurs in this case before you spend any more time or money."

"Of course, Theo."

I wanted him to leave so that I could stop being afraid.

After that, I quit recording my time on the case. I still did the work. I wasn't going to shortchange Smith, even if he was a multiple-times convicted drug user and thief.

My fear turned to anger.

This is my client, I thought to myself. *I have to do what's right. Fuck you, Forsythe.*

I managed to get through the first year at Lewis & Bruce and felt like a real lawyer. I conducted a hundred depositions and appeared in court on a couple dozen motions. At one of my first depositions, the other attorney got up in the middle of my questioning and announced, "We're done, we're out of here."

Max later reported that the attorney hadn't prepared his client for my thorough questioning.

"Good job, way to make them sweat," he said. The walrus on his lip was turned upward.

By then, I was simultaneously working forty or fifty cases. Some cases were small, like the male model who had a nickel-sized second-degree burn on his foot when a shower hose ruptured.

Others involved death or grossly disfiguring injuries. With Max, I represented a railroad company. Very few people ever tangle with trains without grave injuries or death, like the kid who had tried to hop a slow-moving train, only to slip under a wheel—pictures showed a bloody arm lying on the track. In another trespasser case, the victim was cut in two.

Max and I tried a death case that involved a subway worker who had been drinking; off balance, he was struck by a passing train. When his wife broke down on the witness stand and talked about their three kids, I looked at my notes.

It wasn't the railroad's fault, I told myself.

As Brendan Lewis had instructed, I attacked. "Isn't it true" became my mantra, like a hammer striking an anvil. I weaved through facts and looked for inconsistencies and weakness. I learned that my voice, especially when slow and deliberate, took on the quality of a hard, blunt object. I watched witnesses—men, women, and children, I didn't care—squirm as I pointed out discrediting statements they'd made to doctors or friends or loved ones.

"You're like Batman and Robin," a judge told Max and me during a trial recess one day. "One of you hits 'em high, and the other hits 'em low. I'm impressed."

I couldn't stop grinning. In the background, I heard the murmur of someone crying.

At my first review, Max and Richard glowed; my work was considered to be of quality. It furthered my resolve; if I could do well on the job, I could do just as well in my marriage.

That meant keeping thoughts about clean lines at bay. Yes, I was back to cross-dressing again, but no, it wasn't a problem. I rationalized it was my way of coping with stress. Someday, once I had the ropes down as a lawyer, the stress would go away. Then I'd stop dressing as a woman and fantasizing about goateed men.

On a Friday afternoon, I met Lydia on the Blue Line near Boston Commons where we headed to Logan for a flight to Denver. Thap had moved there after law school. He lived in a fifth-floor apartment with Julie, his very pregnant wife.

We landed at Stapleton. I heard, "Hey Kruggie and Lydia!" and saw Thap with arms outstretched. "Welcome to Denver! I couldn't wait for you to get here."

"What do you have planned for us?" I asked.

"The only thing I know," he beamed, "is a lot of beer drinking. After that, it's anybody's guess."

That night, while our wives visited inside, Thap and I sat on the apartment balcony. I took in the Colorado night as daylight dimmed against purple snow-topped mountains. Then, one twinkle at a time, dots appeared in the night sky. From galaxies a billion miles away, an invisible hand stitched a blanket of stars above us.

A chill settled in, but it didn't matter; the beer and Thap's mere presence were enough to keep me warm.

Thap retreated for more beers. I tried to count stars, but something else shot into my head. At that precise moment, I couldn't care less about pretty lingerie or being adored by men.

Quickly, I talked to myself.

Notice how the crap in your head goes away when you relax. Just remember how you feel tonight and you'll never want to dress as a woman again.

After midnight, Thap hauled a mattress onto the balcony so that he and I could sleep under the stars.

It was perfect.

Lydia and I saved enough money to move to Easton, a small town in the woods south of Boston. We bought a townhouse-style condo in a newer development named "Gaslight Village." In 1985, mortgage rates were 10.5%, but we didn't care; we finally had our first real home. My commute tripled to an hour and a half one way.

"We're the cat's meow, Bo," I cooed one golden June afternoon. We sat on the deck behind our new condo.

Lydia raised her wine glass to mine.

I leaned in for a kiss. I felt alive, contented. Our *Grand Plan* for a forever life was right on track.

Most of our fellow condo owners were in their thirties too. Like us, they loved dinner parties and cocktails in pretty glasses. I watched these couples interact, sometimes not pleasantly. I noted that Lydia and I had a different marriage.

One by one, the couples fell to the side, some the victims of cheating, others doomed because the wife or husband lacked sufficient economic power for an equal say.

"That'll never happen to us," Lydia whispered one night after we had witnessed a couple fighting. "I know you'll always tell me what's on your mind, what's bothering you, Bo. That's why we'll make it."

Her head was planted on her spot. I felt the gentle weight of a unique love and single-focused devotion.

"You're right," I answered. "That's what makes us special." I softly rubbed her head until she drifted off.

I didn't even think about the plastic bag flattened underneath the bottom drawer of my dresser, where I had stashed my pretty lingerie, all bought in the last couple months.

Four years of Brendan Lewis memos took their toll.

A temporary secretary had mistakenly erased a cassette tape that contained hours of dictation—time that I couldn't get back. There was no way I wanted to do the work over.

"What do you mean you erased the tape?" I fired from my office doorway.

"I'm sorry, Ed," the secretary said. "I made a mistake."

"You're an idiot!" I yelled. "I don't have the fucking time to redo this!"

I felt my arm move, and next I knew, the tape shattered against a wall, a foot from the horrified secretary's head. She shot me the same kind of look I gave Lewis when he came after me.

A friend from Coe College, Joshua Morse, had moved to Boston for his medical school residency in psychiatry. Joshua was one of the smartest people I knew and hailed from common-sense Nebraska.

I talked about the pressures of trying to make partner. "I'd like to get another, less intense job," I said, "but the pay's too good."

"It's called golden handcuffs," Joshua answered nonchalantly. "You get to a certain point where you can't change your life, because it costs too much."

I laughed. "Golden handcuffs. Who came up with that?"

"Someone smarter than you or me," he said dryly.

We moved on to other topics.

I told Joshua about my secretary—newly assigned after the temporary one quit—who was gay. Lionel, a leather-vest-wearing punk rocker, was the only male secretary at Lewis & Bruce. He didn't care if anyone knew that he dated men.

Incredibly, I grunted, "What a queer."

"You know, Ed," Joshua said, "The literature is pretty supportive that people who make fun of homosexuals actually have homosexual tendencies."

I laughed nervously. That was the last time I ever gay-bashed anyone.

Not long afterwards, in the spring of 1987, I was in a movie theater, only it wasn't just any theater. It was in Boston's Combat Zone, a slice of downtown filled with decaying porn shops, fetid strip clubs, and dirty single-person movie booths. The grimy theater reeked of urine and, I feared, dried sperm.

I wore a gorgeous cream lace bra and panty set under my male jeans and sweater. I'd been at the theater for twenty minutes. On the screen was a jumpy, grainy movie about two men sharing a motorcycle in the French countryside. They stopped to picnic under a tree, and things quickly progressed to kissing and undressing. The images certainly stimulated me, but still, I had trouble focusing. Almost like clockwork, every couple minutes, men walked up to the front of the theater and veered off to the right, down what looked like a hallway.

I thought, *What the hell?*

After a while, I figured it out. *That's where you go for a blow job.*

By then, there were regular newspaper stories about what had started as a mysterious pneumonia-like illness among gay men in New York and San Francisco. Soon, doctors would call it AIDS.

The absolute last thing I wanted was to have sex with a man and then have sex with Lydia. I wasn't about to kill my wife.

Earlier that day, I had shopped for lingerie along Washington and Newberry Streets. I stopped at Filene's and Jordan Marsh, and small specialty stores. Lydia was on a buyer's trip to New York for the weekend, which allowed me the freedom to roam and pretend that I was available for a sexual liaison.

"Pretend" was the operative word.

Everything I did was pretend. As I walked down Newberry Street with its fragrance of wonderful spring flowers, I fantasized that I was a woman out for an afternoon of shopping. I imagined being attractive enough to interest a goateed man, who would take me back to his high-end condo for sex. I pretended that I wasn't Ed Krug, a mustache-wearing guy with an unforgettable deep voice.

Most of all, I wondered, *What would it be like to be free? To be whoever I really am?*

I had barely started thinking about who was inside me; it was still too large to comprehend all at once. However, month by month, weird thoughts about being female crept into my brain.

I pushed the thoughts to the back of my consciousness. I loved Lydia and that was all that mattered. Still, visiting gay movie houses was proof that I had to escape Boston's temptations before I lost a grip on myself. I feared that I wouldn't be able to pull back from the brinkmanship of pretending. I worried that soon, I'd cross over into *real,* breaking a lifetime of promises to Lydia and myself.

Lydia and I had talked about returning to Iowa for a less complicated life, where the commute to work was measured in minutes instead of hours and where houses with real lawns were reasonably priced.

Iowa would be a good place for an escape. If we lived there, I just knew I'd be able to get things right in my head.

———————

On a Thursday afternoon, I received word that Eugene Smith's case would start trial on the following Monday. I immediately thought of Theo Forsythe's admonition to report when the case was called for trial. I feared that he'd tell me not to prepare, to just show up and wing it so as not to waste valuable billing time for paying clients.

Smith's case would be my very first solo trial—no other attorney would assist me—a seminal event in any trial attorney's career.

I didn't want the added pressure of Forsythe nagging me about billable time. I decided not to let him know about the trial.

Monday quickly arrived, and we got through jury selection and opening arguments. Eugene Smith, on temporary release from prison, took the stand and testified that he had repeatedly asked for a doctor when he started to feel sick from heroin withdrawal. The government's attorney then cross-examined, and showed that over the course of his several imprisonments, Smith had single-handedly filed more lawsuits against the government than any other prisoner in the United States—several hundred cases. It was a record that even merited a *Penthouse Magazine* story.

Smith hadn't ever mentioned this to me, and I hadn't thought to ask.

Yet, despite credibility problems, the day went well enough for Smith to exclaim, "Why haven't my other lawyers been as good as you?"

For the first time in my life, my confidence spiked.

Maybe I won't get sued after all.

On Tuesday morning, just before I left for the courthouse, I asked Lionel to let Theo know the case had been called for trial unexpectedly. On that second day, I cross-examined the federal marshals who had refused Smith medical treatment. Both admitted knowing he was sick from drug withdrawal, and both admitted to not getting him medical help.

"He didn't look sick enough," one of the marshals said with a glare.

With adrenaline racing through me, I returned from the courthouse.

I walked into my office and found a note from Theo taped to my chair. It read, "Come to my office immediately." This meant trouble.

I knocked on the door frame of Theo's office and found him yelling into the telephone. He motioned me to shut the door and sit down. He ended the call and looked ready to attack—high-power partner eyeing low-on-the-letterhead associate.

"Didn't I say to immediately report if Smith's case was called for trial? I sure as hell remember telling you that."

"Yes, you did."

"Then why the fuck didn't you tell me about the trial? I goddamned told you not to spend a lot of time on this file, and now you're doing just that."

I had never seen Theo so angry. I wondered whether he might fly across his desk. I didn't care. After all, Eugene Smith had said I was the best lawyer he'd ever had.

"I did what I had to do, Theo," I said, without even trying to tamp down my cockiness. "As soon as I got the call about the trial, I started preparing. I'm sorry if you're upset."

"Upset? You little prick, you're goddamned right I'm upset. From here on out, for the rest of the trial, I don't want you to make even a single photocopy without my express permission. You got that?"

What the hell?

I was in the middle of a trial where you pull out all the stops and do whatever is needed to win. Lewis had taught me that much. I wasn't about to handicap my client and break my oath as an attorney.

I blurted, "Theo, don't you think that's a bit unrealistic?"

I watched Theo's face change from red to crimson to purple, all in a second's time. He jumped out of his chair. I clenched my fists.

"Get the fuck out of my office!" he screamed. "Get out and never set foot in here again!"

I sauntered up and strode out. The confrontation boosted my ego a couple more notches. Flying now, I bobbed and weaved all the way back to my office, where I grabbed my trial bag, and left for the train station.

A couple of days later, I gave my closing argument in Smith's case. I invoked Bobby Kennedy and paraphrased, "The true measure of a right and just society is not how it treats the privileged, but instead how it treats the lowest of its people."

After they deliberated way longer than I expected—lending hope—the jury came back in favor of the defendant, United States of America.

Notwithstanding the result, Smith thanked me. I was pretty sure I'd be the first attorney he didn't sue.

Good enough, I thought.

Weeks later, close to September, 1987, Richard Finch asked me to lunch. Just before the food arrived, Richard let me know the reason for his invite.

"The partner retreat is next week," he said. He hunched and looked around to see who else was in the restaurant. "We're going to discuss associate raises and who's on track to make partner."

Yes, I knew that.

"Word has it that Theo Forsythe is going to do a hatchet job on you. He's really got you in his sights."

That didn't surprise me, either.

I told Richard what had happened with Smith's case.

"I'm sorry you had to go through that," Richard replied.

"Okay," I said. "So what happens next?"

Richard leaned in closer, almost within kissing distance.

"I'm willing to go to the mat for you. I just need you to tell me to do it. I don't want to expend the capital if you have other plans."

Oh, my dear Richard. I hadn't ever met another boss that kind, so willing to sacrifice for me.

As luck would again have it, I had sent out many Iowa-bound resumes by then. I wasn't going to have Richard do something needless. However, I didn't feel comfortable telling him my plans.

"Uh, no." I said. "I really appreciate your willingness to do that for me, Richard, but it's not necessary."

Richard nodded. We were simpatico.

Two weeks later, Richard and Max gave my review. Their report: I had a good skill set and promising career as a trial attorney, but there was a problem. Theo believed I had disrespected him.

The pronouncement?

"You have six months to apologize to Theo," Richard summarized. "We believe that if you do that, you'll continue to have a future with this firm."

I looked at my mentors, two men I admired greatly. It was obvious that neither had his heart in this. They were simply the messengers.

We each knew how this would play out.

"Oh," I said, "I'm from Iowa. I don't apologize for doing the right thing."

I wrote down the six-month deadline in my new 1988 calendar. Two weeks short of the deadline, and with a job offer from Cedar Rapids in hand, I walked out the door of Lewis & Bruce for the last time.

I thought, *I'll go home to Iowa and leave the temptations of Boston behind. Finally, I'll be able to stop thinking about clean lines.*

By then, Lydia and I had been together for seventeen years. With luck, there would be another fifty before I made her a widow.

The weekend before we packed the U-Haul for Iowa, Lydia and I visited Uncle Ed and Rita and Rich in Connecticut.

Uncle Ed was getting along well—way better than anyone would have imagined. I asked if he'd visit Lydia and me in Iowa someday soon.

"Fly-ink remind me of beeing on a DC-3 trooop plane," he said. "It wadn't too comf'table, ya know, Beeter."

Rita prepared a nice ham with puffy rolls and silky mashed potatoes. We remembered the good days in The Country. Everyone smiled when I offered, "And maybe this time next year, Lydia will be pregnant."

After dinner, I drove Uncle Ed back to his place. Lydia followed in our car. I didn't know how many more times I'd have with him before it would be too late.

As we pulled off the interstate, I told him how much he had mattered.

"Thank you, Uncle Ed," I said, with a cracking voice. "You saved me. I'd never have made it without you."

I looked over as I slowed for a stop sign. In his own understated way—the only way Ed Graney knew—he answered, "It wat da least I culd do." His eyes were moist. I grabbed his hand and held.

We parked next to the mobile home. I heard Stubby barking to be let out. I held on as we hugged. "I love you," I said.

"I love yuu ta, Beeter."

His eyes were still wet. So were mine. Using the cane that had become a necessary appendage, he went to tend to another love.

I wondered whether my dear uncle wasn't thinking, *Couldn't you have stayed around just a little bit longer, Beezer? I don't have much more time.*

I tried to ignore the thought, but it stuck with me all the way to Easton.

SIX: *Too Much*

There's one more thing Mark and I have to do before we can head to Cedar Rapids for my father's memorial service.

We need Dad's personal things from his work cubicle. I call Avionics, Inc. and talk to a guy named Rod, who gives me the building address. He tells me to come at two o'clock.

I hear a sorry-your-father-killed-himself-how-did-he-do-it sound in his voice, a ring of sympathy tinged with curiosity. I shake it off.

In the last three days, I've realized there's a sort of death hierarchy; some ways of dying have far better social stature than others. At the top, rightly so, are people who die for their country. A notch below is cancer and the awe factor for those who see you battling it. After that, you've probably got stroke and heart attack, deaths you don't consciously bring upon yourself.

People know what to say about that kind of dying.

Suicide, on the very bottom rung, is totally different. Unless you're terminally ill, it's unnecessary, avoidable, and selfish. Survivors are left with feelings of inadequacy (*Why didn't I see it coming?*), guilt (*Was I one of the reasons?*), and shame (*Hmm. Does depression run in your family?*).

With my father, there was one more feeling: painful, isolating, embarrassing *relief* that a tragedy strung out over fifty years was finally over.

I didn't doubt that people would show up for my father's memorial service. I rightly predicted that in the months afterwards, everyone would avoid talking about him or about how he died.

If you're a suicide survivor, you're on your own to sort out the inevitable questions: How could someone I love decide life isn't worth living?

Does it mean there's a point where it's okay to throw in the towel?

Then there's the big one: What if that familial osmosis thing also includes a predisposition—some would say weakness—to suicide?

I wondered where those questions would lead me.

———————

Mark and I take another trip in my father's ash-filled Nissan. This time, I drive. We go down roads that didn't exist five years ago when I last visited Dallas. We buzz through intersections with 7-Elevens that repeat like a woven pattern of modernity, one on the north side, the next to the south, another back north, past townhouse after townhouse, supposed sanctuaries of alleged sanity. The sameness makes it impossible to get my bearings at any given moment. I wonder if this new-but-same stuff lulls you into believing everything is okay.

The shallowness reminds me why I don't like Dallas in the first place, something that goes back to Kennedy, the Presidential one, being murdered there.

Dallas = Death.

The Big D.

Mark and I find the office building easy enough. I pull into the parking lot and nudge the car toward the front entry. I see three Dockers-clad men on the sidewalk. One holds a white banker's box.

I look at Mark; he looks at me. I say, "Uh, these guys aren't for us, are they? No way do we have a greeting party." Mark shrugs.

From nowhere, shame creeps up my spine. Deep in my brain a neon sign blinks, *Tainted Tainted Tainted.*

It sounds with the *dzzzt* of electrical current changing pulse: *Your genes are weak; that makes you weak.*

Mark and I aren't even out of the car before Rod, the one with the banker's box, walks toward us. He thrusts the box at me, as if it contains something radioactive.

"Hi, I'm Rod. We wanted to save you the trouble of going through your father's cubicle. Here's everything. Let me know if we can do anything else for you."

A quick rehearsed speech. No handshakes, no words about the kind of worker Dad was, no oral record to hold on to.

I want to punch Rod in the face.

Mark holds the box on his lap as we drive back to my parents' condo. Both of us wonder what kind of stuff my father kept. He was someone who always surprised you, like the time he joked, "Incest is better than no cest." I thought, just maybe he meant it.

There's no telling what secrets the box will offer up.

We make camp in the living room, where I smell a faint Clorox odor. I park a Heineken on the coffee table.

Mark opens the box. He pulls out office doodads and a calculator. I remember that in 1970, Dad came home with one of the first high-function calculators, a Texas Instruments wonder. He loved being the first on the block with something new.

It's quickly apparent the box lacks any personal items. There's nothing memorable—no family pictures or pencil holder by any of us kids or crude watercolor by Jacki or Mark. Nothing other than usual office stuff.

I reach into the box and pull out several thin calendars that were lying flat in the bottom. As a lawyer, I'm trained to look for paper. All kinds of things are written—good things, bad things, but most of all, things of one's essence. This is especially true when people believe they're writing in a secret place, a safe dwelling for the honest soul.

The calendars, 8 x 11 books with black covers, have larger daily date blocks for writing multiple appointments. They're just like the cheap calendars I get from vendors every New Year's with the company name inscribed on the front, "Courtesy of Joe Schmoe, Court Reporter."

The calendars span *1985* through *1990*. I scan and find that a few date boxes have appointment notes, but most boxes are devoid of text. Still, each box has a dot of color—every day of every month has some color. Some days are red-dot days; some are blue, others are yellow. Even the weekends have dots.

"Mark, what the hell was he doing with these colors?"

Mark grabs *1987* and looks for a minute.

"I don't know; I have no idea," he says as he tosses it on the coffee table. He's distracted—maybe he also thinks the banker's box should have more in it.

71

I'm sorry, but I want to know what these colors mean.

Since it's Dad we're talking about, the guy who drank from *Playboy* glasses and who unfolded centerfolds in the Kent Drive living room, I'm guessing the colors have something to do with sex. Does the blue represent days that he didn't have sex, and the red, days that he did? Was it vice versa? What's the yellow?

He was fifty-three and married to my mother for thirty-four years when he died, so I don't think his sex days would outnumber his sexless days. There are a lot more blue dots than red dots.

Of course, this doesn't take into account the days he had sex with himself.

I open *1989*, the end of my father's last complete decade; he almost made it a full month into the next. Two folded sheets fall from the back of the calendar.

I unfold the sheets and see that they're actually graph paper. Each sheet contains a list of names and a graph with lines and dots. Everything is in my father's handwriting.

On the first sheet are two columns of women's names, some first— some first and last. Each name is followed by a geographic location or abbreviation: "CR," "NY," "Calif," "Dallas."

Preceding each name is a calendar year—" '66," " '68," all the years of the '70s, and most of the '80s.

I count the names and come up with a dozen. With some, several years are jotted next to the name.

I recognize a few names, like "Sarah Rosen," from the New York home office, who had moved to Cedar Rapids in the early 1970s. She was tall and shrill, high on herself, and seemed to get along exceedingly well with my father.

There's "Kelly Jamieson"; I knew her as the wife of my high school football coach. My father had become friends with Coach Larry. They were even on the same Tuesday night bowling team. Mrs. Jamieson, a real beauty, had once helped me with a social studies project. Even to a fourteen-year-old kid, she seemed unhappy in her marriage, with an air that she could do better than a high school coach. And she probably could.

Wait a minute.

A synapse fires in my head.

Suddenly, my gut hurts. I reach for the Heineken and take a deep drink.

I slam the near-empty beer on the coffee table.

I yell, "Jesus Christ, look at all the women's names that Dad has here. They're women he fucked!"

I can't believe what I just said. Hell, I don't want to believe that even Tom Terrific could do this volume of cheating on my mother—cheating on *us kids*. I start to feel nauseous, as if I'm on the Tilt-a-Whirl at the Iowa State Fair.

Mark scans the list. I take in my little brother, the clean-up artist's reaction. His face scrunches as he processes.

"Well, one or two, I can understand," Mark answers way too calmly. "But not this many, no. I don't think Dad would be *that* unfaithful."

I think, *Since when does infidelity have a threshold number?*

At the bottom of the sheet is a graph running from 1966 to 1989. My father has plotted a sort of infidelity time line, with peaks and valleys that correspond with the years of his affairs. He specially noted, "Turn 40" in 1975, the year I got out of high school. After that, there's a huge peak covering about five years—I'm guessing, his most productive period. From there, the line slants sharply downward, probably his age catching up with him.

The trophy list is both fascinating and sickening.

That's my Dad.

I remember something from the early 1980s when my parents lived in Commack, on Long Island—another job hop, another Willie Loman-like dream—when Lydia and I were still in Boston. Tom Terrific went missing, PMIA once more, early one Thursday. He never made it to work. Instead, he got on a plane at JFK and flew to Dallas, where some brunette from his earlier Dallas days picked him up. He was with this woman for twenty-four hours until he got sober. Massive guilt set in. On Friday afternoon, Mark (who was living in Dallas at the time) retrieved Tom Terrific and took him to his house.

Hours later on that Friday night, at like eleven o'clock, Mark telephoned and sprang the story on me.

"Mom begged me not to call you, but I felt that I should." He paused, and added, "She's beside herself. I think you should be with her."

I didn't want to hear about my father cheating on my mother. I also didn't want to deal with Mom's drama over a man who had treated her like crap for most of her life. Plus, there was no way I'd get on the road close to midnight for the four-hour drive to Long Island.

But since I also suffer from the same always-do-the-right-thing affliction as Mark, I called Mom.

The phone in Commack rang only once before I heard my mother's voice. I could see her shaking hand trying to grip the phone from 200 miles away.

"Hi, Mom. Mark told me about Dad. I'm so sorry that he's putting you through this."

"Oh, my god, I told Mark not to call you," she near-screamed. "He promised. I don't want you involved."

I interrupted. "Mom." I tried to pull a strand of empathy from my heart. "Mark was right to call me. I'm in Boston, after all. You're alone. We're coming down. We'll be in the car in fifteen minutes."

My mother quickly relented.

"Oh, Eddie, yes, please come. Your father has hurt me so much."

We got to Commack at four o'clock on Saturday morning. Surprisingly, my mother answered the door smiling.

"Your father called a couple hours ago. He's very sorry, and he's flying home," she said ecstatically. "I'm going to pick him up at the airport at noon. You really didn't need to come."

Lydia and I looked at each other. *Can you believe the denial?*

After a few hours of sleep on an inflated mattress in the living room, we left for Boston at nine that morning. Mom and I never talked about the incident again.

As I sit here in Dallas with Mark, it's clear that my father's quick fling was only a small part of a larger pattern, the kind from which legends are made.

I say, "Listen, Mark, there's no reason for him to list a dozen women's names unless it was to remember who he had slept with. Some of them are women we knew, like that Sarah lady, who was so obnoxious. I remember how she and Dad used to go drinking together."

Mark's eyes fall back into his head. He registers: Tom Terrific the *really big cheater.* Even bleach can't erase this kind of intimate knowledge.

I pick up the other sheet to figure out if I know anyone else. It's a shorter list, but the format is the same. I scan: "'70 Bob—CR." "'75 Don Jones—Dallas." "'83 Mickey—NY."

I don't recognize any of the names but certainly these were places Dad lived and worked.

What the hell?

It's *so* obvious. Tom Terrific created a separate sheet for the *men* he had fucked.

Shit!

"Uh, little brother, you'll want to look at this other sheet." I hand it to him.

"What?" he says, grabbing. "Was he having sex with animals?"

"Not animals, but men. He was sleeping with men, too, Mark."

Mark grins, a hint of relief, like he thinks I'm kidding around, big brother trying to cut the tension, and make little brother feel better.

"I'm not shitting you. Look at it."

Mark forces his eyes toward the paper. Grin turns to grimace. We lapse into more silence, until Mark sighs—there really isn't a sound that can precisely capture someone's utter disappointment in another person.

I wait for something else from Mark and start to assemble my own response, my heart trying to muscle my brain. I'm cut off when Mark laughs. It's not a "that's hilarious" laugh but a "this is way too bizarre" laugh.

Surveying calendars and lists has changed us from novice archeologists to accidental voyeurs.

It's one thing to be a voyeur, gazing at a stranger who lights your libido. It is a completely different thing to be a voyeur—no, make that a witness—to crimes committed by someone you're supposed to love and model yourself after.

Obviously, Tom Terrific couldn't pull off the good character act. Instead of going down Do Right Boulevard, he took dark side streets, ones that I can't believe he'd want us to ever travel, with names like Liar Avenue, Cheater Parkway, and Fucker Drive.

It's too much.

I think, *Why did you even keep these lists?* I can't believe that this guy, someone who went to the trouble to Ziploc his jewelry and wallet, would forget trophy lists at his office.

Did he want my poor mother—*my mommy!*—to find the names on

75

some rainy metallic gray day after mourning him? Was this cruel record of DNA deposits and receipts intended as payback, to let her know that she really never mattered?

As bad as cheating is, to tell us about it, especially when we have no way of telephoning back with questions or commentary, well, that's just real shit.

And these are my genes at work, in a man whom I look like?

"No one other than the two of us will know about these calendars. Not even Jacki," I insist. Mark nods. Still in a fog, he gets up and heads to the bathroom, leaving me with Tom Krug, *en literature.*

Alone in the living room, my mind goes into overdrive. The problem is that this isn't the end of it; these secrets aren't all that I'll have to deal with. I now understand, infinitely well, there's a part of me, something deep inside, that mimics Tom Terrific.

Those men's names. Bisexuality. The need to explore sexually. Thinking on the edge. All of this is me too. Maybe my father even liked being adored while he wore women's lingerie.

Like father, like son. Fucking goddamn.

I think more.

Krug, you've spent twenty years dreaming of clean lines and men adoring you. You love imagining you're a woman. You compartmentalize, just like he compartmentalized.

You're just like him.

No I'm not.

Sure, I also know that dirty side streets beckon me. I refuse to walk them. I've fought myself with bare knuckles in the mud and it's kept me from cheating on Lydia. Still, in my heart, I know the tugs won't go away. Every time I beat them down, they come back stronger. Before I know it, I'm wearing women's clothes again, dreaming of having a vagina. And even though the tugs and pulls have waned of late, I know they'll return.

What then, now that I know this about Tom Terrific?

Am I destined to be like him? To give in to myself and destroy what I've achieved? To destroy myself?

I quickly do the math. I'm thirty-three years old, and statistically, I could live to be eighty.

That's another forty-seven years of fighting myself.

How the hell are you going to do that, Krug?

I fall back against the cushions on a hideous yellow and brown Mediterranean-style love seat. It all seems so impossible—my father's failed past and my questionable future.

I'm not him, I say to myself. *I'll never be him.*

I wish I believed me.

SEVEN: *Knollwood*

It was the ugliest house in the neighborhood, if not in all of Cedar Rapids.

"I know there's a lot to be desired about it," Lydia said.

We stood on a long, cracked driveway and looked toward a two-story monstrosity of peeling paint, broken windows, Amazonian evergreens, and curled screens.

Without taking a breath, she added, "But, Bo, it has *character.*"

"*Character?*" I moaned. "That ain't character. That's a bottomless money pit."

"Can we buy it anyway?"

I moaned again. We had looked for weeks without finding anything close.

Aw shit.

"Yes, if that's what you really want."

"Yippee!"

In May of 1988, we dived into restoring the seventy-year-old former farmhouse. It was hardwood floored and framed by towering shag bark hickories, resting on three-quarters of an acre on Knollwood Drive, the ugly duckling among gorgeous swans in the city's most exclusive old-home neighborhood.

Together, Lydia and I stripped wallpaper, sanded walls, rehabbed windows, and ripped out carpeting to make Knollwood a solid manifestation of our dream for a life done right—where Lydia and I cherished each other, where our children would be loved and attended to, and where Daddy would come home every night on time, sober.

I found new energy and fell into *us,* Krug and King, the high school romance that had made it. Knollwood was a fresh start, and I mustered amazing strength—call it prairie stoicism—to stuff any thought about clean lines.

One side of a dilapidated front porch soon became a stunning sunroom; the other side, an extended living room with curtain-free floor-to-ceiling windows. A cracking red kitchen turned into a blonde cooking and eating space. A few years later, we transformed a rutty backyard into a two-story 1,200-square-foot addition, with master bedroom and fireplace-adorned family room.

By the time we were done, Knollwood had been transformed into a beautiful bird, with its own nest of red, yellow, and pink wildflowers in the front yard, lovingly tended to by Lydia.

"Isn't it beautiful?" Lydia said one day, stepping back to admire our work.

"Yes. It damn well better be with all we've spent."

Lydia found work as a women's clothes buyer at a downtown department store. I went with a ten-attorney firm, Littleton & Davis, doing car accident whiplash cases. This was a far cry from the death-and-maiming cases I had handled in Boston.

"It's like going from driving a Cadillac to riding a bicycle," I complained.

"Give it time, Bo. You're a great lawyer, and they'll give you better cases once they figure that out." Lydia grabbed my arm. "It'll work out. I just know."

I quickly discovered just how small the Cedar Rapids legal pond could be. The local attorneys—most of them University of Iowa Law School alums, the place I had passed up in favor of BC Law—weren't impressed by my pedigree.

I was a month into the job when I visited another law office for the deposition of my client, a woman who had run a red light and banged into the client of Jack, an attorney at another law firm. We were fighting about whether my client had to cough up a document that had nothing to do with how the accident happened.

"Counsel, you may have done it that way in Boston," Jack said, "but that's not how we do it in Cedar Rapids. It would do you well to brush up on how we practice law *here*."

"I don't care what *your* practice is," I shot back. I whipped off my glasses, one street dog staring down another street dog.

This only made things worse. Jack strutted to my side of the table and stopped a half foot from me.

"You know, we have twenty-six lawyers in this firm who can't wait to take you on," he said.

"That doesn't impress me." I glared back.

I reported the incident to Darwin Rudd, the lead partner at Littleton & Davis. Darwin, bald and soft-spoken, was a respected elder in the city's legal community.

"Darwin," I urged, "this wasn't my fault. I can't help how that asshole reacted."

Darwin winced at "asshole."

"I know it wasn't your fault," he said, frowning. "Still, it could affect our relationship with that firm. You need to be less aggressive in how you handle things."

Oh boy.

The message was clear: back off, blend in, don't make waves. All things contrary to my nature and something that lawyers at Lewis & Bruce wouldn't go for in a million years. I left Darwin's office wondering if I had made a huge mistake by escaping to Iowa.

Then I got lucky.

A new railroad in Iowa, the Midwest Railway Company, called Littleton & Davis in search of a railroad lawyer willing to go for the jugular.

"I can do that," I assured.

Before long, I was defending lawsuits against the MRC and winning. I tried five cases in six months, and won four of them outright. I settled the fifth on great terms.

"Ed, I think you care more about this company than just about anyone who works here," MRC's president said as we basked in the victory glow of a favorable verdict.

I had found my groove, but it came with a price. I was back to ten-year-old kids playing around railroad cars that suddenly moved, kids who ran home screaming, "Mommy! Mommy!" with one less arm. There were teenagers who lost feet and hands because they cut through railroad yards at three in the morning.

In one case, I deposed the father of a fourteen-year-old amputee and asked an adroit question: "Who were you with when you received the telephone call about your son's accident?" Both his wife and I discovered that he'd been cheating with an office secretary. The wife later left him—a chain reaction family tragedy, courtesy of Krug's quality interrogation skills.

I don't care, I thought. *I can't control what people do.*

I even tried a case against one of those twenty-six lawyers that Jack had advertised were lying in wait, ready to take me on. This time, however, I represented MRC against another railroad in a big business dispute. I kicked the other attorney's ass and won $7 million for MRC.

"You're brilliant!" Lydia cheered as we drank champagne.

Having a good client like MRC helped convince Littleton & Davis to make me a partner. No longer on salary, chasing time took on a different dimension. Now, I was working for *me.* After paying firm overhead and taxes, every dollar I billed and collected went into *my* pocket. Since most civil trial work involves preparing and examining paper—letters, depositions, expert reports—I could make money anywhere, at any time: at home, on a plane, even at the beach, twenty-four hours a day if I desired.

Krug, the sky's the limit on how much you can make.

I smiled. Having money was one more degree of separation from Tom Terrific. Besides, time spent working meant my mind was occupied with something other than thoughts of clean lines.

I told myself a thousand times, *An idle mind is the Devil's playground.*

Suddenly, I had the answer: I'd beat clean-line urges and gut tugs by overloading on work.

In the process, something went missing. I stopped quoting Bobby Kennedy and started reading mutual fund reports. I nodded in agreement as clients, all white men with money, bemoaned the government. I slid the election booth curtain shut and pulled the Republican lever.

It's okay, I told myself. *This is how success looks. It's all about the* Grand Plan. *The fucking* Grand Plan.

I met Drew Bloom at a neighborhood dinner. Like me, he had grown up in Iowa, moved away after college, and returned for a less pressurized life. He was married with two children and headed a local charity.

Drew was the nonprofit version of Ed Krug: driven, sometimes abrupt, but otherwise very personable, especially when the bottom line depended on glad-handing potential money sources. We both wrote as a hobby. Soon we were close platonic friends and good for a lunch or after-work drink. He wasn't a Thap—no one could be—but it was nice to have someone other than Lydia around to talk, or whine, to.

Over lunch one day, Drew confided, "My wife has an anger streak that borders on abuse. Most of the time, everything's fine, but then something, like the kids, or her job, or me, will set her off. It could be the smallest thing. It gets pretty ugly."

I felt for him. "Have you tried counseling?"

"She won't go."

"What are you going to do?"

"I don't know. My parents divorced when I was my son's age, and that was hell. I don't want to put him and my daughter through it."

I couldn't imagine being stuck in a marriage where your spouse's behavior was unpredictable, and where divorce was a constant consideration.

Lydia and I would never have that kind of marriage.

We couldn't get pregnant, so we consulted doctors. One ultrasound and a laparoscopy later, Lydia remained un-pregnant. We never found out why.

As a stopgap, I surprised Lydia with a puppy. A dog was absolutely the last thing I wanted in a newly remodeled house with refinished wood floors. Lydia had been asking for months, but I resisted until it looked like she'd start to mother *me*.

"You got me a puppy!" Lydia yelled as she walked into the house on a Saturday evening after work. In a second, she was on the kitchen floor wrapped around me, crying. She hugged a yappy golden retriever pup that jumped, jumped, jumped.

"You're the best Bo that I could ever ask for," she said between tears.

She named the dog Kelsey.

Kelsey worked as a child substitute only for a short while. Soon we were back to the desperate desire for a small human in the house.

By then, we had gotten to know our next-door neighbors. They had a beautiful black-haired daughter, Erica, three years old. Both Evan and Shelly were blonde-haired Norwegians, so I figured something was up.

"Erica's Korean; she's adopted," Shelly said matter-of-factly one afternoon as we raked leaves along a chain-link fence line.

Adopted? I hadn't ever considered it; no one in either the Krug or King families was adopted. It seemed so radical: bringing someone different into your home, a genetic stranger. As your child? Loving them forever?

I watched Evan play with Erica in their front yard. He did it all— dancing, tickling, and carrying her on his shoulders. An ecstatic dad and his adoring daughter. They were *normal*, just like the Andersons, the five-kid, all-birth-children clan on the other side of our house.

"What if we adopted?" It was out of the blue. Lydia and I were three streets over from Knollwood wrestling with no-way-will-I-ever-heel Kelsey on a chilly fall evening.

The question threw Lydia back. I saw wheels turn.

"Really, Bo?"

"Yes, really. With my genes, I'm not all that crazy about having another Ed Krug running around anyway. Can you say, 'dysfunctional'?"

Lydia laughed. "I don't think so; it's only your father who has that title."

By early January, 1990, we had initial paperwork from the same adoption agency that had placed Erica with Evan and Shelly. After an application and references, there would be a home study by a social worker. If we were accepted, we would need to attend a two-day adoption orientation class.

Then January 31—a day of infamy for the Krug family—happened. We had barely started the paperwork when my father killed himself.

A month after the suicide, I sat in the sunroom filling out a family history form, a part of the adoption application. I got to the question, "Please tell us about your parents and how they shaped your ideas of parenting."

I hadn't expected such a simple and straightforward question. It threw me.

I felt a sharp knife cut in the shallow of my chest. I tried to keep a tight hold, but lost it to wetness, then tears, and finally, uncontrollable sobbing; my first since the suicide.

Lydia, in another part of the house, came running.

"What is it, what's wrong?"

"It's my father again," I choked. "His suicide could ruin everything. What if they think that I can't handle the stress of parenting or the stress of life, like him?"

I couldn't get my bawling under control.

"Oh, my Bo."

Lydia pulled me in and rocked gently. "You're going to be the best dad. You aren't your father and you'll never be him. It'll be okay and we'll have our family, I promise." She was crying now too.

I buried myself into her. I prayed that she'd hold on forever.

"I just don't want to be like him," I whispered, near-confessing.

"What are you talking about? You're the most opposite person from your father I know," she answered. "That's the last thing anyone would ever say about you."

I thought, *If she only knew.*

By the time my crying died down, I had realized that at some point I'd be asked something like, *Is there any reason why you might not make a good parent?*

How would I handle that with my do-right character?

Yes, remodeling Knollwood and pushing my career had occupied my mind—for now—but those damn clean-line fantasies were still under the surface, lurking, killer fish-like, waiting to attack.

It wasn't as if I could casually admit to the social worker, "Sure, let me tell you about the heap of lingerie from Boston that I've got stashed in a box at the back of a cabinet in the far corner of the basement."

Yet, I was certain that loving Lydia, and her love for me, and our love for a baby, would trump anything in my head.

It had to.

Love conquers all, I assured myself.

As Lydia and I embraced in silence, with our hearts beating in perfect rhythm, I resolved that I wasn't going to screw everything up by telling anyone, especially some social worker, that I often dreamed of having a vagina.

The adoption agency assigned a social worker, Lisa, who set an appointment for the home study. Lydia and I cleaned and shined, vacuumed under beds, and displayed family pictures.

Lisa showed up more hippie than social worker. With flowing blonde hair, wire-rim glasses, and ankle-length floral skirt, she exuded compassion and cheer.

After a tour of the house, we settled in for the big interview. We insisted that Lisa take the most comfortable chair. With Lydia and me on a newly scrubbed white couch holding hands, Team Krug was ready.

Lisa wanted our life stories. She brightened at hearing that we started as high school sweethearts. From there, Lydia detailed a strong Lutheran family that lived by clear and unambiguous rules demarcated by black-and-white lines.

"My parents were always there for me," she said, projecting.

Lisa jotted in a notebook. She beamed.

Next it was time for the black sheep, the Krugs. I got Tom Terrific on the table first thing.

I confessed, "My father committed suicide six weeks ago."

Lisa's pen went still. "Oh, I'm so sorry, Ed. How horrible." She reached for my knee. "I'm sure this has been hard for you and your family."

"Thank you, it has been difficult," I answered. "Most of all, I'm afraid that this will disqualify us."

Again—damn it—I started to tear up.

Lisa shook her head. "No, it doesn't work like that. We know families are made up of a lot of different people. Just because someone robs a bank doesn't mean everyone else in the family is a bank robber."

I felt a rush of cool air.

Pen resumed, Lisa said, "Let's talk about your parents and who else may have been important in your life."

I cautiously poured out the story about my father and mother—his drinking and her denial and extravagancies—and quickly added the contrasts. "I've worked hard not to be like them. I got an education, we don't use credit cards, and I talk with Lydia about everything."

Well, maybe the last part wasn't entirely true.

Lisa looked up from her pad. "Other than your father, who else was important in your life as you were growing up?"

I thought for a minute. Something clicked: *Uncle Ed.*

How could I have forgotten?

"I had my Great-Uncle Ed; I'm his namesake," I said. "He's still alive, in Connecticut. When I was a kid, we spent a lot of time together. One of the things I loved about him was that he didn't drink."

Lisa penned intensely. In my near panic over Tom Terrific, I had almost overlooked Uncle Ed, my savior.

I told Lisa about The Country, and even mentioned the dirt-pile lesson. "Uncle Ed's like my real father," I said.

Lydia squeezed my hand.

After twenty minutes of back and forth on Uncle Ed and Nan and Poppy, and even Rita and Rich, Lisa pronounced, "I don't see a problem with your father's suicide. It looks like you've had many good people in your life. I'm comfortable going forward."

I breathed her words in. *Maybe Tom Terrific wouldn't destroy the* Grand Plan *after all.*

The questions continued for almost three hours. How did Lydia and I resolve our differences? What would we do for child care? Were we willing to take a child with special needs?

Each answer garnered more ink and smiles.

Finally, Lisa started to gather her things. I thought we were home free. Ten seconds later, she sat back down. Notebook and pen appeared once more.

"I almost forgot," she said, as she uncapped the pen. "Is there anything you've not told me, good or bad, that if you were in my shoes, you'd want to know?"

Not quite *the* question I had dreaded, but close enough.

In a split second, a hundred memories went through my head—me in my bed at Kent Drive plotting an escape from alcoholic quicksand; kissing Lydia for the first time; giggling with her on the night before our wedding; Lydia and me in a dust fog as we sanded walls in the baby's room, dreaming of *our child.* I thought of how Lydia would make a fantastic mother and how I might be a good father.

The right kind of father.

No way am I going to keep that from happening.

Before I could say anything, Lydia replied, "You've got everything."

I looked at Lisa and added, "No, there's nothing I can think of."

I felt like I had just lied to my second grade teacher.

Lisa recapped the pen with extra gusto. "Great," she replied. "I don't think there'll be a problem. Assuming there aren't any surprises, we could have a baby placed with you in five or six months."

Lydia gripped my hand so hard that it hurt. "That would be wonderful!" she said. I gripped back so that she wouldn't float off the couch.

We walked Lisa to her car and exchanged hugs. As we waved goodbye, Lydia and I exhaled. "That wasn't as bad as I expected," she said.

"You're right," I answered. "It wasn't bad."

"Kruggie, it's not working with Julie anymore," Thap reported in a worn-out voice.

We were parked next to a field of corn stubble in the middle of Nebraska on a pale October day. We had roamed for hours with beers hidden on our laps, not far from a Holiday Inn, the midpoint between Cedar Rapids and Denver.

"But Thap, you've only been married six years," I answered. "Don't you think you need to give it more time?"

By then, Thap and Julie had a son, Justin.

"I *have* tried," he argued back. "She wants to control everything: how Justin dresses, what he eats, how much time he's outside playing. It's driving me crazy."

"Have you talked to her about this?"

"Yeah, but it doesn't do any good. Being married isn't anything like I thought it would be."

I felt for Thap. He had always been a free spirit, and now he was caged. Still, he had made a promise to Julie when they married; I was a witness, I reminded him. He was supposed to hang in and make it work.

"I think you need to give it more time, Thapper." I chugged the rest of my beer. "Try marriage counseling, take a trip just with Julie, have more sex, whatever."

"Don't even talk about sex," he shot back. "That's nonexistent."

"Well, you need to try harder." I wasn't about to let him off the hook.

"I don't know, Ed. I don't think I've got it in me."

He was hurting in a way I hadn't seen before.

Thap took my advice and did try again. He and Julie went to counseling and gave each other more time to adjust to marriage and parenthood. In the end, they weren't a good fit and Thap moved out. By then, there was a second son.

A part of me felt bad for Thap. The other part was less forgiving. *Jesus Christ, Thap, how could you let this happen?*

———————

In late August, 1990, I was at my office when Lisa, the social worker, called. I felt excitement as soon as I heard her voice.

"Ed, I tried Lydia but I couldn't get her. I've got wonderful news: we have a daughter for you, four months old. You'll have her in a couple weeks."

I jumped out of my chair and shouted into the phone, "Hooray!" My secretary came running, wondering. "That's absolutely fantastic, Lisa!" I happy-hollered.

Fifteen minutes later, I tracked down Lydia at work. "We've got a baby girl!" I yelled. I wanted to jump through the phone so that we could touch.

"Oh Bo, I can't believe it! I can't wait!" She repeated "I can't wait" a hundred times in the five-minute phone call.

On the night before our new daughter came home to us, I drove to Beaver Park in Cedar Rapids. I stopped next to a battered green dumpster and made sure the coast was clear. From the trunk of my car, I took a box filled with my lingerie stash—everything going back to Newberry Street in Boston—and tossed it into the dumpster. I slammed the lid shut.

I won't need this anymore now that I'm going to be a father. This shit's over.

The next evening, we met an agency escort at the Des Moines airport. She gently handed Lydia a smiling black-haired girl, whom we named Emily.

"Oh Emily! You are so beautiful," Lydia said softly.

I'd never seen Lydia happier. It took ten minutes of gentle nudging before Lydia let me hold Emily. Cradled in my arms, my new daughter melted my heart.

Two hours later, we stopped at the end of the Knollwood driveway. The car's headlights revealed a banner, "Welcome Home Emily!" strung across the garage door, courtesy of my sister Jacki.

A few days later, Lydia and I agreed that she wouldn't go back to her buyer's job. It would be quite a change for Lydia, who had often proclaimed, "I'll never be a stay-at-home mom."

"Never say never," I offered as I watched Lydia give Emily a bottle.

I approached fatherhood with vigor. I changed my work habits; I didn't work less, but instead adjusted my hours. I got in the office at five in the morning and was home by five at night. I wanted to make sure I didn't miss anything—feeding and bathing, and then as Emily grew, reading to her book after book, many of which she memorized. Before long, Emily rode on my shoulders, as I hopped, "Boop, Boop, Boop!" to belly laughs.

"You're such a good dad," Lydia said one evening, not long after Emily had switched from crib to big-girl bed. When I had an out-of-town trial that lasted two weeks, I took along a picture of Emily on the back-yard swing sporting the world's prettiest smile.

Every morning and evening of the trial, I looked at that picture. I thought, *For you, my beloved daughter, I'll do anything.*

It didn't take much cajoling to get Uncle Ed to fly out for Emily's first Christmas. A Redcap delivered him via courtesy airport wheelchair, with cane in lap.

"Hey big guy, good to see you," I said, as I helped him stand.

Barely erect, my uncle asked, "Where's dat new gret, gret, neese of mine?"

Apparently, my status had changed a bit.

A half hour later, Uncle Ed sat in the Knollwood living room, a glass of skim milk at his side. Emily, asleep in a pink blanket, was curled on his lap. My uncle adjusted from one arm to the other, uncertain about positioning, and worried about dropping. I snapped the picture of a large human with infant, and the beauty of a rare smile across my great-uncle's face.

In that instant, a circle closed.

I entertained Uncle Ed for several days doing what he loved. "Driive mi around, Beeter. Le-t me tee more of tis city of yurs." We stopped for coffee and sweets. We sat saying nothing as Emily napped nearby.

On the last day, at the airport, I waited with him until they called his flight. Slowly, with hand gripping cane, he stood.

"Do you want me to get a Redcap with a wheelchair?"

"Nupe, I'm gud."

I reached up for a soft hug. I didn't want to throw him off balance.

"Thank you for coming. It was wonderful to see you with Emily."

"I woodn't have mit it," he said. He stood solid.

"I love you, you know that." I got near tippy-toe. I squeezed with both arms, and took him in one last time.

"I know, Beeter. I love you, ta."

I pulled back. His face was scrunched and wet, but he was trying not to let it show. He turned and started for the gate, rocking slowly. He glanced back just before going around a corner. It wasn't long enough for me to wave.

Five weeks after that, Rita called. Another stroke. It didn't look good.

I called the hospital room that evening and was surprised when Uncle Ed picked up.

"What are you doing answering the phone?" I was amazed.

"No one's dere," he whispered. "I taught it mit be you."

"Hang in there," I said.

I woke up in the middle of that night and decided that I'd fly to Connecticut. I had a deposition that I needed to cancel.

At eight in the morning, I called the opposing attorney. "My uncle's dying and I need to go to him," I said.

The other attorney growled back, "I object to any postponement. Your uncle's extended family. That's not a reason to delay the case. It'll prejudice my client."

If I could have done it, I would have strangled that guy. Instead, I hung up.

A few minutes later, just before I dialed the airline, Rich telephoned.

"Eddie, he's gone. About twenty minutes ago. Rita and I were just leaving the house to spend the day at the hospital when the nurse called."

I pushed the phone away from my ear. I sighed a Country-sized sigh. I knew this day would eventually come. I knew that I would hurt like hell. And I knew that I'd miss my uncle for the rest of my life.

One other thing that I knew: Rich's call came on January 31, 1991, the first anniversary of Tom Terrific's suicide.

Two years after our trip to the Des Moines airport, we were back; this time to meet Lily.

"She's so small," Emily said when she saw her baby sister for the first time.

"You were that small once," I answered. I poked at Emily's belly and got a giggle in return.

In fact, Lily *was* small, too small. She had serious health problems overseas that required surgery and multiple hospitalizations. She eventually ended up in an orphanage, housed with a dozen other babies in a cavernous room.

"She's going to die before she gets here," I worried to Lydia after reading a medical record from the agency. The diagnosis: "Failure to thrive."

Miraculously, the agency put her on a plane and sent her to us. Lily was five months old and weighed barely ten pounds.

Incredibly, Lydia quickly figured out the problem—lactose intolerance.

A month later, we had a butterball on our hands.

"Your spirit kept you alive," I told Lily when she was old enough to understand. "Mommy helped, for sure, but it was your spirit that kept you hanging on."

Now, there were two girls for bedtime reading. "Read it again, Daddy!" Lily liked to say. Evening baths became giggle frolics—in and out of the tub. No sooner would I get the girls dried off, and they'd bolt out the bathroom door sans Pull-Ups or pajamas.

"Naked baby alert, Mommy! Watch out, there are naked babies loose!"

With a full contingent now, every summer included a road trip to Sister Bay in Door County, Wisconsin. We stayed at the same hotel in the same room the same week of every year.

"The girls will appreciate this when they're older," Lydia said one radiant afternoon. She was sunning on a cream-colored chaise lounge at the edge of a pool. I was spread out as well, enjoying a moment of peace. Both girls were maneuvering in the pool's shallow end. In a second, there would be a call, "Daddy, come swim with us."

In the parking lot, the car was loaded with bikes: Lydia's and mine, and tag-alongs for both girls. On every trip, we rode the canopy-covered trails of Peninsula State Park, racing to see who could make it to a rocky beach on the other side of the park first. Emily, always my shotgun, loved to yell, "Enchilada"—don't ask me why—as we passed the losers.

Lydia never liked second place, and I'd hear a half-serious plea, "Lily, you need to pedal!"

Amid the rocks, we picnicked on Lydia-made turkey sandwiches. There was rock skipping and beach combing. "Yuck, Dad! Come look, a dead seagull!"

At night, we walked into town, with sweaters wrapped around the girls' waists, ready for the night chill. The hotel was a good half mile from the nearest restaurant. The girls didn't mind the walk—there were wild-flowers to pick on the way in and full bellies on the way out. Sometimes, one girl or the other, or both, finagled piggyback rides.

The blacktop wove past flowered fields and through thickets of trees. Big bulbs on weathered poles, not exactly modern streetlights, helped fend off the dark. Our shadows danced from one light to the next, dark-ness-spawned body doubles.

I raced ahead and stomped on Emily's shadow.

"Got your shadow!" I yelled.

An Emily belly laugh erupted. "No, you don't, Daddy. I've got *your* shadow." Emily jumped one way, and then another, vying for my shadow.

"Ouch, you got me!"

"Hey girlie, I've got your shadow." It was Lydia, now into the fray, hopping squarely onto Emily's silhouette.

"What about my shadow?" Lily pleaded. "Aren't you going to chase mine?"

"Oh Lily, I'll always get your shadow," I answer-stomped.

We teased and high-stepped, and giggled and laughed, all the way to the hotel. Our shadows were plain worn out by the time we got to the room.

On a glorious Sunday afternoon in October, 1993, the kind that sticks with you forever, Lydia and I found time alone. While the girls napped, we crawled through what had been a second-floor rear window of Knollwood. Lydia cradled a bottle of chardonnay; I carried two glasses. We were in the midst of building the two-story addition—the final step in transforming the monstrosity. In what would be the master bedroom, near where our bed would go, Lydia and I dusted a spot to sit. We gazed out newly framed window openings and smelled the tangled sweetness of freshly cut two-by-fours. Outside, rakes scraped acorns and crinkly oak leaves as neighbors worked their yards. Every so often, a dog barked in the distance, adding tempo to the moment.

We nuzzled against a plywood wall and took inventory of all that had happened in the five years since we moved to Knollwood. It was a victory moment, a time to savor the *Grand Plan.*

"I love you so much, Bo," Lydia said. She gently planted her head on her spot. "We're so lucky."

"That we are," I answered. I rubbed her leg. "All four of us are the cat's meow now."

Lydia sighed.

Maybe it was the way the sun hit the leaves, or perhaps it was the sense of accomplishment, or simply the feeling of *love* and the idea that we'd built something great, or all of it combined, I don't know; of everything in my life, this is the one moment I'd return to if a magic time machine ever suddenly appeared.

I felt the gentle weight of Lydia's head, and I reached for her hand. Fingers slid between fingers. We didn't speak.

Gloriousness. Truly.

A thought flicked across my brain. White lace panties. I had bought them earlier that week while out of town on business. Now, they were buried in the trunk of my car—the first installment on a new stash.

I had been lingerie sober ever since the night before Emily came home to us. Like some repugnant houseguest, the desire for clean lines had shown up, yet again. This time it came with even greater ferocity and much less mercy. I tried like hell to resist. After months of gut-pounding, I gave in.

Silently desperate, I squeezed Lydia's hand and held. I thought that if we touched long enough, I'd absorb her commitment and fortitude; they seemed to come to her so easily.

Five minutes later, I released. I hadn't absorbed a damn thing.

That left one thought: *You really are like him. You're going to fuck it all up just like he did.*

EIGHT: *Therapy*

Larson Williams had started out as a Lutheran minister. Dissatisfied, he transitioned to therapist.

I found him in the Yellow Pages in late 1993. One small ad stood out: "At-home office, private waiting area." It listed a man's name and number.

Perfect.

A man would better understand another man's sexual issues, plus there wouldn't be a big waiting room where I'd be at risk that someone—a client, a neighbor, or worse yet, one of Lydia's friends—would see me.

I had found a stealth therapist to cure me of my stealth problem.

I said I'd pay by personal check because I didn't want my health insurer knowing. I was certain that, at most, we'd meet two or three times and I'd be fixed. I just needed some good advice and perspective. Any therapist could give that, right?

Larson's basement office was lined with floor-to-ceiling bookshelves. His desk was pushed against a center wall. I sat in a big stuffed chair at the end of the desk where I looked up. I wasn't used to occupying the lowest spot in the room.

I guessed Larson was in his early fifties. Sometimes his head swayed as he talked. It made me think: human bobble doll.

Larson asked, "On the telephone you said something about thoughts that were bothering you. What kind of thoughts?"

Naively, I hadn't prepared for such a basic question. It sent me into self-preservation mode—a red light activated, an alarm sounded, "Danger, Danger."

Suddenly, I was in front of a cold steel door. Was I really going to open it? Would I ever get it closed if I did?

I thought about Lydia, Emily, and little Lily—the girls of Knoll-wood—innocents caught up in the Ed Krug vortex. No, I had to talk. Besides, talking was so unlike my father.

Slowly, hesitantly, the words came.

"I'm here because I can't stop thinking... about... having sex with a man while I'm dressed as a ... woman," I blurted.

I looked for a reaction—a stiffening, a grimace, or even a bobble shift, anything on the you're-fucking-nuts scale. Nothing. I went on.

"I've had these thoughts, fantasies really, for years, going back to law school. I don't want the thoughts anymore. I'm married to Lydia, the greatest woman in the world. We've got two little girls whom I adore. I don't want to do something stupid like cheat on them. I also don't want to get AIDS, and end up killing Lydia."

I paused for breath and rubbed my arm.

"I cross-dress," I said. It was the first time I'd ever spoken those words out loud. "I love the clean lines of panties on my body; they make me feel like a woman, like I really have a vagina. I think about men adoring and wanting me as a woman."

Another breath and my last salvo.

"I want you to give me a strategy to deal with these thoughts, some way to get them out of my head, or to at least control them. I need your help to stay married; I'm not looking for a way to leave my wife and family. Can you do that for me?"

I shuddered. In less than five minutes, I had laid out decades of hidden desires. For a split second, I was proud of myself. More to the point: now I'd get the solution to my problem, and be done with this misery.

Larson, completely mum, scrawled notes on a yellow pad. After an eternity, he asked, "How many times have you had sex with a man while wearing women's clothes?"

"*None.* That's *why* I'm here. I want you to keep me from doing that."

I didn't try to hide the sarcasm. I thought, *What's there not to understand here?*

"When did these thoughts begin and how often do you have them?"

I gave him the story about Jacki's underwear drawer and how things had evolved to where, a hundred times a day, I fantasized about men salivating over a feminine me. I told him about my father's drinking and serial cheating; in my mind, it was all related.

"I don't want to be like my father," I said. "Still, that hasn't stopped me from keeping a stash of bras and panties in the trunk of my car."

Larson wrote. He didn't look up.

I continued. "Off and on, I've bought gay magazines or magazines of men wearing women's lingerie. Once I even rented a video of men having sex with women dressed in lingerie. I imagined myself as one of the women in the movie."

More note taking, more silence.

Then there was my gut. "It keeps tugging at me," I said.

"What's the tug about? That you need to have sex with men?" he asked.

"No," I answered. "It's more like I need a different life, that the life I'm leading now isn't right. The tugging is far worse than the sexual fantasies. It's killing me, actually. How could anyone not love my life?"

"When do you have these thoughts about needing another life?"

"Lately, they pop into my head all the time. Just this morning, on the way to work, my brain derailed. I couldn't stop thinking, *'You've got to have your own life.'*"

"Have you told Lydia about these thoughts?"

"No way," I answered. "Why would I do that? It'd only scare her to death. Besides, her first question would be, 'Now what?' I don't ever want to answer that question."

Larson flipped through pages of notes. I looked away and wondered whether seeing him—or for that matter, anyone—was a good idea after all. Maybe I could have handled this another way.

I heard Larson's voice. "How do you feel when you wear women's underwear?"

Without thinking, I said, "It makes me feel wonderful."

What did I just say?

I finished the thought. "When I look in a mirror, I see someone completely different—not a man, but a woman. I know, that's crazy. I can't be a woman. There's no way."

I told Larson that a couple years before this, I had shaved off my mustache. The public explanation: I wanted to be more likeable to juries. The private one: it made the mirrored views of womanhood slightly more realistic.

I didn't mention one more reason; without a mustache, I looked a little bit less like my father.

"Another thing," I said, now spent. "I feel guilty as hell thinking that I need my own life."

Larson put his pad aside and sat up. He spoke head-on.

"Guilt is a powerful force," he answered. "Don't ever underestimate how it can dictate what you do."

"I love Lydia," I said. "I'm here because of love, not guilt."

Larson sort of smiled. He asked about my law practice and how much I worked.

"I get to the office by five every morning. I'm there six days a week. I go in early so that I can get home to see my daughters."

"What does Lydia say about your work hours?"

"I can count on one hand the number of times she's ever complained," I said.

"How would you describe the amount of stress in your life? How would you rate it?"

Oh boy.

We were finishing the two-story addition to Knollwood. I was the only breadwinner. I had twenty cases scheduled for trial in the next two years. Most clients wanted something done like yesterday.

"Have you ever seen anyone to help manage stress?"

"No, never."

Larson speculated that the fantasies were some kind of relief valve. Maybe it was my way of getting something for me. This theory ignored the question of *why* I started wearing lingerie in sixth grade. Still, it seemed to make at least some sense; for sure the crap in my head had gotten worse as my career had progressed.

Then again, maybe I had just gotten older.

"I think we need to explore how stress affects you emotionally and sexually," he said with a head bobble.

I looked at the clock. We were out of time.

I handed him my check.

Larson summarized. "We'll address stress-reduction strategies when we meet next."

I felt better.

On my feet, I shook Larson's hand. I was almost out the door when I remembered something I had forgotten to ask.

"How many men have you treated who have my problem, you know, who dress in women's clothes and fantasize about having sex with other men?"

Larson paused as if he was mentally reviewing files.

"I don't think any," he said. "I've had some patients who cross-dress, but no one who has ever talked about wanting 'clean lines' on his body."

That's okay, I thought. *Maybe this really is about stress after all.* I turned and walked through the door. It felt like we were off to a good start.

I saw Larson for eight years. Sometimes it was weekly; at other times, I went for months without an appointment.

We tried various approaches to my "issues."

One plan involved cutting back at work and spending more time with Emily and Lily. The girls and I did "double headers": Chuck E. Cheese for lunch pizza and games, and then to the Play Station—a tunnel and slide maze—where I'd be "it," crawling on hands and knees trying to tag either girl. Other days were "triple headers," where we threw in a visit to the local Disney Store, which was always good for an overpriced video or stuffed animal.

Sunday evenings always involved a Dairy Queen run. "Okay, ladies, it's DQ time," I would announce. Emily and Lily would be in the car before I could even put on my sandals.

We went camping. I bought a tent, a sleeps-eight-people geometric maze of poles and rope that I could never completely figure out. Putting it up was a guaranteed forty-five-minute ordeal.

Emily and Lily didn't care; camping was special because I had declared, "Girls, all rules are suspended at the campsite." This meant they could eat whatever junk food in whatever amount they wanted.

Sometimes, we played Barbies. I even had my own dolls, all variations of Ken. "That's how it has to be," Emily said. I went along with whatever story line Emily or Lily concocted, until I fell asleep on the floor of Emily's room, exhausted from everything else.

One summer afternoon, the girls and I sprawled on the backyard deck and watched puffy clouds float by in a crystal blue sky.

"Look Daddy, that cloud's the shape of Snowflake," Emily pointed, referring to the originally iceberg-white-now-gray teddy bear that never left her side.

Not to be outdone, Lily piped up, "There's a cloud that looks like a dragon with steam coming out its mouth."

I gently nudged each girl to a shoulder. Of all the places in the world, Knollwood was where I belonged. It was where I mattered and where I was loved and adored—as a dad and husband.

I smiled and soaked up the sun's warmth. I wanted to bottle that scene and save it for the next time my gut began to tug; then, I'd have something to reach for, something to drink for fortitude to beat back the unrelenting thought that I needed another life.

Later that afternoon, the girls and I drew on the new driveway, another money pit improvement. The virgin concrete was a wonderful canvas. We had big, thick sticks of chalk—pinks, lavenders, blues, yellows— all of life's luminous colors.

Emily shouted, "Daddy, let's draw a rainbow!"

We went at it. One traced lines, the other colored pink and yellow. The third, blue.

"Let me do the yellow," Lily said. She pushed her way into the middle.

My hands were covered with pink chalk. "Keep going, girls," I said. "We've got plenty of concrete."

An hour later, we stood back to admire. A brilliant rainbow had materialized across the entire driveway. Emily and Lily, their sundresses chalk-covered, giggled and danced in celebration.

"Rainbows are God's way of smiling," I said.

In the weeks after that, driveway love letters greeted me when I pulled in after work: "Welcome Home Daddy." "Hugs." "Love."

Instead of television, we had family time: evenings of game playing and children's book reading. We played "Red Light, Green Light" in the foyer, the point where old house ended and new began. Emily stood with her back to us and yelled out, "Green light, green light" as Lydia, Lily, and I crept toward her.

Suddenly, we heard, "Red light!" Emily wheeled around and pointed:

"You need to start all over, Daddy!"

Lydia smirked. I turned back.

Lily—never, ever deterred—kept creeping.

"Come on, Lily, get back here. Emily caught you too!"

If we weren't game playing—sometimes it was also "Simon Says"—
we acted out *The Wizard of Oz*. The girls always fought over who got to
play Dorothy. Usually, I was the Lion, but occasionally, I was Tin Man or
Scarecrow. Lydia made a great Witch: "Come here, my pretties!"

By the end of the night, giggling arm in arm, we skipped down a
Yellow Brick Road that had magically materialized in the foyer.

Spent, Lydia and I collapsed on the living room floor. Emily and Lily
raced with stuffed animals. Silliness rang throughout the house.

My heart pumped emotion. *How in the world could I ever leave this?*
Never. I'll do whatever it takes to stay.

Months into Larson's plan, I learned that the less I worked, the more
stressed I became. The compartments in my life began to collide: Killer
Krug, the attack lawyer; Daddy, the devoted father; Bo, the loving husband;
and ominously, the person hidden inside me—was it truly female?

The gut tugging for another life continued, unabated. *This isn't who*
you are.

I agonized. *Will this shit ever end?*

I saw Larson. "This working-less-thing isn't helping. I still want
clean lines and another life."

We explored my anxieties, like my fear of making a mistake that
could cost a client its case, or worse yet, one that would get me sued for
malpractice. Larson's approach: was the negative consequence "prob-
able" or merely "possible"?

Almost everything fell into the "possible" category.

Whew.

While this strategy helped me manage my stress better, it didn't do
a thing to stop me from wanting clean lines.

"You need to tell Lydia about what you're thinking," Larson said
solemnly one session. "You owe it to her."

"Lars, I can't." I was irritated that he didn't understand. "It would
only scare her. I don't want to do that."

Still, I took a half step and told Lydia that I was seeing a therapist.

"It's so I can deal with work-related stress," I said, which was partly true, but mostly a lie.

"I think that's great, Bo. I don't want to lose you to a stroke or heart attack." She grabbed my hand and put it on her lap, and smiled.

Larson suggested another approach—a Hail Mary personalized "Ed Krug Twelve Step" plan. The First Step: I couldn't look at any more images of women in lingerie. The Victoria's Secret catalog was out. So was the Kohl's ad in the Sunday *Cedar Rapids Gazette*. By then, I had become attracted to all kinds of women's clothing, not just lingerie. I loved the thought of wearing a tight skirt and how it would complement the curves I yearned for.

After that, the target moved again, and I wanted to be the woman wearing the clothes.

Oh, I'd love to be her. She's gorgeous!

Every day, the mail carrier delivered wonderful catalogs—J. Crew, Banana Republic, Express—all with beautiful women in pretty clothes, just waiting for men to adore them.

I barely started the First Step and then gave up. It was no use trying. I couldn't stop lusting for clean lines.

———

I flew to Denver for an expert's deposition in the fall of 1994. I went early and spent the night at Thap's place in Boulder. By then, he was on his second marriage to a lovely woman named Barbara, whom everyone called "Bebo."

That evening, Thap and I walked Pearl Street, first for dinner and then drinks. Emboldened by alcohol, I let slip, "Why don't we find a club where I can dance with cute men?"

A part of me was shocked that I'd be so honest. Another part felt relief, even excitement, as if something deep inside had just seen the first glimmer of daylight.

Thap looked at me sideways. He grinned and let the subject drop. We talked about other things as we passed backpack-clad university students and couples exiting restaurants.

I soon returned to my cute men remark.

"Does it surprise you that I'd want to dance with a man?" I asked. I stopped walking. I was prepared to run in the opposite direction if he responded badly. We were outside a brew pub where band music shook the windows.

He answered with a wide smile, "Kruggie, it's fine with me whatever you want to do. I'm your buddy no matter what. I mean that."

Instantly, I felt a warmth that had nothing to do with the massive amount of alcohol coursing through me.

Thap opened the pub door and we walked in. The place was filled with men and women half our ages. We ordered drinks and found a place to sit. Soon, I was on a packed vibrating dance floor. Thap followed. I worked my way next to a gorgeous blonde-haired man—he couldn't have been more than twenty-two—who had been dancing with a couple of women. He turned toward me and gyrated. I moved my legs, and then my arms, a pathetic Watusi.

I'm doing it, I thought.

We danced for a song until it ended. The pretty man walked off the dance floor and never even glanced back.

I watched Thap dance with two women, having the time of his life. The women were laughing; I was sure at him. He didn't seem to mind.

I went back to our table and ordered another drink, excited by what had just happened. For the first time in my life, I had a glimpse of *what it could be like.* I had told my best friend something shocking and he didn't turn and run. I felt alive, and I wanted more.

By the end of the evening, I had confessed about my secret fantasizing—almost everything. I held back on telling Thap how I dreamt of clean lines; there would be no way he'd understand, and hell, I didn't completely understand it. Drunked up, I ran through Thap's kitchen at two in the morning wearing only white lacy panties, just to prove that I really was as screwed up as I claimed.

Thap laughed. "Put your pants back on and sit down," he ordered with spatula in hand. "The eggs and bacon are almost done."

The next morning we drove to a parking garage to retrieve Thap's car. I knew that I had to say something about my disclosure, but I didn't know what. As we got to Thap's car, I said, "I hope we're still good."

Thap didn't hesitate. "Yeah, we're good. It doesn't matter."

We said our goodbyes and I drove to Denver for my legal business. On the way, despite a head-pounding headache, I felt regret and joy. I was out in the open now and the vulnerability didn't feel good. Yet, I had bravely spoken the truth to my best friend and he didn't abandon me.

I had no clue where it would go from there.

I sat with the girls while they colored at the kitchen table. Emily, then five or six, filled in a *Beauty and the Beast* picture. She was meticulous with Belle's dress in pink Crayola. No hint of color crossed thick black lines. Next, it was onto the Beast, with a heavy brown. Again, one color never touched another.

"Do you think this looks good, Daddy?"

"Great job, honey." I meant it.

Lily colored her own Beast picture. She mixed red with brown. And borders? She couldn't have cared less.

Before Emily turned to the next page in her book, Lily reached over and put a small red smudge on the edge of Belle's dress.

"Lily, you ruined it," Emily yelled, instantly near tears. She tore the page out of the book and crumpled it.

Later, Emily became a wonderful dancer. She had a decade of instruction by the time she was a teen. Tall, beautiful, and flowing, she practiced dance routines for hours, one movement at a time, until there was absolute perfection. Every half inch off target, which wasn't often, bruised her ego.

"I'll never get it right!"

Ever the parent—but a struggling human, too—I thought, *Be happy with all your grace and beauty. You're an absolute delight to watch.*

Lily's personality also showed through. Her time-outs became passion-filled endurance contests: one, two, three, even five, hours of nonstop cry-whining. Years later, this morphed into the fine art of persistence: "Why can't I sleep in my closet? Why won't you let me ride my bike across town? What do you mean I can't apply for that deli job; after all, I'm twelve years old!"

Spirited and single-minded, Lily pushed the envelope and went outside every line. Yet, she remembered key words: "I'm sorry," spoken whenever the heat of the moment passed. It was another form of art: the art of doubling back, of making hearts whole.

"Look at our girls," I said to Lydia one day as they played together. "They're coming along."

"Yes," Lydia answered. "Much of it's because you're such a good dad."

I happy-sighed. She was being overly generous, but still, it was nice to hear.

The *Cedar Rapids Gazette* announced that it wanted to highlight families for a Sunday feature series. I decided to write about Red Light, Green Light and *The Wizard of Oz*. I thought that if our family was recognized for being special, the gut tugging would end.

If the world knows how good I have it, I'd be both crazy and a fool to ever leave.

One Sunday night when Lydia was upstairs helping with baths, the phone rang. "Is Ed Krug there, please?"

I was about to say, "Whatever this is, no thanks," but for some reason, I answered, "This is him."

"Mr. Krug, this is Kent from the *Cedar Rapids Gazette*. The response to our invitation has been overwhelming, maybe two hundred letters, but yours and a couple other families stand out. We'd like to interview your family and see the four of you play *The Wizard of Oz*."

Holy shit.

A few weeks later, a reporter and photographer spent three days at Knollwood. They arrived before dinner and stayed for family time. They snapped pictures as I sat on Emily's bed reading to both girls.

On a Sunday not long after, the *Gazette* contained an above-the-fold front page story highlighting "The Krug Family." There was a picture of the four of us at the kitchen table. The article let the world know that yes, Ed and Lydia Krug were getting it right as loving parents and spouses.

This is it, I thought. *The anchor that will keep me moored to the girls of Knollwood forever. Hooray!*

The article generated accolade phone calls, letters, and handshakes.

Each added to my resolve. I'd be an idiot to let something in my gut, some stupid idea that I needed a different life, dictate my destiny.

Now I'm safe, I thought. *I'll never be able to leave.*

The gut tugging didn't end.

I remembered the Devil's playground principle and decided to overload my mind. I was sure it would crowd out thoughts about clean lines and finding a new life.

I left Littleton & Davis and opened my own law firm. I found space on the third floor of a converted brick warehouse originally built in the 1880s, downtown next to the Cedar River. I used most of our savings to buy office furniture and computers and to hire a secretary and associate attorney. Clients showed up, looking for a lawyer who was willing to attack.

Within a couple years, I had a partner, Marsha. We grew to four lawyers and ten employees. Lydia became our bookkeeper; she worked from home at night so that she could be a daytime mommy.

For a while, it worked exceptionally well. I made a lot of money, too — more than most attorneys in the city, or for that matter, the entire state.

Eventually, working too much stopped working. Instead of thinking less about clean lines, all that work caused me to think about them more.

You need your own life, Ed.

The Internet was very new, and I discovered a website for men who liked to dress as women. Suddenly, I wasn't alone. There were others like me, in varying degrees of struggle, with Yahoo addresses.

Wow.

Now I could communicate with people who actually *understood* what was going on in my head. Like me, most were sexually charged. Instead of having sane, healthy Internet conversations, I exchanged sexual fantasies with other guys in Iowa, and later, across the country. In my lucid moments, I knew this was exactly the opposite of what I needed.

I thought meeting one of these Internet people could be helpful, a sort of one-on-one therapy. Maybe talking would rid us of our common demon.

Darrell was a pot-bellied, graying fifty-five-year-old office worker. We met at a Burger King on the edge of town and sat in an end booth.

I whispered, "How long have you been dressing?"

"Since I was a kid," he whispered back, somewhat nonchalantly. He sipped a Coke through a straw. "I'd sneak into my mother's closet and wear her dresses. And of course, there was her underwear." He grinned as he hit rock bottom on the Coke.

Like me, Darrell was married. And like me, his wife had no idea.

He said, "She'd die if she found out."

His wife worked retail and wasn't home much during the weekends. "I'll go to Kmart and buy one or two pairs of panties and then head home and get online," he explained. "I've got a couple guys that like to exchange pictures and fantasies. I'll jerk off and throw the panties away. I'll be good for a while. Then I'll need another fix, and it starts up all over again."

He said this all so matter-of-factly, as if he knew it would be this way for the rest of his life. Something inside my brain shouted, *Oh my god!* There was no way I could wrestle with myself for that long, Sunday *Gazette* front-page feature or not. I didn't have the strength.

Darrell raised his way-too-bushy eyebrows and asked, "Would you ever like to get together, you know, for a little panty play?"

Without really thinking, I said, "Maybe. Let me figure some things out, and I'll get back to you."

On the way home from Burger King, I yelled at the rearview mirror. "*Maybe?* You dumb fuck! What the hell are you doing, *Tom?*"

I told Larson about my Burger King meeting.

"Did you take him up on his offer?" Larson was seated high at his desk.

"Of course not! I'm here instead."

"I don't have to say that you need to stay off the Internet, away from chat rooms and anything else that fuels your fantasies, do I?"

"I know, but when I have clients and employees bitching at me, the temptation is too hard to resist."

"Have you thought any more about telling Lydia?"

"She knows I'm seeing you," I said. "She thinks it's all about work stress. If I told her what's really wrong with me, I know, in the end, I'll leave her. That can't happen."

Larson bobbled. "But, Ed, you're not being honest with her, or yourself. You just may be wired a certain way, and there's nothing you can do about it."

I cut him off. "I've just got to work harder."

Larson looked down at his notes. "I don't think you're going to get things figured out if you don't tell her," he answered.

You're an idiot, I glared. *You don't understand that love conquers all.*

By 1998, I fought myself every day.

You have to leave.

No, I won't.

You're not living as who you really are.

I can never hurt Lydia and the girls.

I could barely concentrate on legal work, and I had become a human pressure cooker. I raised hell over minor mistakes and false deadlines. I went through employees—secretaries, paralegals, and associate lawyers—like I went through print cartridges. One prospective associate, who called to say he wouldn't take the job offer, reported, "I've checked you out. People say you're the most difficult person in town."

If I was going to be perfect, damn it, everyone else needed to be perfect too.

Finally, fearing that I'd burst, I did something I had vowed never to do: I again told Lydia that I liked to wear lingerie.

We were in bed late on a Saturday night. "Bo," I said, "I need to tell you something about me. It's been a part of me ever since I was a boy."

Lydia's breathing slowed. "What is it, Bo? What are you talking about?"

I gulped. *It's now or never, Ed.*

"I have this thing about women's lingerie. I'm attracted to it. I like to wear it."

Only a second passed between me speaking and Lydia reacting. It seemed like six hours.

"What are you talking about?" She sat up from my shoulder and put space between us.

"It's something that I've always done," I answered. "This is the *real* reason why I've been seeing Larson."

"Yuck."

"You don't have to tell me it's strange. I've tried like hell to stop this stuff, but I can't. I don't want to hide it anymore. I need to start wearing panties. Larson agrees."

Lydia tilted and frowned. "Are you gay?"

"No, Bo, I'm not gay."

I thought I could tiptoe between honest self-disclosure and intentional omission—no way could I tell her how I fantasized about being a woman or men adoring me.

I tried to make my revelation a positive. "I've met a lot of men on the Internet who wear lingerie and their wives actually enjoy it," I said with a lighter pitch.

Lydia wasn't impressed. "I'm sorry, but this is too much."

"Actually, I tried to tell you when we were kids. You freaked."

Another frown. "No, you didn't. I'd remember that."

I let the comment go. There was no point in arguing. Still, I needed to explain why, now.

"I'm telling you because it's a part of me," I said. "I've spent all my life hiding it. I can't do that anymore. I don't want any more secrets with you," I lied.

We went back and forth for an hour. Twenty times I told her that I wasn't gay. I rationalized that my lingerie-wearing could easily be incorporated into our life. "I'll feel so much better if I can do this," I urged.

Somehow, and certainly incredibly, Lydia relented.

"I love you, Bo, so do what you need," she said with a sharp sigh. "I don't know how it'll make me feel. Also, don't ever look for me to buy you panties. That'll never happen."

She crawled back to her spot on my shoulder.

Something in my gut relaxed. *Maybe this will be enough,* I thought.

Understandably, Lydia was confused and frightened. She trusted me, though, and believed that I would always do the right thing. It was my one ace in the hole.

Again that Krug-and-King love, that soul-mate devotion to each other, showed through.

Within a week, the Fruit of the Looms in my underwear drawer were relegated to the bottom of the dresser. In their place were white, black, and pink lace bikini panties from an ecstatic shopping spree at Victoria's

Secret. In no time, I had two dozen pairs.

"Don't you think that's enough?" Lydia asked. "You have more than me."

The freedom to wear lingerie without hiding it ignited me. Suddenly, I felt good about myself; I had been brave, and now I felt liberated. The gut pulls disappeared, replaced by a sense of wholeness, a feeling that finally I was living in some measure as the true person inside me. In turn, I became sexually charged like a fifteen-year-old boy again. Lydia, and not some anonymous man in my head, was my desire. We had more sex—in the kitchen, in a bathroom, in my car, almost everywhere—in the three months after I began to legally wear lingerie than in the three years before.

Slowly, Lydia came around.

"You know, it's not as bad as I had thought it would be," she confessed a few months in. Even more, despite her earlier admonition, she bought me two pairs of women's bikinis for my birthday. "Don't open this present in front of the girls," she warned.

I wanted to jump up and down, a tribute to being accepted by the most important person in my life.

"See," I said. "It doesn't harm anyone, and it makes me feel good. Thank you for being so understanding."

"Of course, Bo. I love you."

There was someone else I needed to self-disclose to: Mark, my brother. I felt a bond with Mark—an allegiance born through mutually surviving a family horror.

I also had a selfish reason: I wondered if he, too, had our father's defective sexual genes.

When he visited Cedar Rapids with his family one weekend, I suggested lunch at TGI Friday's, just the two of us.

"I think I'm gay," I said, freely sharing something that I still refused to say to Lydia. "I'm attracted to men. To top it off, I have this thing about women's lingerie."

Mark cut into a twice-baked potato. My revelation didn't slow him.

"Well, aren't you going to say something?" I asked.

He looked up from his plate. "How do you know you're gay? You're one of the straightest people I know," he said.

"Trust me," I replied. "I fantasize about sex with men all the time."

"Huh."

It wasn't the reaction I expected. I had also hoped this would trigger some revelation of his own. It didn't.

"Do you think this has something to do with Dad?" I asked. "You know, like genetically? That it's something I can't control regardless of how hard I try?"

I needed to know what Mark thought. He was the smarter one, after all.

"I don't know if genes play a role," he said. "I think Dad was Dad, someone fucked-up. You're not like that, you know."

It was nice to hear, even if I didn't believe him. I pressed. I had to.

"So, little brother, be honest with me," I said. "Do you think about men at all? Are you interested in having sex with guys?" I closed my eyes; it was painful to be so blunt with someone I loved.

He answered in between chews. "No, Ed, I only like women. I'm in love with pussies, not penises."

So much for that theory.

We shifted the conversation. Before the check arrived, Mark returned to my revelation.

"I want you to know that regardless of what happens, you'll always have my support. If you're gay or whatever, I'll always love you."

I thought back to Dallas and what we went through, and how Mark rescued me. *I'm so lucky to have you,* I said to myself.

"Thanks, Bro," I answered. "Don't worry, nothing's going to change. I love Lydia too much. I'm sure therapy will eventually work and I'll get rid of this shit in my head."

Mark grinned. I don't know if he actually believed me.

A particularly difficult case took me to San Jose, California. A fire in Davenport, Iowa, had burned much of a multi-million-dollar business. I represented one of a dozen defendants charged with furnishing defective equipment that purportedly caused the fire. We traveled to an electrical expert's laboratory in San Jose for testing. It was a contentious week—I went at it repeatedly with the property owner's attorney. At one point, I screamed, "That's just not acceptable, counselor! Don't push me further."

I wondered if fists might be next.

I needed an escape. By chance, I came across an advertisement for a "spa" where men could dress as women. Of course; this was California.

Impulsively, I made an appointment.

The next day, the spa owner, Susan, greeted me. "You're welcome here," she said with a hug.

The spa was housed in a building that included a locker room. There were racks and racks of women's clothes in another area. At the back of the building, there was a salon with makeup bays, along with a game-television room, apparently for lounging and socializing. I had never been anywhere like this.

I wondered whether I was still on Planet Earth.

"Would you like to try something on?" Susan saw me eye dresses in the clothing area. "The only charge is for hose," she reassured. "Pick what you want, and I'll meet you at the chair."

I was alone with a hundred different dresses, skirts, and feminine tops, not to mention three racks of wigs—blonde, brunette, and auburn. It was a candy store for the gender-challenged.

I picked out a simple black skirt and a V-neck red top. I found a pair of opaque hose and a not-so-attractive pair of flats. I went for a brunette wig with curls that didn't seem too much out of character. In the changing room, I navigated a butt-facing zipper and tricky pantyhose. I walked in ecstasy but a bit askew.

"Come sit down," Susan motioned when I entered the salon. Within seconds, she had a makeup brush on my face.

"You have beautiful eyes," she offered. "Not many people have eyes like yours; count yourself lucky."

I thought of Mom and silently thanked her.

Susan went to work with mascara, eyeliner, and blush. I took no notes, made no record of what makeup component went where.

"I'm a lawyer," I offered. "There's a part of me that says I shouldn't be here," I said. "But another part is telling me that I'm a woman."

The latter statement just came out. Of all the people I'd met on my journey so far, I figured she might understand best.

"Oh, hon. This isn't something you can fight," she replied. "You'd be surprised by who comes in here. I have lawyers, doctors, police officers, even a couple judges. It's just who they are. Like you."

A voice inside me said, *See, I told you so. You're not alone.*

Twenty minutes later, Susan said, "All done." I leaned forward and squinted into the mirror. Looking back was someone I didn't recognize — someone female.

"Oh my god," I said, awed. "I can't believe it. A woman!"

Susan answered, "A beautiful woman."

She said that to every customer, I was certain. Still, "beautiful" vibrated in my brain. I couldn't stop smiling.

I searched out mirrors for more looks at this person, this woman, who had suddenly emerged from Ed Krug.

There you are.

I wanted to savor what I earnestly believed would be the only moment of womanhood in my life. I went to the lounge. There was another middle-aged man-dressed-as-a-woman there, someone who flubbed, "Jerry," when we shook hands.

"She" moaned. "I mean, *Geraldine.*"

I didn't give my name; I didn't have a female one.

Geraldine had also come to town on business. She had been to the spa several times. "I just love it here," she said.

We quickly exchanged stories. Geraldine was married; her wife knew she dressed but wasn't thrilled about it. "I can't help how she feels about my dressing," Geraldine said. "This is who I am. I was here last night, too, and drove to my hotel dressed like this. I was scared to death, but it was also one of the most thrilling things I've ever done."

I knew I'd never have the guts to do that.

"And you know what?" she offered. "I passed a man in the hall, and he didn't give me a second look. I think he thought I was a real woman."

"I'm sure I'll never do this again," I said. "The makeup, the wig, the clothes; it's all too complicated."

Besides, this wasn't *reality*. I was married with children in a career that valued me for being an aggressive male. Nothing I did would ever change that.

Geraldine shook her head. "You never know what the future holds. I used to think like you, but no more. I'm willing to see where this takes me."

I thought Geraldine was crazy.

A few nights after I got home from San Jose, Lydia asked, "Why is there makeup on your shirt collar?" I had put my dress shirt from the day at the spa in the dry cleaning pile. She had spied a makeup spot on the collar. I must have smudged makeup when I resumed male mode in San Jose.

"What are you talking about?" I feigned ignorance.

"Come, look at it," she ordered. Lydia dragged me upstairs to the walk-in closet where she had segregated my white button-down shirt. She held it up. I saw a half-dollar sized cream-colored makeup smudge on the inside left collar.

"Do you see this?" she said, pointing.

"Oh." I paused, vying for a second of thinking time.

With some of the absolute best thinking-on-feet of my entire life, I answered, "That's from sunscreen. I needed to be out in the sun for the electrical inspection in San Jose." It was a total, complete bald-faced lie.

I saw instant relief in Lydia's face. "Okay," she responded. "It sure looks like makeup, but that makes sense."

I turned and walked out of the closet and said to myself, *God, that was close.*

Christmas, 1998. Lily—as the youngest—opened the last present, an American Girl accessory.

Lydia had a funny grin. "Hmmm," she said. "I thought there was one more present. Oh, yes, *now* I remember."

She scampered up the foyer stairs. A minute later, she was back gingerly maneuvering a large, thin brown-papered square that sported a red bow; obviously it was a large picture.

"Here you go, Bo," she said with a beam. "Just for you."

"Can we help you open it, Daddy?" Emily reached for the present.

"Of course." In seconds, the girls had the brown wrapping torn apart, revealing the back of a picture.

"Turn it around," Lydia urged.

I lifted the picture and flipped it from back to front and took a look. It was a pastel drawing of two black-haired girls kneeling on a driveway with thick sticks of chalk. They were in the midst of coloring the words *Welcome Home Daddy*. The scene was highlighted by spots; dapples of light, actually, as if sunlight shone through a tuft of leaves from a tree high above.

It was the very exact way sunlight filtered through the shag bark hickories on the Knollwood driveway.

The scene captured days where I had come home from the office and stood over the girls as they were busy at work, loving me with chalk.

In an instant, I felt everything good about my life—love, gratitude, belonging, humility, and most of all, a sense of *home*.

Oh my god.

I started to cry. It was the first time the girls had ever seen me do that.

"What's wrong, Daddy?" Emily worried. She put her hand on my shoulder.

"Nothing's wrong, honey," I said quickly. "Nothing at all. It's just that Mommy has given me the best present I could ever ask for. It's you and Lily, can't you see?"

Emily and Lily peered closer and giggled. "Hooray, Mommy! You've made Daddy happy!" Emily yelled. Lily joined in, "Yay, Daddy!"

I hugged Lydia. "Thank you, Bo. How did you know?"

"Oh, come on. I know you better than anyone," she said in a breaking voice.

"I don't only love it," I said, "I cherish it. And you."

Lydia smiled and returned the hug. Even after she knew a part of my secret—the lingerie wearing, the part that I *could* tell her—she hadn't held back. She still loved me with all her heart.

I was amazed.

"Okay everyone, who's ready for hot chocolate?" Lydia asked.

Lydia and the girls went off to the kitchen, leaving me with my pastel daughters, a magical reminder of how good I had it.

———————

Weeks later, well into 1999, I saw Larson again. I told him about my trip to San Jose, and the close call with Lydia. "And then Christmas was fantastic," I said. "I felt so loved by Lydia and the girls."

"Yes, Ed, that's good to hear," he responded, "but let me remind you it doesn't resolve the underlying issue. Aren't you still having the fantasies and that tugging you've talked about?"

"Yeah," I said. "My gut's still telling me I need my own life."

"So when are you going to tell Lydia?"

"Never," I barked. "I love her too much. I would never hurt her like that."

"You're acting like you have a choice," Larson retorted.

"I do," I answered. *"I do."*

Larson put pen to paper. I saw bobble become unmistakable head shake.

NINE: *Seat 13A*

Lily wanted to see a "real" baseball game. I ordered two Cubs tickets.

We drove to Chicago on the afternoon of the first Friday in September, 2001 and checked into the Westin just off the Miracle Mile. On the way to dinner at a nearby restaurant, Lily grabbed my hand amidst office workers rushing for after-five drinks or last-minute shopping.

I looked down and saw my happy nine-year-old daughter with a nervous smile, excited by everything different from home. We even made it through a half-hour wait and an entire meal of chicken fingers without a single "I miss Mommy."

Saturday morning was golden and crisp. We explored before the game and rode up to the John Hancock Observatory, one hundred stories high. By then, the sun was in mid-climb. A million diamonds shimmered on Lake Michigan.

I saw the subdued bustle of weekend Chicago, still busier than Cedar Rapids on its best day.

"Look, Lily," I said. "There's Navy Pier with the Ferris wheel." I pointed out other landmarks, trying to keep her interest. She had a better idea about wonders in the Observatory gift shop.

I asked a woman to snap a picture before Lily ran off. In that photograph, there's a baseball-capped Dad with an arm around his smiling and contented daughter. In the background, a wonderful blue sky— eternity—abounded.

We were half the all-American Family, fifty percent of the *Grand Plan*, on a making-memories expedition.

Wrigley Field was our first "L" ride. At our seats near the third base line, I heard, "Can I have candy, Daddy?" By the seventh-inning stretch,

117

Lily had wrangled almost one of everything from the hawking vendors. I heroically resisted pleas for cotton candy, only to give in at the top of the ninth.

With the sun's tour of a glorious day done, Lily and I got to my car. In short order, we were pointed toward Iowa. Lily was curled asleep in the backseat with Fred, her basset hound stuffed animal, before the first 'burb.

I drove west and glanced in the mirror, thankful. I had just lived some of the best thirty-six hours of my life.

Three days later, everything fell apart.

September 11th started as an idyllic Iowa morning of infinite sunshine and sweet early fall smells. No one could have guessed that it would become a day of numbers—one terrorist leader, nineteen hijackers, four planes, three buildings, nearly 3,000 dead.

A million thoughts raced through me as events unfolded. I ran backwards to a memory burn of when President Kennedy was shot. *Did everyone feel this kind of panic and fear then?*

I tried to not let it show. When Emily asked, "Why is smoke coming from those buildings, Daddy?" I stumbled to explain without scaring her.

"Some bad men have done some bad things. We're safe here. Nothing ever happens in Cedar Rapids. Don't worry."

I walked into the office and found Marsha. She looked up from papers on her desk and spoke a single word, "Tyler." She was thinking of her only kid, a draft-age high school senior.

I hugged her. "Don't worry," I said, "the Democrats will never agree to a draft."

At a mid-morning office meeting, I attempted to lead. "Remember, we're a resilient country," I offered to fourteen co-workers. "Bad things like this have happened before. Our parents and grandparents had such days and survived. Americans don't give up. We'll get through this."

The day blurred with bulletins, rumors, and misinformation. The White House was a target; the president had been taken to a secret location; the Sears Tower was evacuated because radar had spotted a plane.

At five o'clock, I crept up the driveway listening to tinny Washington politicians end a press conference by singing Woody Guthrie's "This Land is Your Land." It put me over the edge. I cried in the garage for ten minutes.

I picked at dinner with the television on as I tried to anticipate what would happen next. I heard that people, maybe as many as 200, had actually jumped from the burning towers, where they rained onto fleeing pedestrians and traffic-choked cabs.

Then, *Oh no, it can't be*—I saw a helicopter camera shot of a man and woman as they pushed off from the 94th floor, with thick black smoke at their backs. I saw a tie flutter and dress billow. With hands held tight, they fell through the Manhattan sky, fatal swan divers-in-arms.

I turned away from the television.

I couldn't stop myself; suddenly I was with Lily, one hundred stories up in Chicago. The ledge of the John Hancock Observatory was two feet away. Lily and I peered from behind broken glass; our hearts raced as wind whipped at us. We choked on suffocating acrid smoke and felt the murderous heat as it marched toward us floor by floor. I could feel the death grip of little Lily's arms tight around my waist. In my head, I heard Lily sob—wait, that's not right; it was a desperate plea with every ounce of her spirited essence—*Daddy! Daddy! Save me, Daddy!*

My soul shifted. There was no way to avoid feeling helpless and condemned.

What if? Could I really say, "I love you, Lily," and then hug her tight as we stepped into nothingness? Did I have that kind of courage? Or coldness?

Could I kill my daughter to save her?

The death images in my head were too much. I shut them down and pushed my dinner plate away.

We dressed for church. The parking lot at Saint Matthew's looked more like Easter Sunday than a Tuesday evening in September.

An usher led us to the second pew from the front. The choir started. Father Christopher, an energetic plain-speaking priest, entered. The girls clutched at Lydia while she pulled at my sweaty hand. I clasped back, with no idea of how long I could hold on.

We got past an unmemorable Gospel passage and a short homily on the need to persevere and love our enemies.

119

A lay minister led the general prayers.

"Please, dear God, protect our country and our service members."

Sheeplike came the response, "Lord, hear our prayer."

"Please, dear God, look after the people who have died today, the innocents, and give them everlasting life."

"Lord, hear our prayer."

"Please dear God, send a message to the world's people that terrorism isn't the answer. Instead, respect and love are the true path to peace."

"Lord, hear our prayer."

Somewhere around the third refrain, my gut hijacked my brain and heart. I stopped listening and again imagined. This time, I was on Flight 11, one of the two planes that originated in Boston. It was easy to fall into; I had taken several early morning cross-country flights to see Thap when I lived in Boston.

I pictured myself in Seat 13A, a window seat. I heard the mechanical *hrrrrrr* of wing flaps as they took hold against the city sky; the terrorist pilot adjusting altitude. I pressed against the seat as the jet's engines revved. There were a thousand office buildings now, their shadows blanketing smaller structures. In the distance, I could see the two towers, the tallest of the tall, obvious targets. In my mind's eye, I looked down at Manhattan streets and spied ant people and city bus specks, knowing I was about to die.

My heart tried to pull me back from this imagining. *Please stop it, Ed. I beg you.*

I couldn't. My gut was at the controls.

I huddled in Seat 13A, crazy with fear, thinking last thoughts and flashing heartache-wrapped memories. I thought of Lydia, for sure. There was Emily and Lily too. Mark and Jacki popped into my head. And Thap. Yes, of course, dear Thap.

Then—completely out of left field—there *it* was, my final, just-before-you-die thought: *You coward. You fucking coward. You're going to die without ever getting to be yourself—your true self.*

Coward?

Goddamn right.

Kneeling now—a mechanical Catholic movement—my stomach churned. I couldn't get off that plane. I couldn't avoid being murdered.

American Airlines aluminum blasted into New York City steel.

A flash of bright light and a zillion-degree heat. Blackness.

Last chance lost.

I turned to see Lydia wrapped around Emily and Lily.

You're a coward.

I thought of my love for the girls of Knollwood. *How could I ever put myself above you? No, never.*

I tried to focus on Father Christopher. He held the Eucharist aloft. He called on us to believe it was the body of Christ. My faith in that, as well as in anything else intangible, had vanished long ago. I'll be honest: the only body I thought of at that moment was *my body* as it vaporized along with everything else on Flight 11.

You're a coward.

My terminal thinking—call it final enlightenment, maybe—continued.

Ed, unless you do something radical, you're going to miss your only chance to live as you. For once, love yourself. Stop being afraid. Otherwise, you really will die.

A hundred thousand times before 9/11, I had told myself, *You need your own life.* I hadn't ever linked the mantra to the idea that I might *die* without ever getting to be *me.* The sacrifice of 3,000 innocents instantly taught me one crucial thing: unless I did something to change my life, I'd *never* be *me.* It didn't matter that I barely knew who or what *me* was. Whoever it was needed to crawl into the light.

She had been in the shadows long enough.

I got in line for Communion. The big clock in my head illuminated. I would die someday, and no one could predict when. The time for waiting was over.

A Communion wafer melted in my mouth. I did something that I hadn't ever done in my life: I prayed for me, Ed Krug, the lost soul.

Lord or God or whoever you are, please help me be true to myself. I don't want to die without being me.

Everything shifted. In that moment, I began to cry. It wasn't for my country. No, I sobbed for Lydia, Emily, and Lily, knowing that now I was going to horribly hurt the three people I loved most.

Finally, I understood. *I have to leave. For me.*

Lydia and I took a short vacation a week later. It was a bicycle escape to Lanesboro, Minnesota, and Madison, Wisconsin.

The area around Lanesboro, with thick forests and huge rock formations, reminded me of New England. Red and orange leaves, fallen reminders of an innocent summer, made parts of the trail difficult to follow.

On the first day, I was my usual false self, a boy in love with a girl, cajoling Lydia into kisses and pets. I concentrated on the gorgeous scenery and my beautiful wife, grasping for anything that would keep me with her.

We had fish dinners at a local VFW that night. I looked around the room of couples twice our age and wondered, *How many of you ever left the love of your life? Were any of you ever torn too?*

Our motel was rooms-in-a-string, the Uncle Ed kind. There was order to the room: a towel rack perfectly placed next to the sink; a television squarely centered for the bed. In no time, Lydia was asleep with her head on her spot.

My heart temporarily broke free of my gut, its captor.

You can never leave this. Ever.

The next day, we started side by side on a dew-covered trail. I soon pedaled far ahead, where I lost sight of Lydia. Alone, I talked to myself with every pedal push, back and forth.

Push: *Can I really give up Lydia's love?*

Push: *Her love doesn't matter if you don't love yourself.*

Push: *I'm afraid of being alone.*

Push: *You'll never respect yourself if you stay. Besides, you're already alone.*

Push: *How could I ever hurt Lydia and the girls? I love them too much.*

Push: *It's just like Larson said: you don't have a choice about who you are. All the love in the world can't change that.*

Push: *I'm just like Tom Terrific.*

Push: *If you stay with her, for sure you'll be like him. Dead in some bathtub.*

I fantasized what it would be like to be *me*. I'd have a huge Pottery Barn-furnished house, with leather couch and chairs, an immaculate white rug, and wispy sheer drapes. Yellow freesia would sprout from a chiseled glass vase. It would be my space, where nothing would hold me back. I saw myself standing at the window in a pretty crimson sundress and wonderful white lingerie, waiting for a goateed man.

The image ended abruptly when Lydia caught up with me. Her soul-mate instincts had kicked in; she knew something was wrong.

"Why are you so quiet this morning?" We stopped near a gas station for our standard breakfast—Diet Pepsi and granola bars.

"Oh, I'm just taking in the beauty of the day."

Lydia flashed an I-don't-believe-you-but-I-won't-push-it look.

We drove to Madison. From our hotel room, I saw Lake Monona adorned with small white sails cruising in circles. The room should have been a place to giggle and play. Instead, I withdrew more.

"Aren't you having fun, Bo? Is it the office? You know, we're on this trip to have f-u-n. What can I do to get you in the mood for a little fun?"

She began to stroke my crotch. I pulled away.

"I've got a lot of office stuff in my head. Give me some time and I'll pull out of it."

At dinner, I forced myself into small talk. We agreed we were tired. Back at the hotel, I turned on the television only to find a movie star telethon for 9/11 victims.

It was more horror and an additional reminder of my new trajectory.

Lydia fell asleep. I had remembered seeing an adult bookstore a couple blocks from the hotel. I knew it was a place where I could see images of naked men—surely some would be goateed—and women with their clean lines.

I slowly edged off the bed and looked back to see Lydia still asleep.

The front door of the bookstore was heavy. It took extra effort to open, which in turn sounded a loud electronic ping that announced my arrival. The man behind the counter was obese, balding, and high-pitched in voice. I asked how much the movies cost and he answered it was a card system; you pay $5 and get fifteen minutes.

I wouldn't be there long. I bought the cheap card.

I went to a well-lit booth that had a bench but no door. I didn't waste a second. An image of two men in a locker room came up. One man grabbed the other, and they kissed. My body reacted and my imagination ramped; it was me being kissed. The scene progressed to where one of the men took off his sweater; I clicked to another channel. I wanted something more immediate.

I kept clicking until I found a man enjoying a woman. Fantasizing, dreaming, hoping—*I* was on the screen being adored as the real *me.*

It wasn't long before a man, maybe thirty years old, showed up in the doorway. He leaned against the door frame with a Cheshire cat smile. I knew what the smile meant. I shook my head and mouthed, "No, no." I went back to the screen. The stranger moved on.

My fifteen minutes were up in no time. It was enough for then.

I walked through the chilling night to the hotel parking garage and pulled a pillow from the car, my excuse in case Lydia had awoken. I quietly opened the hotel room door and felt relief when I saw that she was still asleep.

The next morning, we followed a not-so-clear bike trail through much of Madison. Again, my heart and brain angled for escape, this time with fading resolve. By the end of the ride, any lingering doubt about leaving Lydia had completely evaporated.

My gut had won the war.

As I tied down the bikes for the trip home, my heart sent off one last *SOS,* a final gasp.

Mayday! Mayday! You're a fucking idiot.

Two months later, on a Wednesday heavy with clouds, Lydia and I had a day date in Iowa City. After a mall excursion, we stopped for a drink at our favorite bar.

I fumbled with the usual topics—the girls, the office, what we'd do over the coming weekend—until our wine came; in a minute, both of us would need alcohol. I looked at Lydia with her wispy golden hair and perpetual smile. It was the last minute of normal we'd ever have and I wanted to remember it forever.

It was time. I started to speak, but didn't believe the words could actually come out of my mouth.

"We need to talk about what's in my head," I said. "I had thought I could keep this stuff inside me, but I can't."

Lydia's smile evaporated.

"Okay, what is it, Bo? What's wrong?"

Here you go, Ed. The point of no return.

I breathed deep and jumped.

"Well, I think I'm gay, and if not that, I'm something else. For years, I've thought about having sex with men while I dressed as a woman."

Lydia's jaw dropped. She pulled her hand out of mine and joined it with the other around the stem of her wine glass, the only available anchor.

I knew what she was thinking and wanted to head it off.

"I've never cheated on you, if that's what you're worried about. I've never had an affair, and you're safe." Then, wanting to get all of it out before I lost resolve, I said, "This is the real reason why I've been seeing Larson Williams. Yes, he's helped with my work stress, but mainly it's been to help me stop having these thoughts. It hasn't worked. Since 9/11, it's gotten much worse."

Suddenly, I talked in slow motion. It was as if I was at the next table over, witnessing a marriage implode, Twin Tower-like.

Lydia tightened, but only for a second. She leaned forward and put one palm against the edge of the table.

"How long have you had these thoughts? Is this some kind of midlife crisis thing?"

I pushed back against my chair; foolishly, I hadn't expected an interrogation.

"I wish it was as simple as a midlife thing," I answered. "I've been fantasizing about men adoring me as a woman since I was in law school. I can't keep it out of my head any longer." My heart thumped a thousand beats a second.

"But you swore you weren't gay when you made your big disclosure about wearing women's underwear. Did you lie to me?"

"I thought telling you about the lingerie thing would be enough to keep me from needing anything more. I was wrong. There's something else inside me that has to come out. I can't fight myself over it for the rest of my life."

Lydia bent forward even more. She needed a closer look; surely an imposter had hijacked her husband.

"So what are you telling me? That you want to have sex with men while living with me? That you want to be a woman? Or is it that you want to leave me? I don't understand what you're saying or even why you're confessing this right now."

Her words and tone shook my resolve. Suddenly, I didn't know *what* I was telling her. Was I *really* saying that I'm leaving?

In classic Krug fashion, I defaulted to lying.

"No, I don't *want* to leave," I said, yearning to mean it. "I love you and our girls with all my heart. It's just that it's gotten so hard for me. There's this thing in my gut tugging at me to have my own life. I don't *want* another life; what I do want is to be your husband and have a happily-ever-after. That's what I told Larson."

The love part was absolutely true. Hence it had taken a national calamity and recognition of my mortality before I could ever get the guts to talk to her about this.

Lydia reached into her purse for a tissue. She dabbed at her eyes. It was sinking in, her own residual 9/11 moment.

"So, what does Larson say about all of this? It doesn't sound to me like he's done you much good." I couldn't blame her for the sarcasm.

"If you really want to know, he's been telling me to talk to you about the stuff in my head for years. I didn't want to do that because of the hurt and worry. I thought I could just bottle it up, but I can't any longer. I feel like I'll die if I keep it bottled any longer."

Lydia cut a look. "I feel like I'm going to die, now that you've told me this."

We were quiet. I reached for her hand and she gave it. I tried to find footing on what had become very muddy ground. I grasped for something to better explain, a hook for *why*.

A thought shot into my brain: *Tom Terrific.*

I gulped wine.

"Listen," I said. "Do you remember when my father died? Remember I told you about the calendars and the list of women he slept with?" (Despite my oath to Mark that I'd tell no one about my father's trophy list, I had quickly disclosed to Lydia that Dad had volume cheated with a dozen women.)

Lydia answered, "Yeah, so what?"

"Well, he didn't just sleep with women. There was another list, one that I never told you about. That list had men's names on it. My father also had sex with men."

Her expression stayed solid.

"It doesn't surprise me," Lydia said deadpan. "Your father was so oversexed, he was gross."

She had a come-on-don't-shit-me sound in her voice too. Before I could get in another word, she added, "So what? You're telling me this because you think there's some kind of genetic link with your father? Oh, give me a break."

Again, she pulled her hand from mine.

"Yes, that's exactly what I'm telling you," I said. "This is too weird, too coincidental, for my father and me to both have the same thoughts going on in our heads."

I wanted her to know that I was fighting something inside me, that it wasn't some kind of choice, where I could simply be one way or another. And really, if I could take a pill to be normal, to not love clean lines, I would have done it in a New York minute.

"So, have you been like your father, having sex with men?" She looked ready to jump up and bolt.

"God, no, Bo!" I almost yelled it. "I told you—absolutely not! I'm not like my father. I never cheated or put you at risk. And cheat on the girls? Only to have them grow up feeling about me the same way I feel about Dad? No way."

"Well, how do you know you're gay if you've never had sex with a man? Maybe you won't even like it."

"I know," I said. "But I have this attraction to men, and a deep need to be seen as a woman, so I'm thinking that yes, it's something that I'd like. Still, I don't want to do it. I don't want to have gay sex and I don't want to leave."

Lydia finished her wine and snapped the empty glass down. "What do we do now?"

It was the golden question that I had wanted to avoid forever.

I tapped a finger against my wine glass. *This is a disaster. No way do I want to continue hurting her.*

I lied some more.

"I'll tell you what. I'm *not* leaving. I'll find a new therapist. I'll make it work."

Lydia wiped tears one last time. She shook her head. "If that's the case, I wish you wouldn't have told me," she said. "I really didn't need to know about your stupid fantasies."

At that point, the server appeared.

I forced a smile and said, "We'll take the check."

TEN: *Leaving Lydia*

On a stone-cold evening in January, 2002, I walked into a Victorian-style house turned offices and meeting rooms in Iowa City. It was home to the University's Women's Resource and Action Center, also known as WRAC. A thin, worn reception desk stood in what had been the living room. A redheaded coed—as in flaming red—looked up from a magazine. I guessed it was *Ms. Magazine*.

"Gender Puzzle meeting?" Nervous, I barely got the words out.

I wore a blue androgynous women's sweater and tight Victoria's Secret jeans. I hoped the coed wouldn't notice my age or maleness or the obvious five o'clock shadow working its way across my face. I was out of place in so many other ways, too, but most of all, I didn't want her to flash a look that she was judging me.

"In the back room, beyond the hall," Red said coolly before she went back to *Ms.*

I walked down a bright yellow hall, past small office doors adorned with the remnants of a bygone movement—posters of bracelet-wearing fists proclaiming "Women Power," pictures of Gloria Steinem and Janis Ian, and oddly angled bumper stickers, "If Only Women Ruled the World!"

The place felt part Communist, part earth mother, and completely foreign.

I started to sweat.

At the end of the hall, I peeked around a door frame. I saw people occupying a few stuffed chairs and a couple couches.

A short-haired brunette with bright silver rings protruding from her right nostril and lower lip spotted me.

"Welcome to the Gender Puzzle meeting! Come on in and grab a seat."

I shuffled in and found a couch spot next to a heavyset woman who wore Army boots. She sported one of those wallets-hooked-to-a-chain. My sofa companion moved to make room for me, certainly a nice gesture.

There were about a dozen people in the room, all young women of varying shapes and sizes; college students, I assumed. I was the oldest by at least a decade and a half. Before long, I was rubbing my arm.

The pierced greeter, Eleanor, headed the group. She described herself as bisexual and polyamorous, a word that I'd heard maybe once in my life.

"I'm happy that we have such a large group," Eleanor beamed. "And with such diversity," she said with a glance my way.

I rubbed my arm faster.

Eleanor continued.

"Our goal for the next eight Tuesday nights is to explore gender: what it means, how it applies to us individually. We want an open and safe discussion where everyone is comfortable regardless of their location on the gender spectrum."

I stopped rubbing and caught my breath. In forty-five years of living, and except for stilted therapy sessions with Larson Williams, I had never talked to anyone about gender—theirs or mine.

Eleanor gave the ground rules. Respectful, nonjudgmental discussion was mandatory. Only first names could be used, assuming you were comfortable with even that. Finally, no one could meet one-on-one after class. She ordered, "If someone wants to get coffee afterwards, the entire group needs to be invited."

I interpreted the last rule to mean that Eleanor sought to avoid hurt feelings. It may also have been that the University didn't want WRAC to become known for hook-ups.

We started around the room introducing ourselves and, if you were inclined, describing what you wanted out of the class.

Lisa, a way-too-thin art student with tattoos on both arms who smelled of stale cigarettes, went first.

"I don't know what I am," she whispered with a barely raised head. "I only know I like wearing men's clothes. I don't want the restrictions of a culture that tells me what I have to be or how I have to think."

Eleanor nodded and looked at the next person, a curly blonde-haired doctoral candidate in music composition named Arlene, by far the prettiest of the bunch.

"I'm bisexual and questioning whether I want to be the more masculine one in my relationship," she explained. "I hope this group can help me figure it out."

Eleanor answered confidently, "Maybe we can do just that."

Holy shit, I thought. *If nothing else, this is going to be damn interesting.*

We got to a deep-voiced woman who wore a loose Army-green tee shirt and torn jeans. I guessed she might be twenty. She didn't give her name, and reported that she'd dropped out of school and was cooking at one of the bars up the street.

"I don't own any feminine clothes," she said. "And I pack whenever possible."

Pack? What the hell is that? I was afraid to ask. I didn't need to; a second later, my sofa mate clued me in.

"Hi, I'm Mel," she said as she leaned forward. "I'm majoring in women's studies and consider myself a gender queer." Then, with a nod to the throaty cook, she added, "I pack, too, but I've decided that I need a more flexible dildo; this one is too uncomfortable."

She pulled at her crotch, like she was trying to adjust something.

It hit me.

I'll be damned. They're walking around with fake penises in their pants! Real fake penises!

Eleanor motioned. My turn. I gulped a gallon of air. I had come to the Gender Puzzle for a reason and swore that I wouldn't chicken out.

"Hi, I'm Ed," I said.

I looked at a couple faces, not knowing what to say next.

Ten seconds and two "Ahs" later, I pushed on. "I'm married with two kids. I'm trying to understand some things that have been eating at me for decades. I love to wear women's clothes, particularly pretty lingerie, but I think I'm way more than just a cross-dresser. And to tell you the truth, from what little I know about this stuff, I'm surprised I'm the only man here."

I heard a loud "tsk" as Eleanor cut in.

"'Man' is disfavored in group," she said coldly. "We prefer 'person,' without reference to traditional binary gender markers."

I grinned but shut up. Even with nineteen years of education and a hundred-some courtroom trials to my credit, I didn't understand a word of what she had just said.

After a pregnant pause, Eleanor asked, "Is there anything else you'd like to share?"

I thought for a second. I had a whole history, maybe a generation's worth compared to these people, that would take too long to explain.

"No," I answered. "Not right now."

We continued around the room. I soon understood I was with lesbians, bisexuals, and just plain confused people who, like me, were wrestling with gender and sexuality issues of one degree or another. On second thought, "wrestling" wasn't quite the right word; *struggling to survive* was more apt, at least for some. Before the night was out, I heard about suicide attempts, drug and alcohol addictions, family members who'd turned their backs, and depression so severe that it required hospitalization.

It made me think I'd had it pretty easy.

Eleanor summarized.

"In the coming weeks, we'll discuss gender and how we fit as male, or female, according to our brains and not our bodies or physiology. You can attach any label you want: 'transgender,' 'queer,' whatever. Regardless, you're *normal*. You aren't the problem; it's society at large that has the problem."

Wow.

No.

Wait.

Fucking Wow.

It was the first time anyone had ever said I was *normal*. And that word, "transgender"? It, too, was new, but I didn't need an explanation; instantly, I knew what it meant: *me*. Dreaming of clean lines, desiring male adoration, hungering to be the women in clothing catalogs that showed up at the house in everyday mail.

Finally, I had a hook—*something*—to make sense of the gut pulls and tugs that had spread to my brain and heart.

I'm transgender!

Until the Gender Puzzle, I had thought the fantasies in my head were something I could control. *I know I'm really a man. Dreaming of being female is just a harmless fantasy that I can stop anytime.*

For thirty-some years, I told myself that. For almost three-quarters of my life, I had lied to *me*.

Now, my gender thirst had taken me here, to this room in Iowa City with a dozen women who hated their clean lines and who desperately wanted what I didn't want, a penis and scrotum glob.

Slowly, glacially actually, it had become clear that I was wrong: the fantasies about my body having something different *down there* were way more than masturbation fodder.

I drove away from Iowa City and my first Gender Puzzle meeting beaming, an unexpected sense of relief pulsing in my brain. If the night was still frozen, I didn't notice.

A part of me, the Lazarus part that had promised Lydia I'd be hers forever, thought I'd still be able to defeat it. *Maybe I can get past this transgender thing if I just understand it.*

Another part—this one barely breathing—had hope. Hope that, finally, I'd get the *real me* figured out and find my way to freedom.

Lydia had reluctantly agreed to let me go to Iowa City. "If it will help you get this figured out and keep us married, then do it," she resignedly said when I raised the subject for the tenth time. She added, "Maybe it'll help you remember that our marriage and family are more important than some stupid women's underwear." We were thirty years in with each other and despite 9/11 and the hurt I had inflicted, both of us were desperate to hold on.

With the car parked in the garage, I walked into the house, where Lydia waited. "So, how did it go?" She was smiling, pulling on a separate set of hopes.

"Pretty good," I answered as I took off my coat.

I didn't give her a chance for follow-up. "Did you know that some women walk around with dildos while wearing men's underwear?"

Lydia's mouth gaped. "You've got to be kidding me," she said.

"No," I responded. "I think it's great. They're being themselves." My excitement was palpable.

Lydia shook her head. "Ed, that's weird. Normal women don't do that."

I laughed. "That's your definition of normal. Not mine."

Lydia's face went sour. She turned and walked upstairs. Our conversation was over.

By the time I attended my first Gender Puzzle meeting, Lydia and I found ourselves on the opposite ends of no-man's land.

It was precisely where I had feared things would end up.

On my side, I scrounged for anything to help me stick it out until I discovered a magic bullet that would rid me of gut tugs and pulls. Hence the Gender Puzzle and my thought that the answer to the thing tugging at me was to better understand what fueled it.

Over on her side, Lydia fretted that everything she had assumed about me was a lie. Naturally, she worried that there might be other surprises too.

Just as Larson had predicted years before, I felt tremendous guilt. To top it off, Lydia wasn't about to take things lying down.

She announced, "I don't want to limp along for ten years, only for you to tell me you're leaving when the girls are out of high school."

We were at the Tic Toc, a Cedar Rapids restaurant. Dead clocks — cuckoo, kitchen, even art deco — lined the walls.

Lydia continued, "I'd rather you go *now*, that we deal with this *now*, so that I have time to meet someone before I get too old and wrinkly. I'm sure the girls will be able to survive this. They love you. Together, we can make it as easy as possible."

Her clarity shocked me. I wondered whether she had already talked to a lawyer.

"Bo," I said sheepishly, "I told you. I don't want to leave. I love you. I'll get this worked out in my head."

My gut did somersaults.

I went back to Larson Williams, scraping for wisdom and praying for solace. I got one but not the other.

"If you continue this hesitation, you'll end up like your father," he said coldly. "Emily and Lily are better off with you out of the house and alive, than with you staying put and eventually killing yourself. You know this."

"But, Lars," I pleaded, "I have everything a man could want: a gorgeous sexy wife, two wonderful daughters, a beautiful house, money in the bank, and a successful law practice. Why isn't that good enough?"

Larson looked up from his pad with a flushed face. "Ed, you're talking about what a traditional man would want in a traditional life. That's not you. Heck, I don't know exactly what you are. All I know is that you can't be married."

This was license, a green light to leave and something to hold on to when I doubted myself. However, I remained very much in love with Lydia and hated to hear it.

I left Larson's office still conflicted, wanting one thing but needing another. He didn't have the magic bullet. I didn't know if anyone did.

As promised, I found a new therapist, Steven, who advertised in a gay newspaper. I thought a real gay person would better appreciate what it meant to be torn.

Steven was rock-solid handsome: tall, fit, and dark-haired. We met weekly. By our fifth session, he theorized I was the victim of "chaos" in my childhood.

"You never got the basic nurturing that kids are supposed to get from their parents," he said. "You're stuck at age twelve and don't know how to deal with yourself."

"Chaos?" I had never heard that word to describe someone's upbringing.

"You've overcompensated by trying not to be like your father," he explained. "No wonder you can't get beyond square one to figure out who you are."

"You mean it's possible I'm not gay?"

"I can't say." He pulled at his tortoiseshell glasses. "You haven't ever had the chance to know who you are."

The idea that my childhood kept me from progressing as an adult sounded like a real answer. What Steven also said but what I either didn't hear or understand at the time: fear about life in general and my inability to process the tugs in my gut—both owing to Tom Terrific—had held me back. It would take several more years, and much more pain, before this fundamental insight sank in.

Instead, my immediate takeaway was that I needed to work harder to get order in my life, so as to chase away the chaos from my childhood.

If I can get rid of the chaos, then I'll be able to stay married to Lydia.

I drove home from Steven's office fighting tears. After all the hurt I had caused Lydia, I finally had something solid. I called from the car.

"Bo, I just had the best session with Steven. I think I've got it all figured out. It's my damn father. He created chaos when I was a kid and I've been lost ever since. Steven says I'm stuck at twelve years old. I've never been able to grow into the real me. Besides that, I need order in my life."

I heard a skeptical, "How are you going to do that?"

"I don't know," I said. "I'll figure something out."

Later that night, I sat in the sunroom with my journal and created a list of things I wanted to accomplish, like work less, take violin lessons, and enroll in a photography class. Most of all, I'd spend more time with the people I loved.

I was certain this would chase away any lingering chaos.

I also would stop wearing lingerie. I would no longer think of that other person inside me. I'd stick to being a man and I'd enjoy masculinity; what wasn't there to love about it? It would make Lydia happy again.

Somehow, maybe because it was one last gasp, I shut out my gut. *Don't ever bother me again,* I warned. Surprisingly, for a long while, my gut obeyed.

I pursued this latest and greatest modification to the *Grand Plan*. With my lingerie boxed up in a closet, I bought a violin, attended weekly lessons, and practiced daily in the sunroom. I took a photography class at a community college and told everyone at the law firm that I'd be working less. I even treated myself to a brand-new BMW, thinking that I deserved a reward for my hard work—both at the office and in trying to be a heterosexual man.

I didn't shave on the weekends and bought item after item of camping gear, including one of those eighteen-function knives, which I carried around thinking that it might come in handy. We tore down the garage at Knollwood and built a four-car version, complete with a real man's workbench, and all the space a guy could need for man-toys. I even shopped for a Rocker, the coolest macho Harley ever made. Luckily, I didn't buy one.

We took family vacations to Chicago, Colorado, Cape Cod, and South Carolina. There was always Door County too. Lydia and I had more daytime "dates," which meant lunch and drinks, followed by a movie or afternoon sex, which I still enjoyed. Once, we overslept past the pick-up time for Emily and Lily. We rushed to their school, feeling like terrible parents. The girls were completely alone at the front door, long after the last kid was gone.

In short, I became a better husband, father, and manly man. Too bad it didn't work.

By the fall of 2003, two years after I told Lydia I was gay, I was back at it: wearing pretty panties and bras, dreaming of clean lines, and fantasizing about goateed men.

I confessed to Lydia that I had fallen off the wagon.

She was incredulous and screamed, "Why do you have to do this? Why can't the girls and me be good enough?"

I didn't have an answer. I only knew that I had to wear pretty things. Then, before I fully realized it, I jumped another fence: I bought a non-androgynous woman's top, a pretty crimson knit sweater with a full V-neck. The tag, the validation I sought, read "Women's Medium." In no time at all, I had a wardrobe of androgynous—and some not so— women's clothes: sharp Gap chinos, buttery Victoria's Secret tops, and vibrant socks from Kohl's.

Even worse, except for days when I had court, I stopped wearing men's clothes to the office and after work. Now, everything I wore was feminine in one way or another.

Lydia grimaced every time I walked into the house with a shopping bag. Each purchase was another notch of hurt, another reminder of where I was headed.

For me, it was self-preservation.

I told Steven about dressing again and how it had progressed. His response: chaotic upbringing or not, I needed to live as me. "You'll never find peace unless you do that," he cautioned.

"But I love Lydia," I argued back.

"Can you love her any more than you already do?"

"No."

"You have your answer." I watched him put his glasses back on.

"What do you mean you're thinking of leaving your wife?" Arlene screeched as she took a hesitant sip from a steaming cappuccino. "You told me she was your soul mate. People don't leave their soul mates."

I sighed. This wasn't what I expected from Arlene, my Gender Puzzle buddy. We had quickly become conversationalists during recesses at the weekly meetings. Now, a year and a half after the last group meeting, we didn't need to worry about breaking Eleanor's rules by getting together without inviting the rest of the group.

"Hell, you're one to talk," I answered. "You left Kevin—who you said was the soul mate of all soul mates—for Susan. Aren't you much happier?"

Arlene put down her cup and straightened. "Actually, no, I'm not. I miss Kevin a lot."

"But you said you needed to be with a woman because Kevin hated it when you wore men's clothes, especially those Fruit of the Loom briefs you love so much. Doesn't Susan adore you for that? Don't you love that you're finally getting to be yourself, a masculine-butch-bisexual-queer?"

"I don't know, Ed," Arlene whispered. She frowned. "There was something about Kevin that I'll never find in anyone else. I'm not sure wanting to be the man in a relationship trumps what I feel about Kevin."

My stomach hurt. I had relied on Arlene to stay the course, to be a diligent comrade on my gender march, a real-live breathing example for me. I needed some role model if I was going to make an escape, even if she was fifteen years younger.

Oh god, I thought. *This doesn't help me at all.*

"I know you'd never guess it, but I'm gay," I said.

I caught Drew Bloom, my best friend in Cedar Rapids, in mid-bite. He swallowed hard—he didn't want to spit out Mongolian noodles.

"You've got to be kidding me," he said finally. "You're the last person I'd ever think of as gay. How did this happen?"

"It's been a long time coming," I answered. "I've been in therapy for years. Two therapists have told me that I need to leave Lydia."

"I'm blown away," Drew answered. "So, are you going to do that, are you leaving her?"

"No, I don't want to," I said. "I'm trying like hell not to. I love her way too much and I don't want to hurt my daughters. Plus, the entire Cedar Rapids legal community would shit if they knew."

Drew put down his fork. "You know, Ed, if you really are gay, that'd be fine with me. I work with a lot of gays and lesbians, and I've never had a problem."

"Thanks," I said. "I hope I can avoid any big coming-out. I tell myself to stay focused on all the good I've got."

"I'd say that too," he said. "First off, you've got one hot wife. If you ever left, there'd be guys lining up to date her in no time."

I grimaced. It was obvious.

"Oh, sorry, Ed." He tried to recover. "I didn't mean to make it worse."

I put my fork down. My appetite evaporated. I couldn't fathom Lydia in bed with someone else.

I started with yet another therapist—now No. 3—a woman named Charlene, from Steven's office. Steven had moved out of state unexpectedly, and she was his replacement. We met a couple times before I asked if Lydia should also come in.

"Maybe you can help her to understand," I said.

Lydia and I sat next to each other on a tapestry-covered couch as Charlene got right to the point.

"It looks like Ed has tried to live as a traditional married man, but it doesn't appear to be working. I know that's not what you want to hear."

"You're right about that," Lydia replied.

Charlene looked at me.

"I can also say that if Ed lives as his true self, there's a real chance things will escalate. He could end up wearing dresses and women's make-up. I can see him living as a woman in public."

"Oh, I don't think so," I interrupted. Charlene hadn't even told me this. I couldn't imagine the kind of guts it would take to live as a woman.

Lydia turned to me and rolled her eyes. "Ed, I don't think you have a clue about what would happen if you left." She was crying. I handed her a tissue.

"I swear to you that I'll never walk around in a dress," I said.

Lydia softly blew her nose, and changed the subject. "You tell me you love me, but in the next breath you say you need to have a different life. One day you promise to stay and the next you're looking out the window."

I let her talk.

"All of this back and forth, the uncertainty, is killing me. The girls and I will survive if you leave. But if you're looking for me to be the one to make the decision and tell you to leave, I won't. You'll have to decide if you love us enough."

The words stung. "Bo, I love you. You need to understand that. It's why we're here."

"Well, apparently, you don't love us enough," she shot back.

Charlene jumped in. "I'm sure you love each other greatly, but in the end, what we're talking about is accepting that some things have to be a certain way regardless of love, regardless of the fact that the two of you have created a wonderful family. Some things can't be changed no matter how much love exists."

I grabbed Lydia's hand; she pulled it away.

Charlene asked, "Lydia, is there any way that you could stay with Ed if the process went full course as I predict? Could you love Ed as a woman?"

Lydia shook her head. "No. I've told Ed that I want a man as my partner. I can't love a woman. It's not who I am."

I accepted that, but wondered: *How is this any different from me wanting to live as a woman, adored by a man? Isn't that who I am?*

I was hurting. I needed to talk to Thap face-to-face.

In January, 2004, I drove to Colorado under a gunmetal gray sky on salt-soaked I-80. As the highway pushed away from Omaha on the flat snow-covered prairie, I talked out loud.

"Tell me your story," I said.

I started at the beginning, vocalizing about the wonderment of Christine's clean lines. From there, over the course of three hours, I re-counted everything, the whole sordid mess, in chronological order: my sister's dresser drawer, inaugural masturbation, my first male-attraction fantasies, Cleveland and Boston, yearning for a vagina, and now, constantly dressing in androgynous women's clothes from head to toe. I ended with how I had flipped, then flopped, and then flipped again, on leaving Lydia.

It was the first time I had ever put things together from start to finish. There was no escaping that the thing inside me—call it a gut tug, an urge, or maybe truly a female spirit—had always existed. As far as I could tell, it would be with me until the day I died.

I thought of Max English, my mentor from Lewis & Bruce. I had single-handedly boxed myself in on I-80. There was no way to squirm out of the obvious.

Admit it: You're a woman caught in a man's body. You can't go on without being yourself. It's not fair to Lydia, and it's not fair to you.

By the time I got to my hotel in North Platte, I had again, maybe for the three-thousandth time, resolved that I would leave Lydia. Only, this time would be different: I wouldn't look back; I'd be strong, and I'd go forward despite all the pain and hurt I would cause.

Screw the guilt.

As proof, later that night, I stood in front of the bathroom mirror and raised my right arm, exposing an extremely hairy armpit. With shaving cream and razor, I chopped until there was nothing. I stepped back from the mirror and raised my arm again, this time in victory.

There they are—the clean lines of a woman's underarm. Beautiful.

I did the same to the other underarm and my chest.

I drove to Boulder the next day and met Thap for lunch. I didn't waste any time.

"I talked out loud to myself all the way from Omaha to North Platte," I said. "I realized this has been in me all my life. It will never go away. I've got to leave Lydia. I don't see how I could ever think I had a choice."

Thap leaned closer. "Kruggie, don't beat yourself up. Lydia's a great woman, but it's like I've been telling you all along, you have to be yourself. I know it's hard. Still, you'll make it. Lydia will too."

"I'm probably going to lose everything," I said. "With what I've done to Lydia, I feel like I should walk away and say 'you can have it all. It's the least I can do.'"

Thap righted up and stopped smiling. He donned his divorce lawyer hat.

"Now, don't talk nonsense. I know you'll be more than fair, but I'm not going to let you just give everything away. You've worked long and hard, and you deserve something out of this."

"I'll need your help," I replied. "First I have to tell Bo that I'm leaving for sure."

"Don't worry, I'm here for you and for her, if need be," he said. "The most important thing is to recognize what you need to do. I was worried that you'd never get to a real decision, and worried even more that you'd keep beating yourself up and get further depressed. I didn't want to think about what it could lead to." His voice trailed off.

"I'll be okay, Thap." It felt good to know that he cared enough to worry about me.

I got what I needed from Thap. We spent the rest of the day enjoying best-friends company.

The following day, feeling empowered for the first time in my life, I made an appointment at a spa in Denver. Now I was willing to do almost anything, short of surgery, for clean lines.

The spa, on the edge of downtown Denver, was housed in a chic-looking rehabbed storefront. I waited nervously until a tall, long-haired platinum blonde named Janice escorted me to a third-floor studio.

She asked, "What are you looking for?"

I answered hesitantly. "A bikini waxing."

Janice didn't react. "Take off your clothes and get on the table."

I was shaking; maybe I didn't want this after all. Somehow, I pulled together the courage. I said, "Okay, but I need to warn you. I'm wearing a bra and panties under my clothes."

Janice adjusted the dial on a wax heater. She didn't even look up. "Please. You're not the first cross-dresser I've ever seen," she said. "I'm very used to it, so don't be uncomfortable."

I immediately felt something that had been missing since those three hours at the spa in San Jose: the cool breeze of acceptance.

An hour later, I walked to my car, beaming but quite sore at the crotch. I stopped at the first rest area on the interstate back to Iowa and looked down while standing at the urinal. I saw a million red bumps but complete smoothness, the first footprints on a journey that seemed to have no end point.

Almost woman-like, I thought.

———————

We knew it was just a matter of time before the next shoe dropped. In true coward fashion, my decision to leave came in the form of an email to Lydia in early April, 2004.

I tapped, "I'm sorry, I love you, but I need to have my own life." I hit, "Send."

I called Thap and told him what I had done. "Good," he said reassuringly. "You've been miserable. Now go forward and don't look back."

I packed a small bag and checked into a hotel. I needed to figure out where to go next. For the time being, Emily and Lily would hear that I was out of town in a trial.

I wasn't gone two days when I attended a fundraising meeting for a non-profit where I volunteered. Seated around the table were a dozen people, all professionals, all married heterosexuals and, I was sure, all people who were very happy with their lives. I felt a burn in my throat; suddenly I was jealous of these straight, flawless people.

Why can't I be like you?

It was enough burning that once again—unbelievably—I told myself I needed to try even harder. *You can't hurt Lydia anymore. And the girls? You've got to be kidding. Ed Krug is better than that.*

Besides, I needed to fulfill the *Grand Plan.*

I drove to Knollwood with boxes from the office. Lydia was out of the house with Emily and Lily for dance classes. I went to the walk-in closet and filled five boxes with every piece of feminine apparel I owned. Lydia came home just as I finished.

"What are you doing here?" She was pissed. "I thought you had decided..."

I didn't let her finish. "Yes, I had decided, but no, I'm not going to be without you, the person I love more than anyone else in this world. I'm so sorry for what I've done to you, but now I know what I want. It's you I want, not me."

Lydia's face turned sour. For a second, I thought she might take a swing at me (something that neither of us had ever done). Her heart was

on life support. I had put her in our own private hell—that put it mildly—
and there I was, dragging her through ground glass once more.

"I don't know," she finally said. "What's suddenly happened? You
were pretty set on leaving me."

"I'm serious, Bo," I said. "It's a matter of me changing my life even
more, of being less obsessive and enjoying what you and I've made here.
I don't want anything but you. Please believe me."

Lydia was quiet for a few seconds. Then I saw it—the beginning of
a smile. Soon, the smile widened. I was back in.

Hallelujah!

"Okay Bo, but this is it. You can't leave again and then think that
you can come back."

"I know," I said.

To prove that I was serious, we carried the banker's boxes to her car;
she would take them to Goodwill the next day.

We went back into the house for celebratory glasses of wine. It was
great to see Lydia smile and re-center.

I called Drew Bloom and told him the good news.

"Sometimes you need to get to the precipice before realizing where
the pathway is," Drew said enthusiastically.

*Finally, I'm done with this nonsense. It's a good thing we never told
Emily and Lily.*

We took the girls to dinner at a brew pub a couple hours later.
Somewhere between the drinks and food, my gut wrenched again, but I
ignored it. I watched Emily and Lily write trivia answers on their place-
mats and reminded myself of how much I loved them.

Parents always self-sacrifice.

Soon, though, I was back to thinking about the lacy lingerie and
tight-fitting jeans boxed up in the back of Lydia's car, clothes that I'd
never wear ever again.

My gut churned: *Buyer's remorse.*

I avoided looking at Lydia because my eyes would give me away.

I reasoned with myself. *Just ride it out, Ed. Make it to bed. In the
morning you'll feel better.*

We headed back to Knollwood as the Krug family: a confused,
weak-willed husband/father, a beat-upon wife/mother, and two middle

school-aged girls oblivious to anything wrong in their worlds.

Lydia and the girls settled in the family room to watch a movie. I went to the sunroom, my sanctuary, and tried to read the newspaper. The chatter from my gut interrupted.

This is your last chance, you coward. Love yourself.

It was too much. I quietly went upstairs. Quickly, I grabbed my bag and tossed some clothes into it, along with my shaving kit and the girls' picture. I walked downstairs, dreading what would come next. I got to the entryway near the family room and opened the closet door for my coat. Lydia looked up with innocence, unsure of what I was doing. In an instant, her eyes registered horror, as if she had chanced upon a murderer in a darkened hallway. I spoke before she could say anything.

"I can't get beyond it, Bo. I'm sorry," I said. "I love you, but I have to go."

I didn't wait for her response; I couldn't take the chance. I walked out the door and opened her car. I put the boxes with their pretty contents in my BMW and drove away one last time.

In the middle of the night, after a couple hours of hotel guilt-ridden sleep, I got up and went back to Knollwood. The house was dark; Lydia was in bed. I tiptoed into our bedroom. She was in a fetal position, crying softly with a crumpled tissue in one hand.

"What are you doing back here? I don't want you here," she moaned.

"I came back because I love you."

"How can you say you love me? With what you're putting me through? I believed it when you said you wanted to stay and would never leave again. God, why did I believe you?"

I climbed onto my side of the bed. I pulled her toward me; I wanted her head on her spot. She came willingly. It surprised me.

I whispered, "I'm so sorry, Bo. There's a part of me that believes I have to live my own life. I don't want that—I love you and the girls—but I think I need to be this person who's inside me. I can't explain it any other way."

"That I can understand," she answered. "What I can't take is the inde-cision, the back and forth. That's far worse than you just leaving. Why do you have to do that to me?"

"I know," I said, "It's just that I'm so torn. We have the best marriage and I don't want to hurt the girls." I rubbed her head and listened to her weep. I hoped that she'd fall asleep so that I could feel like I did something *for* her instead of *to* her.

"That's fine, but now you can't come back. And we're going to tell the girls. *Tomorrow.*"

The words pierced my heart. I was worse than Tom Terrific; I'd be walking out the door to never come back. At least he returned home at some point.

This isn't how my life is supposed to work out, hurting the people I love. How could I destroy the Grand Plan?

I went quiet. Five minutes later, I sighed. "Aw shit. I agree, we'll tell them tomorrow. Now, get some sleep."

Lydia's crying drew down until she was asleep. I stopped rubbing her head and looked at the ceiling, thinking of the crimes I had committed and those yet to come. It was hopeless.

The next day, Lydia, Emily, Lily, and I sat in a circle on the living room floor. Emily, then fourteen, and Lily, twelve, hugged their favorite stuffed animals. Both nuzzled Lydia, each vying for an arm.

Lydia went first.

"Girls, you know Mommy and Daddy love you? Right?"

Each girl nodded. Lily squeezed Lydia's arm.

"And you know that Mommy and Daddy love each other, too, right?"

Again, two more nods.

Lydia looked at me and took a deep breath.

"Well, even though two people love each other so very much, sometimes there are things that keep them from being married, things that prevent them from being a husband and wife."

I focused on the girls as Lydia's words hit their mark. Lily kept smiling, attached to Lydia. Emily's demeanor shifted to shock.

"Why are you saying this, Mommy?" Emily asked. She pulled away from Lydia to hear the answer.

That was my cue. *This is my fault after all.* I felt a burst of self-hatred.

"What Mommy's saying," I answered, "is that while we love each other so much, there's something about me that means we can't be married. *I'm gay.* It's something that I've dealt with for most of my life, ever since I was a little boy."

The words dropped onto the living room floor, like busted cinder blocks. Emily sat up, erect, and clutched her stuffed bear. With a terrified voice she asked, "Are you saying that you're getting a divorce? A divorce!"

The cold tin sound of "divorce" caught me by surprise. My mind moved too slow, and things on the ground were happening too quickly.

I blurted, "I don't know if it means a divorce, but it does mean that I can't live here anymore, I have to live on my own."

Emily collapsed into Lydia's arms and sobbed. Lily looked at me and cried as she grabbed Lydia. All I heard was stereophonic bawling.

It was a massacre.

One last time, Lydia did a cheer for me. She heroically held it together and understood that we needed to finish and get through this gruesome moment, one that would be etched into everyone's hearts for the rest of our lives.

"You girls need to know that Daddy and I have really tried here. We're still in love and still best friends, but Daddy can't be my husband. That's not who he is. He's still a great dad for you girls and loves you very much. None of this will change that."

I was so incredibly thankful for her kindness.

"Mommy's right," I joined. "I've tried very hard. I've seen many counselors about this, and all of them have told me that I have to figure out who I am."

I quickly switched to something positive. "I'm going to get my own place to live, but we'll still have family dinners and do things as a family," I said. "I'll just be living somewhere else. You guys will have a second place to stay, kind of like a hotel."

"But it won't be the same!" Emily yelled.

Lydia responded, "No, it won't be the same, but it'll be close. We'll make sure of that."

I watched Emily bolt upstairs. Her sobs echoed throughout the house and into my soul. I had mortally wounded my first-born daughter.

I could tell Lydia was surprised, but had we thought about it, Emily's reaction was predictable. She was the perfectionist, after all.

Suddenly, I was the ultimate imperfection.

Lydia followed Emily upstairs. This left Lily. She leaned into me and stopped crying. I was numb and out of words.

As I listened to the distant sound of Lydia comforting Emily, Lily nudged me. When I wrapped my arm around her, in a clear and solid voice, she said, "Dad, I understand."

What did I just hear?

I quickly calibrated. Was Lily really only twelve years old? Or was she thirty? How could she understand any of this?

I didn't try to figure it out. I took the gift and breathed easier for a moment. We sat and hurt together.

Later, I went to Emily's bedroom and relieved Lydia. The tears continued. I rubbed Emily's head and whispered that everything would work out eventually.

This was yet one more lie. I knew things wouldn't ever be close to the same. It would be a crude Rube Goldberg contraption of emotions and compensations that wouldn't ever equate to the spectacular family we had been just an hour before.

Emily slowly quieted. I went downstairs to the kitchen, where I found Lydia. Lily had retreated to the family room, at least superficially content to watch a video.

"Well, that went over like a lead balloon," I said.

"Yes, but they will get through it," Lydia answered. "They're more resilient than you give them credit for."

"Maybe, but still, I feel like shit." I fished for an acknowledgment that this was unavoidable.

"You *should* feel like shit," she shot back in a tight voice. "You destroyed something great here."

ELEVEN: *Into the Gray*

Late March, 1990, almost two months since Tom Terrific's suicide.

I'm on the phone with Mom's quick-talking Texas lawyer whom I don't like or trust. He's been fighting with the mortgage company over my parents' Dallas condo.

"I let 'em know they won't get a dime. Your mother's distraught and there's no way she can make payments," he reports. "I'll get your mother out from under the mortgage by the end of June at the latest. She can just walk away."

Whatever, I say to myself.

It's true that Mom is distraught. Yes, she's settled into reconnecting with old friends from her earlier Cedar Rapids days. She's even found a bookkeeping job. Yet, my mother's barely dealing with the fact that her husband of thirty-four years killed himself. It was only a couple weeks ago that Mom came clean about how they had gotten behind on their mortgage and had failed at debt counseling. Except for the suicide, bankruptcy would have been next.

That still didn't stop them from taking a credit card-financed trip to Vegas last fall.

I've been fielding calls from MasterCard, American Express, and Visa for weeks; they want their money, nearly $45,000. I'm the one—the lawyer in the family—who has to convince them to take a whole lot less. Some of the cards are only in my father's name, so that makes everything easier.

"He was broke!" I yell into the phone at the Visa representative. "There's nothing left to give you."

I try to be supportive and spend time with Mom. It's not much. Lydia and I don't want her smoking in our house, and she doesn't like to stand outside.

"I'm sorry, Mom," I say for the fifth or sixth time. "The smoke gives Lydia and me headaches."

My mother frowns. She walks out the back door with her cigarettes and lighter.

I learn about a life insurance policy my father had through his employer, Avionics, Inc., worth $70,000. I start the paperwork, but things aren't moving as quickly as I want. Avionics isn't returning my calls, either.

A few hours after my conversation with the Texas lawyer, a woman in the Avionics benefits department telephones.

"Hello, Mr. Krug, this is Bethany from Avionics, Incorporated in Dallas. I have your messages, and I apologize for not returning your calls sooner." She sounds nice enough, with just a hint of Texas drawl.

"Thanks for getting back to me," I say. "I'm acting on my mother's behalf and trying to place the life insurance proceeds with a broker. Can you tell me what's needed to get her benefits finalized?"

The other end of the phone goes silent. I think that maybe we've been cut off.

"Hello, are you there?" A few more seconds pass before I hear the drawl again.

"Ah, yes, that's what I wanted to talk to you about. It appears your father had indicated a desire for a doubling of the insurance benefit, meaning that the beneficiary, your mother, would be entitled to $140,000. Unfortunately, the increased premium wasn't ever taken out of his check."

The lawyer in me quickens. I only think in black and white: someone screwed up, and I'm going to have to sue to fix the mistake. *God.* It will be more time out of my life dealing with my father's mess, more resented loose ends to tie up.

Before I can posture, Bethany continues.

"However," she says, "I've talked to my boss and the company has decided this was our mistake; we should have deducted the premium."

She pauses for a breath.

"The reason it's taken so long to get back to you is that we needed to hear from our life insurance vendor. I wanted to be able to tell you what we're going to do."

I'm still ramping up; I can't help myself.

"Okay," I answer. "And that would be what?"

"That would be we're going to pay the double benefit, the additional $70,000. Your mother will get a check for $140,000. I assume this is acceptable to your mother, yes?"

Wow, I think. A company that actually owns up to a mistake and makes things right. I almost can't believe it.

"Well, Bethany, of course, that would be acceptable." I worry that my giddiness will show. I say, "I think that's pretty honorable. It sounds like that's what my father wanted, and it's great that we don't have to make a big deal out of the mistake."

"We thought this was the right thing to do," she answers. "You know, especially after your father had called."

Whoa. What did I just hear? I put giddiness on hold.

"Did you say my father called about the life insurance?" My mind starts to race again in a zigzag pattern.

"Yes, he did. I was the one who talked to him, actually."

"Well, when was that? How long before his death did he call?"

How long had he been planning?

Did he call a month before? Had he been thinking about this for a year? Could I have done something about it? Could anyone? How blind were we?

I detect a hard swallow as Bethany clears her throat.

"Well, uh, the application for the benefits increase was signed a couple months after he started with us in 1987. There were several years that we should have been taking the extra premium out of his check and we didn't," she says.

Okay. So this is simply a paperwork glitch.

"You remember talking to him in 1987, way back then?"

It's hard to believe he would have contemplated suicide that far back, but then again, this is my father we're talking about.

There's another pregnant pause. I'm not getting the easy closure that I think this should take.

"No, you misunderstood me. Your father filled out the paperwork in 1987 asking for the increased benefits. But he called our department more recently."

She speaks with deliberate effort, choosing words carefully. It's the kind of thing I've encountered countless times when I've sat across from someone in a deposition playing attack-dog lawyer. My instincts tell me something really important isn't being said.

Something that I suddenly need to know. Now.

"Well, *how* recently did you talk to him? How close to his death?"

At the moment, nothing in the world is more important than getting answers to these questions.

In a word burst, Bethany says, "I talked to him on the thirty-first, January thirty-first, the day he died. He called our department that afternoon and asked about his life insurance. He was transferred to me. Your father asked if the company life insurance policy had a suicide clause. I quickly checked and told him it didn't, that there wasn't an exclusion for suicide."

I hear her voice break. I detect a sniffle and the beginning of tears.

Her words get to my brain. I feel a black metal pipe smash against the right side of my head.

Oh, fuck.

"Let me get this right," I start. Testosterone turns the word, *right,* razor sharp. "You mean to tell me that out of the blue, an employee calls and asks whether his life insurance policy will pay out if he commits suicide? And you do nothing about it? Nothing at all?"

I can't hide the incredulous tone. I'm human. And an attorney. And a son. Make that the son of a recent decedent.

"Well, he didn't say that he was *going to commit* suicide!"

She jumps to more words without giving me a chance to speak.

"I didn't know what to think of that call. Of course, now I wish I had done something differently, like ask why he was calling about suicide. Please, please, believe me, I've thought about that conversation a hundred times since then. I wish I had reacted better. I'm sorry, but I just didn't think...."

Her voice trails off. The drawl goes silent again. For sure, she's crying now. I imagine her holding the phone in one hand and reaching for a box of tissues with the other.

Aw shit.

I realize I'm hearing a stranger's haunting guilt. Even without looking

152

this woman in the eye, I get it. Remorse, regret, even scarring. Suddenly, and surprisingly, I back off.

"Okay, okay, I understand," I say softly. "I know this isn't easy, and no one ever assumes the worst case."

That's exactly what I think too. No human ever wants to believe another human will pull the plug on their life. At least you don't make that assumption without some beyond-a-reasonable-doubt evidence. A random phone call about an insurance policy probably isn't good enough to get someone to veer into the gray; that uncomfortable place where you actually ask, *Are you okay? Would you like to talk? I'll make the time.*

Besides, I doubt Tom Terrific would have been honest with her. Why would he suddenly start then?

Her report of my father's telephone call also sounds like something he'd do. Cross the t's and dot the i's. He had the attitude that he deserved what he paid for. If he gave up beer money to buy life insurance, he damn well wanted it to be there.

It's time to end the call. I thank Bethany for what she's done and tell her not to feel guilty. I'm sure it won't erase how she feels. Maybe her conscience will forever hit the replay button on that telephone conversation.

A few days later, I receive the $140,000 check from Avionics. I tell my mother they paid double because Dad had intended for her to get that much.

I don't tell her about the conversation with remorseful Bethany.

What good will it do?

TWELVE: *Gay Lite*

I moved into a house on Durango Drive. It was a half mile from Linn-Mar High School, where I had roamed as a hormonal teenager in love with Lydia. Now I was forty-seven years old and starting over. Finally, I had gotten to *it*, the thing I had dreamt of and resisted like hell for so long: my own life.

There was only one small problem: What did that actually mean?

A few things confirmed that I had turned quite a corner. First, my gut—the nag that demanded I take a chance on myself—suddenly quit wrenching. When I pulled up to Durango for the first time loaded down with clothes and pictures, I saw a ghost walk out the front door past me, with luggage in hand.

See you later, the ghost said with a smile-smirk. As it ducked into an imaginary yellow cab at the end of the driveway, it yelled, *I told you so*.

Then there was the euphoria I could taste. I gulped it down the first time I came home with bulging Victoria's Secret and Express bags. I put my purchases on the kitchen counter and left them there. It was liberating. No more did I need to hide the bags and their pretty contents from disapproving eyes. I was done living out of the trunk of my car, one lingerie stash at a time.

I was free to be *me*, even if I didn't exactly know what that meant.

I also discovered that Lydia was right about Emily and Lily. They seemed to quickly recover from the seismic shift in their lives. They settled into a Durango-centered routine of Friday night movies and Saturday morning waffles. Without Lydia as their primary default, the girls even competed for sofa space next to me.

Lydia and I agreed we needed consistency from old to new lives.

Every Sunday was a family dinner, alternating between Knollwood and Durango. I started cooking, something that I had secretly contemplated but never explored while living with Lydia.

"So *now* you decide to become a chef," Lydia said dryly.

One large compartment remained in my life. I didn't want the girls to snoop and find my lingerie and small but growing wardrobe of women's skirts and tops. I installed a lock on my walk-in closet door and limited my dressing to when the girls weren't around.

At the same time, Lydia and I agreed on what we called "the story," as compared to "the whole story." To the girls and pretty much the entire world, other than Thap and Mark, I was just "gay." In Cedar Rapids, the scandal of married family man turned gay man was more than enough. To disclose that I was transgender—the "whole story"—would have been far too much.

"Let's not create even more of a freak factor," I said one afternoon. Lydia nodded.

I announced to friends that I was gay. "Really?" another lawyer asked. "Are you sure?"

No, I wasn't sure. I was certain of only one thing: I wasn't a heterosexual man who could be married. Larson Williams had said as much. After eleven years of therapy with three therapists, I finally agreed with him.

Lydia broke the news to her parents, Barbara and Samuel, who wanted to meet with me alone. I went to their house on a Sunday after their church service. We sat in the living room with a clock that ticked as loud as a passing freight train. The worn family bible sat next to Barbara's chair.

I rubbed my arm. "I know you're disappointed," I said. To show both respect and resolve, I added, "I love Lydia with all my heart, but this is something I have to do."

Barbara answered, "You're right. We don't understand. We'll pray for you." Samuel looked at the ceiling.

I assembled the office and gave them the word. By then, my partner Marsha had become a judge, and the number of attorneys and staff had dwindled to seven.

"I'm gay," I announced. "I've been in therapy for years trying to stay married to Lydia. It didn't work."

I saw astonishment in the faces seated around the table. Since Lydia was the firm bookkeeper, they knew her too. Given that I was an ass much of the time, I had no doubt about who'd win a popularity contest.

"I would never have guessed that in a million years," Julie, the secretary, said.

This was typical. No one could understand that Killer Krug might be someone different, and far more human, inside.

Most people were supportive. "I'll be your friend forever," Drew Bloom offered, now resigned that my separation from Lydia was real. My sister Jacki tearfully said she'd love me regardless, something not so easy for a Catholic middle school science teacher.

The attorneys in town treated me no different—at least not to my face. A former colleague at Littleton & Davis confided, "Ed, I never join in when people make fun of you."

Nice. I think.

Michael was fourteen years younger. Our relationship gave new meaning to the phrase, "December to May romance." A couple months into living at Durango, Michael and I sat next to each other at a gay men's dinner. Almost instantly, I was hooked on Michael's jokes and wit. It helped that he was drop-dead gorgeous with short salt and pepper hair, and most wonderfully, a beautiful trim goatee. He was 6'2", and larger than life when next to all 5'9" of me.

I had found a goateed man on my first try!

Michael's cell phone rang constantly. No party was a success without his appearance. Besides humor, he had a genuine goodness that until then I had only seen in Lydia. "I accept everyone," he proclaimed on our first date. In the time we dated, he never voiced an iota of judgment or gossip.

Michael even tolerated that I wore lingerie and skirts. Clearly, though, there was a limit. He wanted me as a man—someone with a penis and scrotum glob—and not as a woman.

I wasn't completely oblivious. I fretted. *What am I doing getting into a relationship with someone so quickly?* Even more, I asked, *Will this be good enough? A man who sees me as male and not female?*

I didn't have answers. Everything was so new now, and I wasn't going to put limits on where life led me.

Just as Michael and I became an item, Jim McGreevey, New Jersey's governor, came out as gay. I watched a press conference with McGreevey and his wife Dina Matos at his side. She had a deer-in-the-headlights expression.

I thought, *This is what it looks like when someone else's* Grand Plan *implodes.*

McGreevey and I had that in common: we destroyed the *Grand Plans* of women who loved us.

I was grateful about the timing of McGreevey's confession. I wouldn't have been able to handle hearing that McGreevey, who had everything anyone could want, was willing to sacrifice it all in order to be himself. Had I stayed at Knollwood, I'm sure the news of McGreevey's coming out would have ratcheted up my self-loathing even more.

I wanted to introduce Michael to my friend Patricia, the mother of one of Lily's classmates. I had gotten to know Patricia after she and her husband divorced. Incredibly, she confessed that she had secretly been attracted to women throughout her marriage. It was one of many times I found that being honest about myself caused someone else to disclose soul-deep secrets of their own.

I set up a lunch for Michael to meet Patricia. He walked into the restaurant with a fistful of flowers, a sweet-smelling collection of yellows, whites, and purples.

"You always bring flowers when you meet a woman for the first time," he explained.

Patricia showed up a few minutes later. The flowers delighted her. An hour later, she and Michael acted like old friends. I smiled and quietly cheered.

Even Lydia wanted to meet Michael. "I might as well get to know who you're dating," she said tepidly one Sunday as I pulled a new chicken-and-mushroom dish out of the oven.

I arranged for drinks at Patricia's. I figured it would help if Lydia had a fourth person in case things got awkward.

We sat in the backyard of Patricia's house on an Indian summer

Saturday night in mid-October. A yellow and orange fire burned in a steel pit.

Lydia and Michael hit it off, and within short order, both focused on the one thing they had in common: Ed Krug.

"Hey Michael," Lydia teased, "have you figured out that Ed has the worst memory in the world? Or that you need to tell him something three times before he'll get it?"

"Not yet," Michael answered. "I've only discovered that he's pretty boring on his color selections: just whites and blacks for most of his clothes. I've told him that he needs more color in his wardrobe."

Michael threw me a wink about our inside joke: he was referring to my lingerie.

The banter continued for several hours. It was as if Lydia and Michael were suddenly on the same team. It was far better than I could have hoped for.

When it was time to leave, I offered Lydia a ride to Knollwood on the way to Michael's. We drove with Lydia in the passenger seat, just like the old days. Only this wasn't the old days, since we had Michael in the backseat, hunched over because he was too tall for my BMW. Ever the gentleman, he had insisted that petite Lydia take shotgun.

The mood in the car immediately flipped upside down. The jocularity from Patricia's instantly evaporated.

As we rounded a corner three blocks from Knollwood, I looked over and saw tears in Lydia's eyes.

My senses piqued. I heard sorrow in her breathing. I caught myself before I reached for her hand—another thing from the old days. With Michael there, I didn't want to hurt him.

Lydia's crying intensified as we drew closer to Knollwood. Suddenly I felt helpless; I needed to do something but didn't know what.

I pulled into the long, pale driveway. At this point in my trajectory, I couldn't possibly hope for a chalked *Welcome Home Daddy!*

Lydia quickly opened her door and said, "Good night, Michael. Nice to meet you." She bolted out of the car and headed for the house. I opened my door and glanced in the rearview mirror. I saw Michael frown.

I caught up with Lydia as she got the rear entry open. I followed her inside.

"Oh, Bo, I didn't know this would be so hard," I said, once more confessing naiveté. I touched her arm gently. "You really seemed to have a good time. I thought you were okay with Michael."

She cried full throttle now.

"You don't understand," she answered. "He's perfect. He is so nice, Ed. You have a new partner for your new life. And me? I'm going to be alone forever, an old hag no one will want."

Oh god. I didn't expect this.

"That's not true," I said. "You're beautiful and you'll find someone, I just know it. I didn't mean to hurt you tonight."

"I know that," she interrupted, "it's just so hard, Bo. I miss you terribly. I miss *us*. Now you're set with a great person."

I wrapped my arms around her and whispered gently, "Shush, shush, it will all turn out okay."

I remembered that Michael was in the car.

"I have to go," I said. I didn't wait for permission. I turned and walked out the door to my car with its red backlit panels. They softly illuminated Michael's face; he had moved into the front passenger seat.

I opened the driver's door and got in, only to see that now Michael's eyes were wet.

"Why are *you* crying?"

"She loves you so much," he said. "That's obvious, even after what you've both been through. It's so intense to be around the two of you. I don't think you have a clue, Ed."

I shook my head and shoved the stick shift in reverse. The car started down the driveway. I got to the street and headed for Michael's house, working my way through the shift pattern, first to second to third to fourth, slamming the stick with each ratchet upwards. I had no answer for Lydia's tears, no response to Michael's crying, only self-directed anger, even hatred, for putting two wonderful people through a meat grinder of pain.

Michael looked at me as we sped through the cool October night.

"Well, don't you have anything to say?"

What could I say? That I still loved Lydia and that if I had been able to choose, it would be her?

Or that I was so inept as to think that getting them together would give me a happily ever after?

Or that I so wanted to take everything back and dive headfirst into a closet, never to come out?

All I had was, "I'm sorry."

Ten minutes later, I pulled into Michael's driveway. The car was silent—no radio, no conversation—just the sound of Michael crying, which had slowed to a soft hurt. I didn't move to turn off the ignition.

"Aren't you coming in? I want you to come in, Ed. I need you."

His words triggered even more guilt and regret. From the moment I had turned the car away from Knollwood, I knew what I had to do.

"No, Michael, I'm not coming in," I said. "I have to go home."

"I'm hurting," he answered. "I need to be with you. Please, please come inside."

I couldn't look at him. I put the stick into reverse and held the brake. Michael opened the door and got out. He stopped and bent down.

"You have to choose, Ed," he said. His beautiful face glared. "It's not what you think, either. It's not a choice between me and her. You're stupid if you believe that. No, it's a choice between you living and dying. Once you understand that, you'll see I'm the one you need."

For emphasis, he pulled back and slammed the door.

Michael wasn't just much younger than me; he was also a hell of a lot wiser.

I let up on the clutch and shot down the driveway in reverse. The engine groaned with increasing speed. I turned the wheel, shifted, and drove away, my mind blank, my soul numb. There was nothing I could do. I was on autopilot, headed to Lydia for another middle-of-the-night-what-the-hell-have-I-done-to-you visit.

I got to Knollwood and quietly opened the back door to the darkened house. I crept up the stairs past Emily's bedroom, the magical place where I had lain on the bed reading to her a thousand times. I heard her snoring softly, my precious daughter momentarily at peace.

A few steps further was spirited Lily's room. The door was closed; there was no way to tell if she was asleep on her bed, or more likely, sleeping on a mat in her closet.

I was back in the place where I had loved and been loved, now a near-stranger.

I slowly pushed open the master bedroom door. In the light of a full moon, I saw Lydia's shape under the covers. My hearing sharpened; she was still crying. Yet again, I climbed onto my old side of the bed and collapsed on my old pillow. I heard the soft hiss of air escaping.

"What are you doing here?" Lydia asked. "I thought you were going to be with Michael tonight."

"I know. But I'm here with you. You're hurting."

"Oh, Bo. I need to get over this. You've started your new life where you've met Mr. Perfect. I have to get used to it."

I pulled her toward me. She didn't resist and put her arm around my chest.

"I don't want you here, you know," she whispered. "It just makes it harder. I have to get beyond you dating someone."

"I know, Bo, but for now, let's simply lie here. You can fall asleep like you used to."

"This won't help me," she said.

"Shush, go to sleep." I rubbed her head.

She drifted off quickly; her body twitched slightly. I lay for a while, bathed by the bleached glow of moonlight that illuminated the impossibility of my journey.

Slowly, I worked myself away. I softly retraced my steps from the bedroom, past my sleeping daughters, down the stairs, and out the back door.

I drove toward Durango and banged on the steering wheel.

Will this shit never end?

Michael was invited to a Halloween party in Mount Vernon, a small college town outside Cedar Rapids. With Van Dunkin for a last name, Michael was one hundred percent Dutch.

"We'll go as the little Dutch boy and little Dutch girl. Guess which one you'll be," he Devil-smiled. "I know where to get you an outfit."

Until then, fear and intimidation had kept me from shaving my legs or trying on makeup. I was afraid that if I went that far, I'd want more and more, just as Charlene, my latest therapist, had predicted.

Makeup in particular was intimidating. I didn't know the difference

161

between eyeliner and eye shadow. And lipstick? I'd look hideous if I ever tried any of it.

Still, a hairy-legged Dutch girl was out of the question. With a pink razor in hand, I went at my very hairy legs for nearly an hour in the shower one morning. I finished with a horrible gash behind one knee; this wasn't like shaving my face, where straight-line strokes worked just fine. I realized too late the need for light-handed deftness.

From that day on, I never again allowed hair on my legs. The silky smoothness was just as I had expected: an intense feeling of freedom.

Once more, I had nudged myself closer to the clean lines of real womanhood.

For makeup, Michael had a friend, John, who had once been a stylist. On the night of the party, I sat in front of a mirror. I wore an authentic orange sash-covered Dutch dress and huge wooden clogs. Michael held a hat that looked more flying nun than Dutch girl.

I watched John go to work. First, he grabbed powder foundation and brushed my face, ever so gently. It tickled. Next came a light shade of makeup. I felt more tickles.

"Close your eyes," John ordered, as he applied eye shadow. My eyeballs bounced inside their lids.

"Now open."

He held a mascara brush at the ready. I fretted as he drew close. "Steady, girl," he said. I stiffened as he moved from left to right eye.

"Okay, you can blink."

Again, I did as directed. I felt small clumps as I opened and closed my eyes. "Don't worry about that," he reassured.

I leaned into the mirror for a better view. John said, "We're not done yet."

I sat up straight as John gently brushed on rose-colored blush. It smelled luscious, like baby powder.

"Okay, now you can take a look."

I went back to the mirror. Big clear bulbs illuminated the face of someone female. I thought of San Jose and my one brief escape to womanhood.

Yes! There you are again!

I felt a rush of excitement; once more I had jumped the big divide separating my inside from my outside. I didn't see a man named Ed; no, I was looking at *me*, the real me, a *woman*.

I looked pretty damn good, too.

"Well, my little Dutch girl," Michael said with a grin, "should we head out to the party?" I flashed a smile that stuck for the rest of the evening.

I hobbled into a large Victorian house in Mount Vernon a half hour later. The place was packed with costumed people—Batman and Robin, a biker bitch and her poodle, even a six-foot tampon. It was a collection of odds and ends, many gay and lesbian and some not. Michael, ever popular, was in great demand. I grabbed a beer and found a place to sit. I scanned the living room and saw a full-sized casket with a fake mummified body propped up holding a beer.

It was the coolest Halloween party I had ever attended.

Oddly, I didn't feel like I was in costume. Instead, I was a woman who happened to be wearing a cute Dutch girl dress.

The McGreevey scandal spawned a cottage industry of media stories about gay married men and their secret lives.

A couple weeks after Halloween, Sunday dinner was at Durango. Lydia handed me a VCR cassette. "I taped this for you," she said. It was an Oprah show. "I learned some things. I think you will too."

I interpreted this to mean that she hoped the tape would make me question my course. I put the tape in a corner on the kitchen counter, where it sat for months until I tossed it.

The next Saturday, Michael was out of town. I took Lydia to my favorite restaurant, an Italian place. The plan was to later hit Club Basix, the only gay bar in town, where Lydia could meet my new gay friends. Even after the debacle at Patricia's, I still believed that debunking the gay mystery would help in the long run.

While we waited for the meal, Lydia brought up the Oprah show again. Her voice got tight, a signal that we were headed back to rehashing things.

She had gone online to a message board looking for comments about the Oprah show. Lydia pulled a paper from her purse.

"This was one of the comments," she explained. "A married gay man who chose to stay with his wife and family."

She pushed the paper toward me and asked full barrel, "Why can't you be like him?"

Something inside me sank.

Lydia had circled the comment. It was entitled, "Gay and Happily Married." The posting was by "Husband," and read:

> My wife knew that I was gay long before we married 13 years ago. I love her and I am committed to our relationship and our love. I am a good husband who cleans, cooks, does laundry and romances my wife. I'm glad that your show has shed some light on this very difficult subject, but please understand there is always another side.

I fumbled for a response. Lydia looked at me impatiently.

Eventually, I said, "Bo, this doesn't say how old the guy is. I'd be interested in knowing if he's had his 9/11 moment, you know, where he thought about dying."

"What does it matter if he's thought about dying?" She reached for my hand. "He loves his wife and doesn't care about her gender. How difficult can that be? I love you, Bo. And I miss you so much."

With exquisite timing, the server showed up with our dinners; I was temporarily saved by a hot plate of chicken Parmesan.

I adroitly changed the subject, which worked until it was time to leave. Lydia suddenly wasn't in a mood to dance with gay men. I inquired—don't ask me why—"Do you want to go back to Durango to talk?"

Lydia answered, "Yes."

At my house, we sat in the dark on a newly purchased living room sofa, a Pottery Barn replica. Lydia got up and flicked on the gas fireplace, igniting a yellow-blue flame. The fireplace, which came with the house, wouldn't have been my first choice. Gas doesn't produce a real fire. I much preferred the wood fireplace at Knollwood where you had to work for a flame, but once lit, it burned much hotter and longer.

Lydia returned to the couch and sat next to me. We shared a small blanket. I had figured we would talk, she would cry, and I would drive her home. On the way back to Durango, I'd stop at Club Basix for some fun—finally.

Lydia leaned into me. Instinctively, I put my arm around her and stroked her arm. Within minutes, we kissed.

It feels so good to kiss my Bo again.

Before I knew it, we were in my bedroom. Part of me, the rational part, was numb. I couldn't find footing in my head. Reason gave way to emotion, to reconnecting with my soul mate and lover. A half hour later, I was on my back, on my old side of the bed, with Lydia's head on her spot.

"I love you, Bo," I whispered, my body spent.

"I love you too." She sighed.

I soon felt an old sensation in my gut, a familiar tug.

Don't you know this won't turn out well?

As I had done so many times before, I reached for an imaginary knob and tuned out my gut.

Leave me alone, I thought.

Lydia fell away, into her own space, asleep on my shoulder. I found sleep after a while; I didn't want to think about what I had done to the two of us.

My last thought before drifting off: *You're so goddamned weak, Krug.*

After that night at Durango, Lydia and I entered a netherworld that I dubbed "Gay Lite."

The ground rules?

I would wear what I wanted, live at Durango, and have my new gay friends. The one prohibition: sex with men. Lydia and I would remain un-divorced as we figured things out, and we'd continue to occasionally sleep together. A part of me, the man part with testosterone in his blood, was completely fine with this arrangement.

Another part, the female grounded in reality, knew this was craziness.

I had dated Michael long enough to realize that I couldn't be with a man who didn't see me as a woman, even if Michael was okay with the clothes I wore. Something, another kind of tugging that had barely begun, hinted that eventually, I'd need to deal with my penis and scrotum glob in a way that wouldn't make any gay man happy.

I gave Michael the news. "I need to pull back and be supportive of Lydia," I said in a telephone call. "I'm also uncertain about where I'm headed with my body. It's not fair to you."

He wasn't entirely surprised, but he didn't want me to leave. "I love you, Ed," he said. "You're making a mistake."

I had no resiliency, no bending left in me. "I need to get some work done," I answered. I didn't wait for a reply and hung up the telephone. More cowardice.

For thirteen months—from November, 2004 to December, 2005— Lydia and I kept one foot in marriage and the other in gray uncertainty and apprehension. Emily and Lily didn't mind one bit; they loved having two parents dote over them in separate houses.

Even Lydia seemed happy with the arrangement. "I have the best of both worlds," she said. "I can paint the kitchen any color I want, but I still have you, my best friend. Not to mention, someone who makes dinner and takes the girls to give me personal time." She raised a ruby red cosmo as a toast to Gay Lite.

I went back to Charlene. "So tell me, Ed, how's it working out?"

"Not well," I answered. "Lydia's getting everything she needs. All I've done is reenter the closet."

Sunshine streamed into Charlene's office. It heated the arm of my chair.

"I'm glad you understand that," she replied. "How do you think it'll end?"

"Badly. I'm sure we'll jump the tracks at some point."

"How will you handle that?"

"Who knows," I said. I looked out the window.

Several months later, I announced, "I'm taking all of us to New York City." It would be Lydia's fiftieth birthday present and a family vacation. Lydia and the girls started planning immediately.

We stayed in a small room at a nice hotel just off Times Square. Lydia and I shared one bed and the girls shared the other. We saw a couple Broadway plays and toured the Empire State Building. We took a cab to Greenwich Village to buy Emily and Lily their first iPods. On the way back to the hotel, we walked through Chinatown. Lily held my arm and nuzzled the entire way.

We stopped at a large cosmetics store. I saw a man wearing eye shadow and mascara. It sealed the deal that New York would forever be my favorite city in the world.

———

Lydia and I slowly realized that Gay Lite couldn't possibly stand either the test of time or my feminine spirit. "You need to date," I said. She reluctantly took my advice.

By late 2005, she had racked up a total of three dates split between two men. One man was too young and the other too old. As for the old sap, she reported, "He's got health problems and too much baggage." She had kissed him, "But I hated it. I only want you, no one else."

While that made me feel good, it didn't resolve the ultimate issue.

We were invited to a well-heeled holiday party in December, 2005, which we had attended for years. A few weeks before the party, I heard about a man named Stephen Johnson whose wife died the year before. The rumor was that he was witty, charming, smart, and most importantly, that he'd be at the Christmas party.

I called a friend and asked what she knew about this Stephen guy. "Oh, Ed, he's really nice and very personable. I've never heard a bad thing about him."

A pretty good review, I thought. I told Lydia that she needed to talk to him at the upcoming party.

"Why would I do that?" she said with a grimace.

"You know why," I answered. "He sounds decent."

"I don't want to talk to someone named Stephen."

On the night of the party, Lydia and I arrived as a couple, which I'm sure confused many people. After all, we were supposed to be divorcing because I was gay.

There was a large table of wonderful finger food and two bars with free drinks. The atmosphere was festive and alive. People were still quite receptive to me, gay or not, and I made the rounds.

An hour into the event, Stephen showed up. Someone let me know this was the man of the hour. From across the room, I saw the younger brother of Neil Young, the singer. Stephen was in his early fifties, tall and solid, with a short gray beard and good-sized graying ponytail.

Jesus Christ, I thought. *A ponytail! Lydia can't even get used to the idea of me in modest women's clothes; how would she ever go for a guy who's got an actual ponytail?*

I walked over to Lydia and pointed out Stephen. "Go talk to him," I directed. "He'll be thrilled that you did."

She looked at me skeptically. "I'll do it in my own good time."

Twenty minutes later, I was in the odd position of watching my wife stand next to a stranger as they talked and laughed, and talked and laughed some more. Lydia was making an impression; how could she not, being the delight she was?

After the party, Lydia and I drove to our favorite bar for an after-party drink.

"So, what did you think?" I desperately wanted to hear that he was a cad.

"He's nice," she offered. "I don't think he's really interested, though. He had a date to leave for. He seems to want someone different than me."

This was nothing more than her filter. I was certain Stephen would call her. I was equally sure Lydia was interested, ponytail and all.

A couple weeks later, I was in Boulder visiting Thap. Lydia called to report on her first date with Stephen the night before.

"It was so much fun," she said. "I met his friends, and all we did was laugh." Her excitement was unmistakable.

I felt something thud against my left ankle and glanced downward. It was my heart.

"So, are you going to see him again?" I hoped against the odds.

"I don't know if he even wants to see me again," she responded.

Right. Unless he's some kind of idiot, he'll see you again. The terminal thinking continued. *This is it. I'm toast.*

Stephen and Lydia dated again. And again. And again.

On Christmas Eve, 2005, Lydia surprisingly insisted that I sleep over in her bed. "Bo, it'll be great to have you here in the morning for the girls." I was reluctant. It would be another reminder of what I had given up. As usual, I surrendered. We had a nice family Christmas.

For New Year's Eve, Lydia and I invited a few friends to Knollwood. Much to my surprise, Stephen wasn't one of them.

Lydia took a picture of Emily, Lily, and me in the kitchen that night, smiling and touching. It was the last picture of the three of us ever taken in that house, the last time we were any semblance of the *Grand Plan* that had once been.

Two weeks after New Year's, I had dinner at Knollwood. It was time to leave, and I leaned in to kiss Lydia. She returned a quick peck. I reached for her again and offered something more intense, a test to see where things stood.

This time, instead of lips and tongue, I kissed a brick wall.

Lydia pushed me back. "No, I can't do this anymore. I need to see where things go with Stephen."

It was the formal announcement that deck chairs had been rearranged.

I knew this was coming. Even so, it was near impossible to hear. I drove home to Durango dazed and hurt. How I could have put into place a plan where my lover and soul mate ended up with a guy sporting a ponytail?

What the hell was wrong with me?

At the end of January, 2006, a month and a half after Stephen's appearance in our lives, Lydia and I went out to dinner.

"Stephen's a lot like you," she reported. "He makes me laugh, but there's a real sensitive part to him. I feel like I've met you all over again."

"I'm glad for you," I lied. Everything—my marriage, my love affair with Lydia, my family, my home—was gone.

I reminded myself, *This is how it has to be, Ed.*

A week later, in the middle of the afternoon, I was at Knollwood to pick up some tax documents. No one was home. I decided to snoop in Lydia's private places and found two unsigned Valentine's Day cards. One was highly romantic, with the printed words, "You've taken my heart, which I've gladly given." The other was addressed to "My good friend." Inside were the words, "I really appreciate how you support me."

Even a moron, which I certainly constituted, could understand which card was for Stephen and which was for me.

Wait. There was a spark of hope. On her nightstand, Lydia still had a picture of me in a frame in the shape of a star. Maybe the relationship with Stephen was rockier than it appeared.

On the next Friday night, just after Valentine's Day, I stopped at Knollwood to pick up Lily for an overnight at a friend's house. She was the only one home; Lydia and Stephen were out on yet another date and Emily was cheerleading at school.

I went to my old bedroom while Lily packed her bag. This time, the room was immaculate. I had never seen it in better shape: pillows and bedding were in their proper places; the nightstand and headboard were dusted; a brand-new candle rested on a window ledge.

Most importantly, the star picture of me was gone, retired to some old lover's drawer.

This will be the night when she will sleep with HIM!

All at once, the weight of loving Lydia for three decades collapsed on me. It was far more than mere hurt: I couldn't breathe as I hungered for the intimacy of our hearts and thirsted for Lydia's laugh. I desperately craved Lydia's touch and sexual energy and wanted her head on my shoulder forever. Most of all, I yearned for how Lydia could ignite me with a single word: "Bo."

In that instant, I also grieved for the lost feeling of *home.* I so missed living with Emily and Lily, the other loves of my life.

A few seconds later, everything shifted. I became angry, even enraged—at Lydia, at life, at me. I had fucked up everything and had no one to blame, not even Tom Terrific. This was all *my* fault. I had voluntarily forfeited happily ever after—the one precious thing I had scraped and clawed for ever since the night Lydia comforted me in the driveway at Kent Drive.

How stupid can you be, Krug?

Lydia's made-over bedroom was proof that I was on my own now, alone. I feared it would be that way forever.

I grabbed hold of myself. In turn, one more thought, this one far cooler, shot into my brain. Despite the hurt, anger, and remorse, a part of me—the one that would love Lydia until my very last breath—knew this was *right.* It was so important for her to have someone. I knew Stephen would treat her with respect and love. For reasons I couldn't explain, that somehow comforted me.

My gut rang up parched words of reason. *You can't have what you want, but now, for the first time, you're on your way to getting what you need.* It was enough of a hook for the moment.

From downstairs, Lily yelled, "Dad, I'm ready." I took another look at the immaculate bedroom. For a second, I thought about creating mayhem. I could mess the bed or steal the K-Y or do something even worse.

I left everything just as it was and closed the bedroom door.

I drove away from Knollwood with a crumpled heart. I dropped Lily off at her friend's and headed to watch Emily cheerlead.

I cried hysterically as I sped down a blackened roadway.

Lydia and I never again called each other "Bo."

It just didn't feel right.

THIRTEEN: *Black Hole*

I fell into a three-mile-deep vinyl-lined black hole.

Time and again, when I struggled to stick to Gay Lite, I had projected that I'd feel relief once Lydia found my replacement. Reality was entirely different. The ache reached all the way to the back room of my soul. A stomach knot became my constant companion. I stopped eating and sleeping and drank cases of Heineken and chardonnay.

When outright exhaustion gave in to sleep, I woke in the middle of the night consumed with Lydia.

How can I go through life without you?

My spirit drained away. All of a sudden, I didn't care about freedom or some stupid journey of self-discovery.

I wanted my soul mate.

The clock in my head quit ticking off how little time I had left. Now it sounded the number of years, decades actually, that I'd be alone without Lydia.

I had completely taken for granted that I was ready for *me,* for my new life.

It was a horrific miscalculation. I hadn't been alone since I was fifteen years old. For three decades, Lydia had been one of my limbs, certainly my best and most functional. In a grand fit of self-absorption, I had single-handedly amputated my Lydia limb.

I thought of those kids who had tangled with railroad trains. At least their losses were visible. Mine was completely emotional, self-inflicted, and as far as I could see, endless.

I wept and grieved. Dreary pessimism replaced abounding optimism. I scratched at black vinyl, but simply fell deeper and deeper.

Thap called frequently. "Ed, you need to focus on the future, not the past. I'm proud of you. You've done what you needed to do."

One of his calls came at seven on a Tuesday morning. "How'd you sleep last night, buddy?"

Weeks before, I had remembered that the camping tent—now collecting dust in my garage—contained fifty miles of nylon rope. The balcony that led to the basement at Durango had a solid wood and metal beam, no doubt strong enough for my weight. I thought of the people to whom I'd write notes, and mentally composed what I'd say. I would tape a sign on the front door, "Don't enter. Call the police and Mark Krug."

I lingered at 4.5 on my own personal suicide scale of 1 to 5 for weeks.

It didn't help that Lydia was so happy. Or that my avoidance strategies didn't work.

One Thursday evening in early spring, 2006, I picked up Emily and Lily for our weekly dinner out. I put on the Daddy face, the one that smiled and joked, and asked Fate to give me a break for a couple hours. I pulled it off through dinner.

We drove back to Knollwood. Emily asked me to stay and watch one of her television shows. Lydia was out with Stephen, and I figured the show would be over before she returned.

My timing was less than perfect. Midway through the TV program, Lydia came in the back door, enlivened. I wanted to melt into the couch.

A minute later, Lydia walked into the family room chewing on half a roll. I said, "The dinner mustn't have been that good if you're eating again so soon."

Reflexively, she answered, "We didn't have dinner." She suddenly got red-faced and then hustled up the stairs.

I was confused until I remembered: Stephen was to leave for a spring break cruise with his son the next day.

Of course!

They had needed goodbye sex.

I felt a gunshot to my heart. I jumped up from the couch.

"Emily, I just remembered that I have a brief due tomorrow and I haven't gotten it done. I love you."

Emily's mouth was agape as I ran out the door.

I drove away from Knollwood picturing Lydia and Stephen in bed with her head on his shoulder—her new spot. The tent rope was an answer to that pain.

Yeah, Krug, just do it. End it all.

I gunned the BMW and blew through stop signs. I tried to remember my Boy Scout knot training and thought about what I'd wear. I mentally composed more suicide notes each mile I got closer to Durango.

End it. You'll never survive being alone. Someone else is getting all her goodness. You fool!

My suicide scale ratcheted up to 4.75.

Everything changed three blocks from my house. Somehow, I remembered the death rainbow in the tub in Dallas. I thought of how Dad had missed out on so much, especially knowing Emily and Lily. There was the hurt from the suicide, which I'd never want to inflict on the people I loved.

I fell back to the most enduring of all thoughts: *I am not Tom Terrific. I've never been my father. All of that will change if I kill myself.*

By the time I pulled into Durango, I shook my head.

No. No way. Never. Ever.

I didn't want Emily and Lily to feel about me what I felt about Tom Terrific. I couldn't put Mark and Jacki through a repeat performance by yet another dysfunctional Krug. And Thap? For the rest of his life, he'd wonder if he could have done something to prevent it.

I ordered myself to bed. Somehow, I found sleep that night, a life raft in a sea of distress.

Fate had given me a reprieve after all.

Our rotating Sunday family dinners ended soon afterwards. I was the reason; it was too hard to sit across the dinner table from the ever-vibrant Lydia. The culminating event was a meal at Durango. I started with Heineken and switched to wine before Lydia and the girls even arrived. I was tanked by the time we sat down to eat.

As soon as they finished their plates, Emily and Lily went downstairs to watch television. The ensuing conversation with Lydia, fueled by my resentment and self-hatred, slid into a screaming match.

"I'm thrilled he makes you so happy," I yelled. "You got what you wanted, didn't you?"

"Stop it," Lydia answered. "This isn't *my* fault."

Emily and Lily's horrified faces poked up from the stairway. It was one of the few times we raised voices, let alone argued, in front of them.

"Come on girls, we're leaving," Lydia ordered. She grabbed her purse and they were gone.

I left the dishes on the table and opened another bottle of wine. I drank until I passed out.

———————

The weather got better and the days longer. With pickaxe and rope, inch by inch, I climbed out of the black hole that imprisoned me.

I signed up for Match.com and began to meet people of both sexes. If I really was going to explore my new life, I wasn't about to restrict myself.

I met many women and men. There was Susan, a struggling mother of seven, who seemed to attract a daily crisis. I had enough drama without taking on someone else's.

I briefly dated Joe Joe, an exceedingly kind gay man with an even deeper voice than mine. Once again, he couldn't see me as female. After that, gay men were off my list.

Next was Robin, who had dropped 200 pounds with the help of surgery. She had plastic stars on her bedroom ceiling that shined at night. "I'm intrigued that you're transgender," she said one evening. "But, it probably isn't for me."

The optimist had returned. I dated someone new almost every weekend. I hoped that I'd find another Lydia, a single-word-igniter, who accepted me as *me*.

Someone had to be out there.

FOURTEEN: *Coming Home*

Janelle Callahan dropped into my life on a Friday in August, 2006. She was a smart, engaging, short-haired blonde with attitude who lived in Minneapolis. Her teenage daughter needed a ride to visit friends in Cedar Rapids and Janelle obliged.

With her daughter delivered, Janelle had free time. By complete cosmic chance, Janelle stopped me on a downtown street to ask for directions to an outdoor café.

"How about a drink with a stranger?" I responded.

Twenty minutes later, we were at the Tic Toc.

It didn't take long to wonder whether Janelle might be *the one*. I was instantly attracted to her looks, confidence, and wit. She had worked as an MBA-credentialed business consultant for many years. Later, she returned to school for a master's degree in social work. Now a therapist, she specialized in helping people deal with emotional trauma.

We were still on our first drinks when Janelle related that she went from dating men to dating women when she was in her twenties. Years later, she returned to men and married Robert. They had two children. When her kids were young, she switched back to women and left Robert for Kathy. She lived with Kathy for several years until she felt the need to date men again.

Janelle sounded as screwed up as me. It gave me hope.

She was also Buddhist. I'd never met a real-life Buddhist before and considered Buddhism a kind of voodoo religion. Still, I wasn't going to let that stop me.

I told her my story, particularly the transgender part. She didn't flinch. She didn't embrace it, either.

The next night, I took Janelle to an outdoor concert at a large public estate in the middle of Cedar Rapids. We got to the entrance and paid our fee. As we started down a long paved walkway through some woods, Janelle grabbed my arm.

"Wait," she whispered. "Do you hear that?"

"Hear what?"

"The crickets. Don't you hear the crickets? Aren't they beautiful? All in harmony."

I cocked my head and listened. She was right. A gazillion crickets were chirp-singing. No one had ever pointed out crickets to me. Until that moment, I never knew that crickets were something you should listen to.

Why has this Janelle woman shown up in my life?

We sat in my car at the end of the night. I said I wanted to visit her in Minneapolis.

"I don't know," she answered. She shifted closer to the passenger door. "You're pretty intense, more than I want. You also don't have peace. I can't get caught up in that."

I wasn't going to let Janelle slip away so easily.

After many telephone calls, which got easier and more jocular each time, I convinced Janelle to let me visit Minneapolis. I would meet her at the Dakota, a downtown jazz club.

At a rest area south of the Twin Cities, I changed from men's business suit and tie to black Express women's slacks and silky white androgynous top. Underneath, I wore matching lingerie.

I found Janelle sitting with a friend at the Dakota. We listened to a female vocalist and the friend left. Janelle and I walked across Nicollet Mall to an Irish pub with dark wood and hand-carved relief throughout. We found a small nook and sat next to each other.

Twenty minutes later, doubt crept in. Was Janelle all that different from other people who refused to accept me? I didn't want to get invested, especially with the long distance involved, only to reenter a closet to make her happy.

Without a plan or script, I veered off course.

"Remember I told you I'm transgender? Well, what about that? Is it something you can live with?"

Janelle paused, obviously surprised by my frankness. She searched for words. Finally, she said, "Ed, I don't know what I think. It's very unusual."

With the alternate lives that we each had lived, and the fact that she was a therapist, I had expected a lot more.

Her equivocation sank in. I looked at my watch. It was almost 1:00 a.m. If I left right away, I could be back to Durango by daylight. At worst, I'd have to get a motel somewhere along the way.

Janelle saw my processing. Before I could say that I wouldn't bother her ever again, she did something totally and completely unexpected.

She began to cry. In no time, it migrated to full-scale bawling.

"Please don't leave," she pleaded. "I really like you. I don't know what you being transgender means for me, but I want to see where our relationship goes. You're one of the most interesting people I've ever met. Please stay."

Aw shit.

On the one hand, it felt good to hear that she wanted me to stick around. On the other, I knew my gut would soon wrench. I couldn't be invisible anymore; the female part of me *had* to be seen.

Still, I couldn't stop empathy from kicking in. I reached around Janelle until her head found my shoulder.

A few minutes passed. I figured that I would scare Janelle away.

I asked, "Do you want to come back to my hotel and talk in bed? We can discuss this and whatever else you want. I promise, no sex."

It was a one-hundred-percent foil. I was certain this suggestion—of all things—would put her off. She barely knew me, and what kind of woman heads into a hotel room with a near-stranger to just lie in bed and talk?

Apparently Janelle Callahan was that kind of person.

She wiped her eyes with a bar napkin, and sat up. "Yes," she said. "I would like that very much."

Awww shittt.

Unbelievably, she had called my bluff and was willing to go into the gray. At that point, something yanked the power cord to my determination. Rationality went with it. Now I, too, was okay with seeing where things would go.

An hour later, Janelle and I were in a hotel bed. True to my word, we didn't have sex, or even kiss. Instead, we talked and giggled. Our stories were shared, secrets revealed, quirks disclosed. She talked about fears, bad memories, and lost chances. I confessed to being an attack-dog lawyer who yearned for something different without knowing exactly what that meant.

We fell asleep at four o'clock, having started something. What it was exactly, neither of us knew.

———

Emily and Lily shifted. They no longer wanted Friday night movies or Saturday morning waffles.

It started with Emily, by then sixteen. "I hate your house!" she yelled one night as we drove to Durango. My leaving, and Lydia's moving on with Stephen, had sunk in. She'd never again have the perfection or nuclear family she needed. It was killing her.

Lily, too, pulled back. "Why did you have to do this?" she asked one day. "Are your friends really more important than us?" She was fourteen and didn't understand what it meant to find yourself.

Hell, I barely understood it at forty-eight.

Underlying this was a million-dollar question: Would my daughters eventually view me the same way I viewed my father?

As I saw it, every reach for a Scotch or grab for a Bud was his choice. So, too, was every missed dinner or decision to cheat on Mom.

Will Emily and Lily think that I've also made selfish choices? That I chose against them? Worse yet, was it actually true: did I have free will every time I slipped on panties or buttoned a woman's blouse?

Will my daughters ever understand — as three therapists absolutely did — that really, I had to wear those clothes in order to be myself?

Where is the line between self-preservation and selfishness?

Paradoxically, what if I had worked just a little bit harder and found one more therapist — the right *therapist? Would I have been able to get "fixed" and stay married to Lydia?*

Did I really give my all to the girls of Knollwood?

I didn't have answers. The questions gnawed at me, corrosively, and fed my guilt. I compartmentalized to find temporary peace. Yet — to have real, permanent peace — I needed answers.

Would they ever come?

If things were bad with Emily and Lily, they were abysmal with Lydia. She had been the Krug Law Firm bookkeeper from day one. Try as I might to limit my interaction with her, I couldn't hold fingers in my ears tight enough to block out giggling from the adjoining office when Lydia phoned Stephen. Her glee made me feel like she had traded up from a Chevy to a Cadillac.

I had had enough.

I said, "You need to find another job. One that's full time."

She looked at me as if I had just reported someone's death.

"But what about the girls? I want to be home for them after school."

"The girls are teenagers who hang out in their bedrooms," I answered. "There's not much you're doing with them anyway."

We soon had a new bookkeeper and Lydia had a new job. It was too bad, too; the replacement didn't measure up to Lydia.

Janelle and I were soon in a real romance that included the word "love." Like Lydia, she appreciated the trench warfare inherent in my trial work. She texted, "Go get 'em," or sent cards assuring me that I'd survive whatever crisis had arisen.

I had found another cheerleader. Only, Janelle was a step above "rah rah": she wanted to teach me a few things too.

Janelle had voluntarily forfeited a six-figure income as a business consultant in favor of becoming a therapist. Life, as Janelle saw it, shouldn't focus on possessions or money. It should be about living free of wants and being open to new things.

"You need to flow with life, not push at it," she said. We were in our usual classroom—a bed.

Janelle sat up, and put a pillow behind her back. She continued.

"Your life is too complicated, Eddie. You have too much fear and you grasp for things that aren't attainable. You operate according to the Krug Plan. The world doesn't care about your plan. You'll never find peace until you understand this."

"I work hard to accomplish goals," I answered. "Look at what I've been able to do—a law firm, a successful career, two great daughters. Now I'm living as me."

Janelle laughed and shook her head.

"No, you're not *living*," she said. "You're holding on to things, like the past—your father, that scared little boy at the window. You're holding on to Lydia too. You suffer because you can't get back some feeling of home. Life doesn't work that way. Everything has its own moment and once that moment passes, it's gone. You need to be mindful of the present. That's as good as it gets."

I frowned. This was Buddhist mumbo jumbo. What did "mindful" and "suffer" even mean? I bounced against my Catholic upbringing. Even though I rarely made it to Mass, I still wrestled with core Catholic principles, like sin; if I sinned, I'd be judged harshly and wouldn't make it to heaven.

Most of all, Catholicism taught that I needed to sacrifice for others; I wasn't worthy as my own person. I had value only if I did for others.

One day a package from Janelle arrived in the mail. It contained a CD box set, *Buddhism for Beginners,* a lecture series by some guy named Jack Kornfield. I wasn't interested in learning about Buddhism. That was Janelle's deal, not mine. I put the package on a bench in the mudroom and forgot about it.

I continued to wear androgynous women's clothes and lingerie. I was encouraged when Janelle borrowed one of my skirts, a wispy white cotton Gap number.

How cool is that? We can wear each other's clothes.

On a visit to Minneapolis, Janelle and I went to a reading by Norah Vincent, the author of *Self-Made Man: One Woman's Year Disguised as a Man.* Vincent had masqueraded as a man for a year, befriending men and entering circles where women weren't welcome. She spoke about gender being both fluid and solid, and how society's unwritten gender rules dictate the way people treat each other.

Janelle nodded again and again as we listened to Vincent. Maybe she would understand my gender journey after all.

Not long after that, while we lay in bed, Janelle whispered, "Eddie, you're a lesbian. I see it now."

Finally, I thought, *Janelle sees me.*

Lydia and I attended parent-teacher conferences at Emily's high school in November, 2006. The tension between us was palpable. Small talk wasn't an option.

I trailed as we moved between classrooms. Lydia stopped in the middle of a crowded hallway and announced, "It's time for the divorce. I found an attorney who's not afraid of you."

I felt nausea and panic. "Divorce" sounded so final. There was also the practical; we had already agreed to a division of assets, which I purposely tilted in Lydia's favor, despite Thap's advice. Why did she need a lawyer?

Ignorantly, I asked, "An attorney? Why? We've already decided on how we're going to do things."

"That money is for me to live on after I retire," Lydia snapped. "I need other money to get me to retirement."

Holy shit.

I didn't want to fight with Lydia.

I hired a lawyer, but I did most of the work myself. It wasn't a long process. Three months after Lydia's announcement, she and I met at the Tic Toc.

"Arguing will hurt the girls in the end," she said. "If you can compromise, I can too."

Of course. In less than an hour, we worked through the remaining issues and agreed on money and other assets.

The last item was the pastel picture of the girls drawing in chalk surrounded by dappled sunlight.

"Can I still have the dappled light picture?" I asked.

Lydia smiled, bittersweet. "That's yours," she said. I could tell she really didn't want to part with it.

"How about if you keep it for now? Just as long as I know I can have it someday."

"That would be great, Ed."

Emily and Lily would feel better, too, with the picture at Knollwood.

In February, 2007, I walked into the Linn County Courthouse holding divorce papers. I knocked on the office door of my former law partner, Marsha.

"You know why I'm here," I said sheepishly.

Marsha answered, "I'm so sorry for both you and Lydia." Her voice was tinged with sadness.

On the way home from the courthouse, I stopped at a bar for a drink and to write in my journal.

Afterwards, I called Janelle.

"It's official," I said. I was driving through the frozen Iowa country-side. "I'm divorced."

"That sucks."

She was right.

Two months later, Janelle and I drove along Florida's west coast and let a two-lane blacktop road lead us wherever.

We stopped at the Suwanee Motel one night. It was another Uncle Ed place: rooms in a string wrapped around a parking lot. Behind the hotel, stairs led to a dock on the Suwanee River. The hotel was owned by a husband and wife, both Indian, who had grown up in apartheid South Africa. As a young girl, the wife knew only one American song—"The Swanee River," which helped fuel her dream to leave South Africa for a better life. It was pure serendipity that she and her husband came to the United States and found the motel for sale.

If you don't dream, it'll never happen.

The next day, Janelle and I drove to Apalachicola, where we found the Gibson Inn, a grand hundred-year-old hotel. A manager showed us several rooms for choice of decor and color. We settled on a gray room with colonial furniture. After checking emails, Janelle and I set out to explore quaint downtown shops.

Lily called. She, Lydia, and Emily were fighting constantly. Life at Knollwood had become dreadful. Previously, Lily and I had talked about her moving in with me, but by the time of the divorce, she had decided to stay at Knollwood.

Lily got right to the point. "Dad, I want to live with you. I don't want to be here anymore."

Oh, man.

"We'll talk about this when I get back in just four days," I said.

"But Dad, why can't I come live with you?"

"I didn't say you couldn't; I said we will talk about it when I get back. I can't talk now."

I looked at sailboats on Apalachicola Bay. I wished I was on one of them, sans cell phone.

"Tell me now," she demanded. "I don't understand why you can't just say 'Yes.'"

"We'll talk when I get back. I love you," I said. I hit "END."

Lily didn't understand that I needed to talk to Lydia; we had promised to cooperate with each other when it came to the girls. Lily moving out would upset whatever order existed at Knollwood, not to mention that it could throw a wrench into how we figured child support in a divorce that was barely two months old.

There was also the fact that I hadn't talked to Lily (or to Emily for that matter) about Janelle sleeping in my bed when she visited Durango.

I didn't want to deal with this stuff while on vacation.

"Eddie, I want you present. Don't get lost in your head now," Janelle said. She pressed her hand into mine, and smiled from behind a pair of funky sunglasses. She was right, this could wait.

We found a place for dinner. It was late when we got back to the hotel. Janelle and I sat on a balcony and looked at a sky awash in stars.

Despite the idyllic setting, I wondered how long Janelle and I would last. Yes, she had called me a lesbian. However, she hated the idea of me wearing skirts. She barely put up with my lingerie. More than once, she said, "I'd marry you in a minute if you weren't transgender."

Not that I had actually ever asked her.

Once again, I had compartmentalized and bided time with the hope that Janelle would somehow miraculously proclaim, "Okay, I get it, and I'm in for the long haul wherever your gender journey takes you."

The next morning, we woke in the gray room. Janelle whispered, "I know you would have rather been in the pink room, but I didn't want it."

Our last stop was a bed and breakfast in the French Quarter of New Orleans. We sat on a patio and took in the city sounds before heading out for the evening. When we got back to the room, there was a voicemail on my phone—this one from Emily.

I heard horrific sobbing.

"I want my old Daddy back, the one who used to take us to Dairy Queen, and who used to play Barbies with us. I don't like this new Daddy," she cried.

My legs went weak. I had to sit down.

Emily didn't answer my return call.

I thought of getting on a plane and showing up at Knollwood to hug Emily tight. I would beg her to forgive me, and I'd tell her that I never wanted to destroy our family or her childhood. I would take back everything and live with her forever as her Dad, a real man.

"At least Emily's talking about how she feels. It's a start toward her getting better," Janelle said, once more the therapist.

That was damn easy for Janelle to say. Her children were much younger when she left her marriage. They had more of a chance to adapt. I left when my poor daughters were barely teenagers. First I told them I was gay. Now I dated a woman. It wasn't only hurtful, it was confusing as hell.

Emily's call was reason to end the vacation early. We got back to Cedar Rapids and I dropped Janelle at Durango. I headed to Knollwood thinking that Lily, Lydia, and I would sit and talk. I'd explain how moving in with me probably wasn't what Lily really wanted since she'd be lonely; I was hardly ever home because of my law practice.

That idea went out the window as soon as I walked into the foyer. At the base of the stairs was everything Lily owned—clothing, books, desk lamp, computer, and Fred the stuffed basset hound.

Lily bounced down the stairs, ecstatic. "I'm coming home with you, right, Dad?"

Lydia looked beat upon. She said, "It's what she wants. It's okay with me." There was no way I could tell Lily anything but "sure."

I loaded the car while Lily said goodbye to Lydia.

Emily, the other reason I ended my vacation early, was at dance practice.

Oh, Emily. I need to see you and say, "I love you, my dear daughter."

In the car on the way to Durango, I told Lily that Janelle was waiting for us. "Oh, that's fine," Lily answered, happy to be starting anew.

"Yes, but you need to know that she sleeps in my room with me, not in the guest bedroom." I thought this would be a big revelation.

Without missing a beat, Lily said, "That's what I expected, Daddy."

————————

Emily's voicemail was the start of a long descent between us. She withdrew and refused to talk to me for several months.

"She'll come around," Lydia assured.

I felt helpless. I knew that Emily hurt—I had wounded her—yet, she wouldn't let me give a hug or even a kind word.

Emily eventually came back, but things were never quite the same. Just as she had predicted.

————————

I traveled to Dallas for a case. The weather felt summer-like. I bought a skirt at a shop in the hotel.

I called Janelle from my room and let slip about the skirt. "It's really cute," I said, in an effort to deflect.

The phone on Janelle's end went quiet. I heard crying when she finally spoke. "I don't understand why you need this," she said. "Isn't what we have good enough?"

That confirmed it. I was back in a familiar neighborhood of walled-off emotions; a ghetto of unfulfilled hopes.

To my surprise, Janelle didn't give up. Instead, she did what she was best at: pondering possibilities and theorizing about how the brain works.

The weekend after my Dallas trip, she visited Cedar Rapids.

"I've been thinking, Eddie. I don't believe you're really transgender. You're all male when you're with me, sexually and in your mannerisms. How can it be that you're really a woman, like you say? I've met other people who are transgender, and you don't fit the profile at all."

"If I'm not transgender, then what am I?"

Janelle smiled.

"I believe you were traumatized by your father's drinking and not showing up. Your dressing in feminine clothes is a reaction to the trauma. I've looked at various studies and several researchers link trauma to gender identity disorder."

"Don't therapy me, Janelle."

"I know this is sensitive for you. Still, from everything you've ever said, your attraction to female things didn't start until after you realized your father drank too much. Think about it."

Given that I first ran into Tom Terrific when I was seven years old, just about everything in my life occurred after I understood he drank too much.

Janelle's diagnosis also ignored what three therapists had said. Each was very experienced. Could all three be wrong?

Janelle had one leg up on Larson, Steven, and Charlene, however: I hadn't slept with any of them. Clearly, they didn't know me like Janelle did. Now Janelle was challenging me intellectually. I respected her smarts.

The challenge didn't feel very good. What if Janelle was right— this was all about my father? It wasn't as if I could walk through the Knollwood front door, the long-lost traveler, and take all the hurt back.

Janelle suggested that I find a therapist who specialized in emotional trauma. She wasn't in Minneapolis more than a couple hours when she emailed with the names of three prospects in Cedar Rapids. I picked the one with the smallest office. I still didn't want to be seen in a crowded waiting room.

I had a reputation to uphold, whatever it was worth at that point.

I walked into Samantha Castle's office on a cool morning in June, 2007. She was late in greeting me, something I detested. When she finally showed, I saw an attractive strawberry blonde with a forced smile.

We sat opposite each other in off-white stuffed chairs. A clipboard with my completed questionnaire, a checklist of a dysfunctional life, rested on her lap.

"I see that you're divorced, the father of two adopted daughters, both of whom are traumatized by the divorce," she said with a glance my way.

She went on. "You're a lawyer, you're stressed out, you work too much. Your father killed himself. He drank too much. You drink too much. You think you're really a woman underneath a male exterior. Have I missed anything?"

If nothing else, this Samantha woman was damn efficient.

"No, you've got the essentials," I answered. I felt an urge to get up and walk out.

"Ed, what do you want to accomplish here?"

Jesus.

I was there only because my girlfriend believed my father's drinking and womanizing had screwed me up into believing I was actually a woman. Is this the kind of thing you tell a brand-new therapist in the first five minutes?

I decided that it was.

I uncrossed my legs and bent forward. It reduced the space between us. I didn't want any confusion about my goal: to avoid any more wasted therapy—or time—in my life.

"Every therapist I've seen said I needed to leave my marriage because I have this gender thing where I view myself as female," I said. "I'm in a relationship with a woman who's convinced I think this way only because of my father. I don't believe her, but if she's right and if I can be 'fixed,' by all means I want that. Can you understand this?"

By then, Samantha was leaning backwards. She held the clipboard to her chest like a shield.

"I don't know what I can do for you, other than offer perspective," she answered. "I certainly can't promise anything. And we'll need several sessions for me to get to know you."

I was sure this was a standard line. I suspected that most therapists can figure someone out in twenty minutes, tops. Yet, they never give pronouncements until at least the fourth or fifth therapy session, if even then. After all, they have to make a living too.

Still, there was something about Samantha's direct approach that I trusted. Maybe it was her desire to stick to a protocol. I was the same way in my law practice.

I settled back in my chair. "Okay," I said, resigned. "Let's get to it."

"Oh, and call me Sam, please. It's more comfortable."

By the time we were done that day, Sam had asked more questions about my childhood and teenage years than all my other therapists combined.

We got close to the hour being up.

"Are you comfortable coming back?" she asked.

"Yeah, I'll come back." I didn't actually know if I'd return. I needed time to figure it out.

As usual, I had one last question.

"Understanding you still need to get to know me better, give me your gut reaction right now. Can an alcoholic cheating father cause a kid to believe they're caught in the wrong gender?"

For the first time in an hour, Sam smiled.

"I don't think so," she said. "I doubt that trauma has anything to do with your gender orientation."

I exhaled.

"You understand, don't you, that your girlfriend probably has an agenda in trying to tie trauma to your issues?"

Now I smiled. "Yeah, I guessed that."

I got up and started for the door. Maybe this new therapist could help me after all.

The most horrific case in my career came into the office just as I began to see Sam. It involved a thirty-year-old man named Ford—a jogger who had been run over by a semi and dragged for a quarter mile. The weight of the truck crushed Mr. Ford's pelvis and forced the amputation of both legs. The accident also destroyed his colon and most of his buttocks.

I received the call from DEF Trucking at 9:00 a.m. on a Sunday morning, an hour after the accident.

"Ed, you've got to get to the accident scene and protect us," David, the company president, instructed. Ten minutes later, I was in the car attempting to break the land speed record to Des Moines, one hundred miles away.

For twelve hours, I walked around pools of blood and patches of skin and bone. I diagrammed the scene, and talked to witnesses. My investigation showed that Mr. Ford, a divorced father with a young daughter, had made the mistake of jogging past a *Don't Walk* crosswalk light.

I took Mr. Ford's deposition several months later. He wheeled himself into the conference room and resisted anyone's assistance. Tattooed on his forearm in large numbers was the date of his accident: "6:12:07." My job was to prove that he alone was at fault, and to deflect any claim that DEF Trucking contributed to the accident by not looking out for a jaywalking jogger.

In the past, I had eagerly attacked plaintiffs, arguing they were responsible for their own injuries, something that plaintiff lawyers call "blaming the victim." I was good at it too. Often, I was able to convince juries that the plaintiff had lied or was mistaken about how the accident happened.

Despite my take-no-prisoners approach, many times I was secretly sympathetic. I saw how serious injuries devastated victims and their families. Many times, accident victims never returned to their former lives or selves.

With Mr. Ford, something changed. Sympathy morphed into real doubt. I started to wonder.

Is this really who I am? A killer lawyer?

Janelle, Lily, and I flew to a hot springs resort in Wyoming in the summer of 2007 for a Thap family reunion. The place was overrun with Thaps — Colorado Thaps, Iowa Thaps, California Thaps. Of course, Thap and his second wife, Bebo, were there.

On the big night of the reunion, everyone gathered in a pavilion near the main hot springs. Bebo wore a pretty top, a brown and lavender Western-themed tee with sparkles.

"Bebo, I absolutely *love* your top!" I gushed.

Twenty minutes later, Bebo excused herself and left the group. I thought nothing of it.

Bebo returned wearing a white sweater. She held the sparkly top out to me and said, "Here, Ed, this is for you. My gift."

My startled look signaled that I couldn't believe her generosity, or more importantly, her acceptance.

"Really, Bebo? It's mine?"

"Yes, it's yours. I want you to have it."

I turned and saw surprise in Janelle's face too. Only, she wasn't smiling.

I hopped and skipped to my hotel room and changed into the top. When I returned to the pavilion wearing undeniably feminine clothing in public for the first time in my life, every Thap, along with Lily, cheered.

Janelle sat stone-faced.

Later that night, Thap and I found a few minutes to talk. We were on the best-friend wavelength in no time.

"How's it going with Janelle?" he asked in between bourbon and Coke sips.

"Oh, not too good," I answered. "She pushes back on my skirt wearing. She says that every time I put on a skirt, I take a step away from her, away from us."

Thap shook his head. "Kruggie, that doesn't sound good. Do you really want another relationship where the other person pushes you to be someone you're not?"

"I know, but I love her, Thap."

"Yeah? That's also what you said about Lydia."

Thap and Bebo saw us off the next day. Thap hugged everyone goodbye. Later, after we ended everything, Janelle said that Thap's hug told her our romance was over.

"He hugged me," she said, "like he knew he'd never see me again."

I saw Janelle only once after Wyoming. I never reported what Sam had said about her using trauma as an excuse to keep me a man.

What I did say: "I see myself as a girl. You see me as a boy. I'm not a boy, and I'll never be a boy again."

I hated hurting her. Mine were honest words, strengthened by some finger-scraped wisdom.

Janelle cried. "I only wanted to love you and for you to love me," she said.

There was nothing more to say. I was done being anyone's *boy*friend.

I prepared for a trial in Omaha on a case that involved a family named Jones. A semi owned by my client, Blonde Walnut Trucking, had blown through a red light into an SUV driven by Mr. Jones with his passenger adult son. Both elder and younger Jones claimed brain injuries. The father denied being able to work after the accident, yet he continued to remodel his house—a new bathroom, siding, landscaping. The son, a school teacher, alleged that his brain injury affected his sense of right and wrong. At least that was the excuse when he was discovered to have stolen from the school milk fund.

The Jones trial was fast approaching. On a Wednesday, I was again in Dallas on legal business. I had to be in Omaha the next day at 2:30 p.m. for a crucial doctor's deposition in the Jones case. Our defense would go out the window without that deposition.

Thunderstorms canceled my 8:00 p.m. flight to Omaha, along with every other flight for the night. The next available flight wouldn't get me into Omaha until early Thursday evening.

I decided to drive the almost 700 miles to Omaha.

I took the shuttle to the airport rental car kiosk and went up to the Hertz counter. "Sorry, sir, we have no cars available," a skinny mustached customer rep said.

I strolled over to the Budget counter. Again, it was the same story—no cars. I sprinted to Alamo, Dollar, and National, and heard the same thing.

Full panic set in. Blonde Walnut Trucking and its driver, a fellow named Alvin, would be screwed if I didn't get to Omaha in seventeen hours.

I rushed back to Hertz. A different customer rep, a middle-aged woman of color named Alma, was at the desk.

"I beg you," I said. "I will be in so much trouble if I don't get a car tonight." She couldn't miss my shaking hands.

"I'm sorry, sir. We're out of cars."

"Please, can you try again? My professional life depends on it."

Alma hesitantly checked a computer screen. She hit a key, and then another, and then soon clicked at light speed. She said, "Just a minute, sir."

I watched her duck into a door. I wondered if she'd come back. Ten agonizing minutes later, Alma reappeared. She was smiling.

"If you're willing to take it, I have a three-year-old Taurus."

"Are you kidding? At this point, I'd be happy with a thirteen-year-old Yugo."

Now I had sixteen and a half hours to make Omaha. With luck, I'd be able to stop along the way and catch an hour's sleep.

My cell rang just as I got on the interstate. It was Lydia. I heard tears; she had broken it off with Stephen.

"But why? You've been going out with him for a year and a half. I thought you were set for life."

Up ahead, lightning ripples coursed through the night sky.

"He couldn't commit to me." Her voice cracked. "He couldn't say 'love.' I have to move on."

"Oh, I'm so sorry," I answered.

I really wasn't.

"Do you think he'll come around?"

I hoped that he'd be gone forever.

"I don't know," Lydia replied. Then, from left field, I heard, "Why can't he be like you, soft and open? You never had a problem saying what was in your heart."

Did I just hear what I think I heard?

I couldn't speak. Other than sloshing windshield wipers doing double duty, there was dead silence on my end. Suddenly, I felt pretty good despite the pounding rain and marathon drive ahead.

"Well, give him time," I offered, finally. "He's a man, after all. They're not real good at processing things until reality hits them in the face."

Lydia laughed. It broke the tears. We moved onto other things—my crazy day; the girls; how Janelle and I were over.

"I'm sorry. I know she meant a lot to you," Lydia said.

"It's how it needs to be," I answered.

Except for talking about lovers gone awry, the call was like old times.

I had to concentrate on my road map, so I said goodbye. I drove north over drenched concrete, ecstatic.

"Soft and open," I repeated. *Words that describe a woman more than a man.*

I made the Omaha doctor's deposition with twenty minutes to spare.

A week later, I was in a downtown Omaha courtroom for the Jones trial.

Blonde Walnut Trucking's corporate attorney, Matt Green, came to watch. He soon became a real pest. Throughout the trial, he whispered in my ear while I tried to listen to witnesses. He demanded that I retrieve documents from my voluminous file and ordered that I ask certain questions.

When I wasn't making particularly good headway with father Jones (something that happens with at least one witness in every trial), Matt wrote notes. Red-faced, he shoved one note at me, "Sit down!," and then another, "Stop asking questions!"

I thought, *Who the hell does this guy think he is?*

I wasn't used to battling the opposing attorney and my own client at the same time.

A jury trial is an arduous process. It requires grit, tenacity, intelligence, and pure luck. The Jones trial turned out to be the most difficult of my career. The volume of witnesses and exhibits had me up at 2:30 every morning to prepare. After nine hours in the courtroom, I returned to the hotel to get ready for the next day. I was in bed by 9:30, drop-dead exhausted. This ordeal went on for a week and a half.

For brief escapes from exhibit piles, strewn files, and scrawled notes, I gazed out my hotel window at Omaha ten stories below. Across the street was a contemporary fountain, very low to the ground, where water spurted sequentially from one end to the other via two dozen nozzles. There was a hypnotic rhythm to the spurts.

One evening I watched two women, early twenty-somethings, take turns at hopping across the fountain. Each tried to stay ahead of the spurts; one woman was way better at it than the other. The slower woman had a long, dark ponytail which lyrically swayed with every movement. She wore a black sundress that billowed on each hop. Fountain water, like an exceedingly public bidet, sprayed between her legs on some of her miscalculations.

A pang of envy shot through me for all that this woman had: the freedom to wear a dress, a shapely female body under that dress, the liberty to be silly and herself in public, and most of all, the wisdom to know that sometimes, one must hop across fountains.

I felt a thirst in the recesses of my throat. I so wanted to be that woman, living her life and free of the masculine armor that imprisoned me.

On the last trial day, we reached a settlement while the jury waited in another room. As the Joneses prepared to leave, Mrs. Jones approached Alvin, the truck driver, and me.

"I don't hold any ill will toward you," she said to Alvin. She turned to me and sneered, "You—you're cruel. I hope you rot in hell."

I closed my eyes in a failed attempt to teleport to another planet.

Two jurors were in the hallway as I wheeled boxes of files.

"What did you think?" I asked gleefully, since Mrs. Jones wasn't around.

A short-haired woman, juror No. 5, replied, "You were great. We didn't believe either of the plaintiffs."

The other juror, a bearded man seated in chair No. 3, agreed. "They weren't credible. You showed that."

I looked over and saw Matt. He had heard every word.

I thanked the jurors for their service. I pushed the boxes half a hall-way length when the woman juror yelled for me. She asked for my card. "If I ever need an attorney, I'll call you," she said.

Again, I looked at Matt. He appeared distressed, as if he had just eaten something that didn't agree with him.

The Jones trial made me question whether I wanted to step foot in a courtroom ever again. I was alone without a cheerleader to urge me on. I was worn out from attacking people. Worst of all, I feared the woman inside me would never see the light of day.

If things didn't change, there was no way I would ever be able to hop across a fountain in a dress.

I saw Sam two days after I got back from Omaha. "I'm way stressed," I said. "It's never been this bad. Life just seems so hopeless."

Sam stopped writing on her clipboard. "So what are you telling me here, Ed?"

"I'm saying I have no idea how to turn things around. I want to simply give up."

That must have scared her.

"I think you should consider a thirty-day voluntary commitment to get your head in the right place," she declared.

What? No way.

The last thing I wanted was to be "committed" for anything. The stigma and lost self-respect would be too much, not to mention the cost. The mere suggestion woke me up.

"No, Sam, I'm not going anywhere for one day, let alone thirty," I said. "It would destroy my law practice."

"I'm worried about you destroying yourself."

I didn't want a sheriff showing up at my office with a court order for an emergency three-day evaluation.

"Don't worry, Sam, I don't have a suicide plan. I haven't written notes. I'm just overwhelmed by everything. I'll get my head straightened out. I promise."

Sam was only half convinced.

"You need to do better than that. I want you to swear you won't do anything to harm yourself without talking to me first. If you can't get me, go to the emergency room. Do you promise?"

"Yes, Sam, I promise. I give you my word."

I thought of Uncle Ed.

"Okay. However, if I don't see some kind of change, I will have to take a different course. Do you understand?"

"I understand." Her message was unmistakable.

We were out of time. She walked me to the door. She reached to shake my hand.

"Can I have a hug?" I felt like crap and needed the touch of another human.

Sam pulled her hand back. "I'm sorry Ed, I hug only women. I've found that men can misinterpret hugs."

Zombie-like, I turned away. I felt worse than when I walked in. Even my own therapist had rejected me.

After that, I gave Sam a nickname: "Sam the Hammer."

It fit perfectly.

Making things even worse, Lydia and Stephen's breakup was temporary. By the end of the summer, they were back together. Just as I predicted, Stephen woke up to reality.

Before Stephen stepped back into the picture, Lydia and I began to socialize again. I found myself in the Knollwood sunroom sipping cosmos and giggling with Lydia. We didn't have illusions of reconciling as husband and wife, or of even returning to Gay Lite. It was a nice respite, but bittersweet, and drove home once more what I had given up and, I'm sure, what Lydia had lost.

One day I cleaned the mudroom and came across Jack Kornfield's *Buddhism for Beginners* that Janelle had given me. I opened the box set for the first time and saw eight CDs and a short introductory booklet.

What the hell, I thought.

I had scheduled road trips on several cases. I could listen to the CDs as I drove from point A to point B. My clients allowed me to bill my travel time. I could get paid while I learned about Buddhism.

Isn't that convenient?

As August, 2007 stumbled along hot and humid, I crisscrossed Iowa and listened to Jack talk about compassion and how all of us are interconnected. He explained the value of living each moment to its fullest. I relearned words and phrases in the Buddhist context: "enlightenment," "mindfulness," "loving-kindness," and Janelle's all-time favorite, "suffering." I started to understand that Buddhism wasn't some voodoo religion. In fact, I realized it wasn't a religion at all, but more a way of living one's life.

Most of all, with Jack's help, I recognized that a root cause of suffering—particularly my suffering—was fear.

I thought of my assorted fears, especially a fear of dying alone, with no one to hold my hand. More immediately, I was scared to death that all hell would break loose if I ever actually got to the point of being unable to live without actual clean lines.

What if I really needed a woman's body? Could I actually have surgery? What if Emily and Lily shut me out? Hadn't I put them through enough already? Could I really take that chance?

Jack said I needed to face my fears head-on. I could get beyond them once I understood that fear was simply grasping for a particular outcome; that if something didn't happen the way I wanted, the outcome was somehow bad. The truth, as Jack explained, is that we control nothing.

This resonated with me; for decades, I had been trying to contort myself into someone that I wasn't. I needed to completely accept who I was. Until I did that, I'd never feel completely free or alive.

By the eighth CD, I was a convert. Buddhism could help me live genuinely, open to the world. It was a path to finding my one true self.

I learned there was a Buddhist center in Cedar Rapids, set up in an eighty-year-old house not far from downtown. An instructional class was set to begin in mid-September. I signed up.

It would have made Janelle so happy.

I walked into the Cedar Rapids Zen Center on a sticky September night. A short, compact bald woman dressed in a black robe greeted me. Zuiko, the resident priest, smiled.

"Welcome," she said enthusiastically.

Four other newcomers sat in what had been the living room. In lieu of furniture, small square black mats with tiny circular cushions were positioned throughout the room.

Barefoot and nervous, I knelt with a cushion under my butt. I faced a wall and tried to clear my mind. Jack had instructed that meditation was a process of eliminating thoughts one by one, to the point of fluid consciousness. For an intense worrier-planner-judger-observer like me, this wasn't particularly easy. I didn't even get close to fluid by the time I heard a soft gong that marked the end of meditation.

We moved to the former dining room and sat at a table where Zuiko lectured on Buddhist concepts. I learned about the "Ten Precepts"— the Buddhist equivalent of the Ten Commandments—and the three "poisons" of greed, hate, and delusion. Zuiko talked about how people "wear a rut" into their psyches; because of thinking a certain way for so long, it becomes near-impossible to change that thinking.

"We each need to step off a one-hundred-foot pole," Zuiko instructed.

Then there were compassion and loving-kindness. "As Zen Buddhists in particular," Zuiko said, "we work to alleviate suffering of others through compassion, even if they are people we ordinarily wouldn't care for." She went on. "Loving-kindness is a way to approach the world, extending good will to all and being concerned about greater humanity."

All of Zuiko's teachings resonated with me in a way like nothing before. They sure trumped fear-based Catholicism.

I went back to Zuiko every Thursday for two months. The number of students dwindled to one—me. Each session provided greater clarity about what was wrong in my life and right about me, the *real* me, the *female me*.

A key Buddhist concept is that we never find inner peace because of ignorance and delusion. I wondered if it was delusional to believe I was actually female.

I finally got brave enough to ask.

"Zuiko, what if a person physically appears male but believes they're actually female inside? Is that a delusion? Wouldn't that person be grasping for something unattainable?"

My journal was open for notes.

Zuiko closed her eyes as she answered.

"No, that's not what 'delusion' means," she said softly. "When someone believes they are too important or better than the rest of the world, that's delusion. We're all interconnected. It's ignorance to think that we're not."

I hung on every word.

"If someone allows their inner essence to surface, that isn't delusion. It's never ignorance or delusion to understand who you are. It's quite the opposite, actually. Knowing your true self is called 'enlightenment.'"

I was certain Zuiko understood that my question wasn't some random intellectual exercise. Her words warmed my heart and hugged my soul.

As our session ended, Zuiko could see me beaming. She said, "It looks like you have come home. I'm so happy for you."

A few minutes later, I opened the Zen Center front door and floated out. Finally, some things were crystal clear.

Despite her refusal to hug me, I continued to see Sam the Hammer. On a windy fall afternoon, I opened the Durango mailbox to find an envelope. It was a note from Sam, along with some plastic cards printed with Zen sayings. Each card had a single word and Japanese symbol: "Courage," "Tranquility," "Destiny," and "Contentment."

In the note, Sam wrote:

Dear Ed: After you left today, I decided to look through my Zen cards for some guidance in our work together; specifically I was thinking about "hope."

These cards resonated with me. You are important; your work is important; I am invested in both.

Peace, Sam

No one had ever said they were willing to invest in me, a confused and quite screwed-up biological male who thought he was a girl.

I had Jack's CD lessons, along with Zuiko's wonderful teachings.

Now Sam believed in me.

Even better, her note was right on.

I had hope.

FIFTEEN: *Going Public*

I joined the board of directors for Connections, an Iowa City gay and lesbian social and educational organization. A dozen people introduced themselves at an orientation meeting in October, 2007. A 6'2" broad-shouldered woman with a slightly strained voice said, "Hi, I'm Elizabeth." She looked around and announced, "I see that I'm the only transgender person in the room."

I thought, *Oh, no you're not.*

Elizabeth and I quickly became friends.

"I've figured out that I'm not a gay man," I confessed. "Sexually, I'm probably a lesbian or bisexual. Gender-wise, there's no question. I'm female, just like you."

"I had you pegged by the second meeting," she said. "Your clothes, how you talk, your mannerisms. *Please.* All feminine. Frankly, you're leaking."

"Leaking?"

"Yes, *leaking.* It's coming out your pores. You have to deal with this."

Is it really that obvious?

After all, not even five months before, Janelle had told me that I was too masculine to be transgender. Did she lie to me? Or, did Jack and Zuiko help open my feminine floodgate? Could I have evolved almost overnight?

"You need to see a therapist who specializes in gender therapy," Elizabeth said. "I'm sure Samantha is a big help, but you should work with someone who treats gender identity issues all the time."

"Who does that in Iowa?"

"No one. You'll need to go to Chicago or Minneapolis."

Despite this nudging, I was wary. Elizabeth had previously confessed that she felt pressured into sex change surgery, technically called "sex reassignment surgery," far too soon.

"I wish I had spent more time thinking about it," she said one night over pizza. She began to cry. "I'm easily influenced. It shows up with authority figures, like doctors."

She had experienced other problems too. Months after her reassignment surgery, Elizabeth visited relatives on the East Coast. On the way back to Iowa, she stayed overnight in Ohio at a hotel with a bar. Security personnel confronted her as she emerged from the women's restroom in the bar. They believed she was a man masquerading as a woman. When she produced a driver's license which identified her as female, the hotel staff fell over each other in apology.

"Right then and there," Elizabeth explained, "I decided to have facial surgery to make me look more feminine."

That surgery, known as "facial feminization," was successful; Elizabeth had an undeniably feminine face.

"That's a whole lot of trouble," I said. "I can't believe I would ever have that kind of courage."

Her tears ended, Elizabeth grinned. "Oh, somehow I know you'll do it," she said. "And when you do, I'll be very envious. With your small frame and natural features, you'll be beautiful."

I didn't believe her. I never imagined that I could step out of my house wearing a dress. Makeup continued to intimidate me. My beard was shag-carpet thick. I hated the idea of the anesthesia and surgery that it would take to get actual clean lines.

Still, afterwards, Elizabeth's words sank in. *Beautiful? Me? What if...?*

———————

I took Elizabeth's "leaking" observation to heart. Two months later, it was time to jump the next hurdle.

Emily and Lily curled into their respective chairs at Durango. It was one of those increasingly rare instances when both were at my house at the same time.

I settled onto the couch and took a deep breath. I smiled and said, "You know how I love soft feminine things? Well, that's who I am."

The girls looked at each other and then at me.

"What are you saying, Dad?" Lily asked. "That you're really not gay?"

"You're right, that's part of it," I answered. "I'm not gay, at least not with gay men. I had to figure out who or what I really am, and that's why I dated Janelle. Now I have a better idea. I'm transgender."

They were used to my androgynous clothes and shaved legs. I didn't think the word "transgender" was a huge shock. Yet, it was one more label, another veer from center lane, added weirdness in their lives.

"What does this mean?" Emily asked. "Are you going to walk around in a dress?" She frowned.

"Oh god, Emily, that's such a big step." I said. "But to be honest, I can't say that I won't ever do that."

The girls again exchanged glances.

"There's been a female spirit inside me all my life," I said. "Mommy knows this. I think it's one of the reasons she loved me so much. But both of us were afraid that the spirit couldn't stay contained in my boy body. That's the real reason why I had to leave three years ago. I had to figure it out."

"Will this affect your job?" Lily asked. "What about college for us?"

"Don't worry," I answered. "You know I always have a plan, I will always protect my girls. Nothing will happen overnight, and I'll be able to save what we need."

I doubted that was sufficient to allay their fears. It was all I could offer at the moment.

Lily shifted in her chair. "What about surgery, Dad? Will you change your body?"

"I don't think so," I said. "That would take a completely different level of bravery, something I don't have."

The living room fell quiet. Emily stared out the picture window.

It was time to change the subject. "Who's up for take-out pizza?"

Two teenagers nodded. An hour later, we were downstairs on the couch watching one of Emily's TV shows while munching on a pepperoni-mushroom pizza.

My daughters had had enough of my continuing saga for one night.

Not long after that, I took Lily to a performance by Scott Schofield, a female-to-male transgender performer who had a one-person show at a Cedar Rapids art venue named "CSPS."

Schofield's show—for which he had won a national artist's grant— was set in his high school years, when he began to transition from female to male. Now he was in his late twenties. With short sandy hair and a voice hinting of testosterone, he definitely appeared male, something that many transgender persons call "passing."

Lily and I took Scott out for burgers at the Tic Toc after his show.

"Gender is between the ears, sex is between the legs," he said, just before he bit into a sloppy cheeseburger.

Scott talked about his girlfriend, who loved him for exactly who he was: a boy who had been a girl. I was jealous. His partner obviously saw life far differently than either Lydia or Janelle.

Lily and I rehashed the evening on the way home.

"You know, Lily," I said. "Lately, I've felt pretty good about myself. I'm starting to like me."

Lily grinned wide. She softly punched my right arm.

"Way to go, Dad!" In the next breath, she said, "I think you look good in those women's sweaters you wear. I don't like it when you put on a collared shirt or man's suit. They're not who you are."

I nearly drove off the road. I replayed her comment in my head for weeks, each time with a little wider grin.

For my fifty-first birthday, I treated myself to a room on the seventh floor of the Hotel Vetro in Iowa City. The room was furnished in exqui- sitely tasteful 1960s chic: Warhol prints, orange chairs, a huge globe light, and floor-to-ceiling windows that faced downtown Iowa City. Outside, big fluffy flakes swirled as day receded into night; suddenly, I was in the French Alps instead of small-city Iowa.

I brought along all my journals, a banker's box load. I laid them out on the bed, side by side, twelve volumes and twenty-five years' worth of my life, on a red polka-dotted bedspread. I started with the first journal— the one from Lydia on the night I left for BC Law—and went to the next, and the next, on and on. I took in a chronology of love, confusion, competing needs, self-sacrifice, guilt, and cowardice. The journals—*my own words*—whispered, spoke, and yelled. I had been learning the same lesson over and over: that no one would love *me*, the *woman in me*, until I loved myself. If I really loved myself, the answer was clear.

I needed to take a chance on *her*, the unnamed woman who had taken up residence in my soul since forever.

She's brave and she'll protect you. Don't be afraid.

A minute later, doubt crept back in.

Did she have the strength and wisdom to survive the difficulties ahead? Was she brave enough?

Out of nowhere, I heard my mother's voice as she paced at Kendall Drive: *"You could end up dead in a gutter."*

I shuddered and pulled the covers over my head.

The next day, I created one of those morbid bucket lists. Item 3 was to write a memoir; Item 5, "Wear a skirt near the ocean on a sunny day with people who love me."

Also on the list: a Sunday *New York Times* subscription and one more Colorado camping trip with Thap. The last item: to live free as a woman, away from Killer Krug, the testosterone-fueled attack lawyer.

It didn't take long to start checking things off the list. Soon, I had a condo in downtown Minneapolis, a city I had gotten to know when I dated Janelle. It was alive with arts and music. Minneapolis also had one of the country's largest gay and lesbian communities, so it was very safe. Plus, my dear brother Mark lived there.

If things really fell apart, he'd be around for clean-up duty.

I would make the condo my second home; a weekend place where I could explore my femininity, and get to know the woman inside me, without the risk of running into anyone who knew a guy named Ed Krug.

An hour after closing on the condo, I stood on a balcony outside my new living room facing downtown Minneapolis. I had peeled off jeans and sweater for pink tank top and casual black skirt. I held a celebratory Heineken; my journal sat on a lawn chair borrowed from Durango.

It was a beautiful spring day. I welcomed the sun's life-giving rays and sighed with relief. I had taken my first big step.

I'm the cat's meow, I told myself.

I learned about the Town House, a Saint Paul bar where cross-dressers and transgender people gather. I also heard that a tall, big-hearted white-haired transgender woman named Nora hung out there. Several Internet acquaintances said she was willing to help others navigate their gender journeys.

I walked into the Town House a little after nine on a Thursday night. I wore my most feminine top, a pink V-neck, and tight Victoria's Secret jeans.

The decor was wood paneling wrapped around a long, worn bar, nothing fancy. A dart board and two lifeless pool tables occupied space. Loud music played to an empty dance floor. A few women grouped around the bar, but dim lighting made it impossible to tell if they were genetic females or men dressed as women.

I sat at a table just off the dance floor. People soon filtered in, filling the place. A DJ ratcheted up the music. By then, my eyes had adjusted. Yes, those people at the bar were guys dressed as women. Each wore a short skirt (what I later learned was a giveaway); some wore cheap wigs. One was Amazonian-like, at least 6'3" tall.

A gorgeous drag queen named "Susie Lee" pranced onto the dance floor. She had long legs, big lashes, a tight-fitting black dress, and four-inch heels. I watched her gyrate and lip-sync to Madonna's "Like a Virgin."

None of the drag queens in Cedar Rapids looked this girl-real.

The audience engaged in a drag show ritual—handing Susie Lee dollar bills in return for quick kisses. I saw flannel-shirted butch women and tight-tee wispy men patiently line up with their offerings.

Compared to the Gender Puzzle in Iowa City, the Town House was in another galaxy.

I spotted an older woman with long white hair in a yellow dress on the other side of the dance floor. She was big and tall and stood out. I watched her receive various passersby, as if holding court.

Nora, I guessed.

I beelined over when I saw an opening. I yelled because of the music.

"Hi! Are you Nora, by any chance?"

She tilted her head and shouted, "Yes. Do I know you?"

"No, ah, you don't. I'm new to town, but I've heard of you. More than one person has said you're the Mother Superior of transgender people. Are they right?"

"Oh, you're funny," she answered. "Yes, I do know a lot of people."

I asked if we could talk. We went behind a door to a small and quiet function room.

"This is my first time to the Town House," I said. "I just bought a condo in downtown Minneapolis, and I'm trying to make friends. I'm told that if there's anyone to know in the Twin Cities, it's you."

Nora blushed.

I didn't want to waste her time. "What advice do you have for someone just starting out? I'm brand-new to this world."

I hoped she'd be kind.

"There's so much to know," she said. "Most of it you'll have to learn on your own. I can tell you a few things."

For the next forty-five minutes, Nora provided a verbal transgender primer—information not easily found on the Internet or in books.

She explained that many transgender people fear losing family or friends and never leave the closet. For most, the cost of surgery is too much. They stop short of actual surgery and live as women with penises or men with vaginas. Many times, the inability to transition to one's true gender leads to other problems, like depression or alcohol or drug addictions.

"Many people find a way to live in two different genders," she said. "I have lots of friends who come here every week. They're not interested in transitioning genders or know they can't. They want to have fun and be themselves, if only for a few hours."

I put my half-empty Heineken aside. This stuff was too important to forget because of alcohol.

"Isn't there an age where people just give up, where they say 'I'm too old to have surgery?'" I needed to know if it was realistic to even consider sex reassignment surgery.

Nora shook her head. "I know of people who have had surgery in their late sixties. One doctor advertises that he's operated on someone in their seventies."

I was amazed. I thought, *The need for clean lines is that powerful.*

It made me wonder if I really even had a choice about surgery.

Nora went on. A surgeon wouldn't operate unless the patient followed the "Harry Benjamin Standards"—named after the first psychiatrist to study people with gender identity issues. One of the standards required that a person live in their true gender for a year before undergoing surgery. Another standard required letters from a therapist and another professional attesting to a person's psychological need for surgery. A similar letter was needed to start hormones, which had to precede any surgery by at least a year.

"Hormones? Why isn't it just a surgical thing?"

"Oh, no, honey. Hormones, mainly estrogen, really are magic. They give you breasts and hips, and softer skin. That, along with a testosterone blocker like Spironolactone, reduces your beard, but promotes hair growth on your head. I don't fully understand why it works that way, but it does."

"Are the hormones in the form of a pill?" I couldn't imagine taking drugs of any kind.

"No. They're either a patch you wear or an injection. There's a higher likelihood of blood clots with injections. Not everyone can wear a patch because they sometimes irritate."

At that point, certain phrases—"surgery," "hormones," "blood clots"—collided in my brain. I thought of another word: "risk," and one more: "death."

If something goes terribly wrong, you could die, Ed.

I reached for my beer and took a long drink.

"What are we talking for the cost of the surgery? Will it bankrupt me?"

"There's a myth about the cost," Nora answered. "People always think it costs more than it actually does."

"Well?"

"A half-dozen surgeons in the U.S. and Canada, like Meltzer in Phoenix, Marci Bowers in Trinidad, Colorado, and Broussard in Montreal, do the surgery. A couple are in Thailand, where it's always cheaper, and a few in Europe. There's competition between these doctors, so that keeps the price down."

She paused, finished her soda, and continued.

"To have sex reassignment surgery in the U.S. or up north, you're looking at about twenty to twenty-five thousand. There's always breast growth with hormones, so not everyone gets implants. If you want bigger breasts, implants cost five thousand or so. Add to that airline fares, hotels, and other incidentals, and you get to thirty, thirty-five thousand dollars, tops."

This was a surprise. "You mean for the price of a Buick, I could get a brand-new vagina and breasts?"

"Yep, hon."

I grinned. It was the only good news so far.

I sensed Nora wanted to wrap up her impromptu seminar. We exchanged email addresses and I got up to leave. Nora stopped me.

"One more thing. With that beard of yours, you better get started on electrolysis. It will take you a while."

Oh great, I thought.

On the way back to the condo, I couldn't stop the doubts.

What the hell are you doing? The cost, the hassle, the risks? Surgery? Are you crazy? And what about Emily and Lily? They'll flip out!

I started electrolysis at a clinic in Cedar Rapids two weeks later. "You really have some growth there," the electrologist reported. It would eventually take four years and 200 hours of electrolysis to clear my beard.

For two decades I had kept my hair crew cut. I decided to grow out my hair and found a salon in Iowa City. I brought along clipped magazine pictures of women with shoulder-length hair.

"This is what I want," I said.

The stylist, a beautiful man named Gerard, studied the pictures. He ran his hands through my bristly hair.

"Oh yeah, I can do that," he said. He grinned as if I had just thrown down a glove in challenge.

I interviewed a twenty-eight-year-old lawyer named Sasha Monthei in the spring of 2008. We met at ten on a Sunday morning; she didn't seem to mind the odd interview time.

Sasha walked into the office in a low-cut top and jeans wearing oversized bracelets on both wrists. Auburn curls overflowed her shoulders.

She was stunning, with the kind of beauty that made men (and women attracted to women) stop and stare.

"I want to learn how to try cases," she said. "I'm not afraid to work."

Sasha had grown up poor in a pint-sized mobile home with an alcoholic but loving father. She graduated from high school a year early and attended a community college. After graduating from the University of Iowa, she started law school in Des Moines, a two-hour drive each way. To make ends meet, she waitressed on the weekends. By then, she had a young daughter.

Despite these hurdles, she graduated near the top of her law school class, earning the highest of law school honors.

I thought, *How could you do that?*

I hired her. By the end of her first week, I wondered if she might be able to take over the law firm if I decided to do something different.

Like change genders.

One afternoon over wine, I told Sasha I was transgender.

"I don't fully know what it means," I confided. "I'm sure things are going to change for me one way or another." I bit my lip. I didn't know how she'd react.

She grabbed my hand. "I may not understand completely, but it's okay with me whatever you are. You're one of the most genuine people I've ever met."

Her words made me feel good. More importantly, she didn't turn in her resignation.

By pure coincidence, I visited my condo on the Friday night of Gay Pride Weekend. In some cities, this one weekend a year resembles an unofficial holiday where every group in the GLBT alphabet—gay, lesbian, bisexual, and transgender persons—gets a let-them-be-themselves pass. It's a three-day license that permits public displays of affection, as in men holding hands and women kissing in public, without straight people mucking things up.

I started to work on myself the moment I realized it was Gay Pride. If there was ever a time to go out in public as a woman, this was it.

For help, I had three makeup books. One of them—*Vogue Make-up*—was a 2005 Father's Day gift from Lydia. Stuffed in my bathroom vanity were a couple dozen unopened makeup vials, mascara brushes, and eyeliner pencils, some high end, some low. I had fashionable age-appropriate skirts and tops. Most importantly, I had all of Saturday to get ready for a transgender party at a funky lesbian bar named Pi that night.

I had everything I needed except for one thing: confidence. I was certain I'd look frightening regardless of what I did with makeup. Clearly, I couldn't move from man to woman without solving my makeup conundrum.

My female spirit pushed and prodded all Friday night until I escaped to bed. *Do it. It's who you are.*

The nagging resumed again on Saturday morning, when I finally gave in. *"Okay, I surrender,"* I said out loud. *"I'll try."*

My nails were first. I went with a soft pink to avoid looking garish. I quickly learned that painting one's nails isn't like painting one's dining room wall. Nail polish requires far more concentration and finesse, both of which I lacked. Even worse, no one had ever told me how long it takes for nail polish to actually dry.

An hour and a half later, and with still-tacky nails, I propped open the three makeup books on the bathroom counter. I flipped through pages in search of "Step One." I couldn't find it. There had to be an order to putting on makeup, but none of the books contained a makeup flow chart.

That left me debating whether foundation or cover went first. I guessed it was called "foundation" for a reason.

Then there was the problem of how much of each. Where was the line between looking good and looking clownish?

I did the best I could.

I got to eyeliner. It took twenty minutes to understand that the sharp end of the eyeliner pencil was supposed to trace—*that would be the "liner" part, Ed*—along the bottom and top edges of my eyelids, micro-millimeters from my eyeball.

One slip and suddenly I'm blind.

Mascara was easy enough—there was a step-by-step description in *Teen Make-up*. It clumped, too, just like when John made me up for Halloween.

I also realized I had eyelashes that spanned the bottom rims of my eyes. How I missed those for fifty-some years, I didn't know.

At the end of the ordeal, I stepped away for a good mirror view. Something hideous stared back.

"*No way,*" I yelled.

I stripped down and jumped into the shower. I knew nothing about makeup remover; my mistake—I hadn't read that far in any of the books.

Another attempt produced another disaster. I showered. A third attempt was no better. My skin became raw.

I gave it one last shot. This time, piece by piece, a woman's face emerged. I made fewer mistakes; by the end, foundation and cover were blotched only slightly, and my eyeliner didn't appear too crooked.

Again, I went for the mirror view. This time someone feminine looked back. For sure, she wasn't very pretty. Yet, she was good enough.

As incentive, I promised myself, *Don't worry, you can stand in the darkest corner of the bar.*

That left my hair. I was two months into Gerard's hair plan. With three inches of growth, I wondered what I could do with a can of mousse, a tube of styling gel, and a curling iron.

I knew I needed some kind of "look" to my hair. Gerard called it "texture," but what did that mean? I gave up on the curling iron after my hand slipped and the scalding-hot iron fell against my ear. For a moment, I thought the burn might require emergency medical attention.

I switched to the mousse, a much safer alternative. It didn't make any difference.

I owned a couple cheap wigs, but I didn't want to wear a wig on this, my first public excursion. In my mind, a wig wasn't genuine. I had come this far. If nothing else, I was going to be authentic.

I gelled my hair into a mini, uneven wave. I thought, *Twiggy.*

Four hours after my makeup ordeal began, I exhaled. *Done.*

For clothes, I decided on a black short-sleeve V-neck top and the white cotton skirt that Janelle liked to wear. It was temperate enough for black sandals. A heart-shaped necklace topped off the outfit. I didn't own any earrings; it would be another year before I'd get my ears pierced.

The final touch: a red lipstick labeled "Trixie."

I stood in front of the mirror one last time. An actual woman reflected back. While she might not have been very attractive, she certainly was so very *alive.* An excitement grabbed me. *I've done it!*

In an instant, an inaugural dose of femininity shot through me. Magically, my DNA switched from male to female. Every gene in my body somersaulted to line up in a brand-new formation, XX, XX, XX.

I curtsied. *"I've been waiting for you,"* I said to the mirrored image.

As an afterthought, I realized I needed a feminine name to go with my new appearance. "Ellen" was simple but elegant. I had met a couple of six-foot-tall, fifty-year-old transgender Brittanys at the Town House. That didn't fit with what parents were naming newborn girls in the 1950s.

Ellen Krug rang true. A year into the future, Rita would remark that both Nan and Mom had "Ellen" for middle names. I had totally forgotten.

I collected my things into a brand-new purse. Ten minutes later, I did something I never thought I'd be brave enough to do in even three lifetimes: I opened the front door of my condo unit and stepped into the hallway as Ellen.

I quickly scanned the hall; thankfully, it was empty. I locked the door and hustled to the elevator. I hit the button and prayed it would be empty when the doors opened. After the longest minute on earth, a completely vacant elevator appeared.

I waited in the lobby for a cab. Another condo resident, a middle-aged woman, appeared with her dog. The adrenaline pump near my heart spiked. I forced a smile and said, "Hello," in a heavy whisper. She returned my greeting and continued on her way without a gasp or laugh.

So far, so good.

The cab driver was a chatterbox. Just my luck. I answered in short word bursts of high-pitched voice. His friendliness disarmed my internal tension. He didn't seem to care that a freak sat in his backseat. Maybe it was that Gay Pride Weekend pass at work.

The cabbie's kindness earned him an extra $5 tip.

We pulled into Pi's parking lot. The bar was bunker-like; I guessed it had once been a warehouse or small factory. Next door, a band warmed up on an outdoor patio.

A muscled white-tee-shirted bouncer guarded the front door.

I exited the cab and paused. *Am I really doing this?* A second later, I pushed myself up the front door steps. "Hello," I said and tried to wring a smile out of utter fear.

"Welcome," the bouncer said, smiling in return. "We're glad you're here."

Simple words, probably even unconscious utterances. They would resonate in my heart for the rest of my life.

Inside, I fished in my purse for the cover. I found a ten spot and raised my head, looking for gawks or finger points. I saw yet more cheerful people. It was exactly what I needed.

With a Heineken in hand, I went outside for the music.

The patio crowd was sparse, which meant I couldn't hide. I stared at the band in an attempt to avoid eye contact. It didn't deter a short older man and younger auburn-haired woman. I quickly heard the woman had previously been a man, something I would never have guessed.

"We went and got married," the man said with a grin. "Fooled the state."

I volunteered that it was my first time as a woman in public. "I'm scared to death," I said.

The woman touched my arm. "Don't be afraid, dear. Everyone's first time is scary. You're among friends here."

Her husband tried to be funny. "Look at it this way; you're a virgin the first time you go public. Once you lose your virginity, things become much easier."

It had been a long time since anyone called me a "virgin." I laughed, only to be jolted at how it amplified my voice.

We were joined by an even more masculine-voiced woman who was maybe twenty-five years old. She was dressed in a tight black bustier with fishnet stockings and big hair. The size of her hair was exceeded only by the size of her breasts; they were easily 42 triple D. Everything on her face was black: mascara, eye shadow, thick eyeliner, and lipstick.

A punk rocker who was lead singer and bass player, she was part of the next band up. She saw me staring at her breasts (how could anyone not) and launched into how she required weeks of "growing out the flap" needed to cover her implants. The rocker then bent forward.

"See this," she pointed at her hair. "It's all real. Took me three years to grow out." She raised and flipped her jet black mane, as if readying for a glamour shot.

Whoa, I thought. *And I was worried that people would think I'm a freak.*

The rocker didn't shut up. She and her girlfriend—the band's drummer who had also undergone "the surgery"—wanted to create the world's first all-transgender band.

It was the weirdest thing I'd ever heard.

I needed to escape. I looked around the patio and saw Nora from the Town House. I thanked my new friends and bolted for Nora. It was comforting to see someone I actually knew, if only sort of.

"Hi, Nora," I said. I caught her by surprise. Once again, we were in the middle of loud music and yell-talking.

"Oh, hello," she said. She gently rocked to the music.

I told her that I had decided on "Ellen" for a name. She responded, "You look like an Ellen."

Even with all the noise, I wanted to talk. "Quite the party. Have you come here before?"

"Every year," she answered. "There was a parade earlier today. We had a couple hundred trans people. You should've been there."

"I would have liked to, but I had a commitment." I passed on explaining about my makeup marathon.

I blurted, "This is my first time wearing a skirt in public."

Nora took a half step back and gave me the once-over. "You look nice," she said. "Cute skirt."

I felt good for a half second until she added, "But your hair. Why didn't you wear a wig?"

I knew this was an honest question and not intended as a critique. The woman inside heard something entirely different. *How stupid of you. Everyone here wonders the same thing. Way to stand out—as ugly.*

"I'm still learning how to style wigs," I offered. "I'll have it down the next time you see me."

Nora answered, "It takes time and practice. You'll get it figured out eventually."

I wanted to take my all-too-short hair and run home. Perseverance prevailed. I walked over to the bar for another beer.

The patio eventually became packed. I found myself near the stage, listening to '80s cover tunes. I danced in place and actually enjoyed myself.

There were so many different people that I didn't feel the odd woman out. For sure, there were envy-evoking transgender women (biological men) in appropriate-length skirts with professionally done makeup and hair. Still, many couldn't have cared less about pulling off the look-good-as-a-woman thing, like the bushy-mustached man in a red bustier and matching tutu walking with a beer in one hand and cigarette in the other.

I felt a tap on my shoulder and turned to see a very familiar face: Beth, one of Janelle's lesbian friends. I had been to Beth's apartment several times with Janelle. I felt instant happiness, and wondered if Janelle was there too.

"Good to see you," Beth shouted. She looked at my skirt and pointed. "Is that Janelle's skirt?"

"It sure is," I yelled. I glanced past Beth. "Is she here?" I hoped so.

"No, she isn't," Beth said with a head shake. "Lucy and Diane are here, and some other people you know. We're back by the tables; come sit with us."

I followed Beth to the group. I saw genuine smiles and heard sincere inquires about how I'd been. There wasn't a single smirk or whisper to the side.

I rode out the rest of the evening with this group. I heard how much Janelle had loved me. "I loved her too," I said, knowing that it probably was a good thing Janelle wasn't there. She wouldn't have been crazy about my appearance, and I wouldn't have been happy with her reaction.

On the way to Iowa the next day, I called Thap. "Guess what I did last night?" I said.

"Ah, you drank too much?"

"No, silly. I did it, Thap. I went out dressed as a woman." Just saying it got me excited again.

"That took courage. How did it go?"

"It went great. I didn't look all that good, but the point was to simply show up. And oh yeah, I've picked 'Ellen' as a name."

Thap rolled with it. "I'm proud of you, Ed... er, Ellen. I know it was difficult, but way to go."

I cut the call short. I wanted to bask in the afternoon sunlight and feel good about briefly escaping from a closet adorned with a Fort Knox-sized lock.

A few days later, I stopped at Hy-Vee, a Cedar Rapids grocery store, wearing women's shorts and sandals, and pink toes. I wanted to savor the pink for just a few more days. I risked everything if I ran into the wrong person, like David, the president of DEF Trucking, my largest client.

The part of me that had barely come out of the shadows was just fine with taking the risk.

Luckily, I didn't see anyone I knew. At my car, I put the groceries in the trunk.

I reached to close the driver's door when I heard a young woman's voice. "I like your toes," the voice said.

I looked up. A teenager with red and black hair and a small nose piercing stood ten feet away. She wore a Hy-Vee smock and had been corralling shopping carts.

"Thank you," I responded. Suddenly, I felt extremely exposed.

"I love painted toes," she said, "but I don't have the time."

"Yes," I answered, fumbling. "It's a lot of work."

"Have a good day," she said. She went back to corralling carts.

I backed out of the parking space. An intensity grabbed me and ten seconds later, I had to stop at the end of the parking lot, away from any moving thing.

Tears came from nowhere. Soon I was bawling and talking to myself. I couldn't believe the kindness of that girl, someone not much older than Lily, and her obvious acceptance of me, *whatever I was.*

A realization shot into my brain. Many people my age, the movers and shakers of Cedar Rapids, would never be that open. Ed as Ellen was far beyond most of my contemporaries' comfort zones.

Out loud I cried, *"I'm fifty-one years old! Do I really have what it'll take to be the real person inside me? To be Ellen?"*

For a moment, it all seemed so impossible. Then I remembered there was something—call it female courage or guts or maybe just plain desperation—that pushed me to step foot outside my condo door dressed as Ellen.

I was certain the woman who roamed within me wouldn't leave the man part alone until she succeeded.

Until she was me completely, all to herself.

With my car perched at an odd angle, I choked out one last thing.

"Don't give up on yourself, Ellen. You're worth the effort."

SIXTEEN: *The Note*

It's sometime in June, 1990.

Lori, the receptionist at Littleton & Davis, buzzes me.

"There's a detective from the Dallas, Texas police department on line two."

I pick up the telephone and tap a button. "This is Ed Krug."

"Mr. Krug, Detective Davis of the Dallas Police Department." He's cop-like: deliberate and sparse. "I called the other day. Sorry that we've missed each other."

I'm not surprised about the call. A month ago, I wrote and asked for a copy of the police report and my father's suicide note. The lawyer in me wanted the complete record.

"What can I do for you, Detective?"

"We have the revolver used in the suicide. It's a chrome-plated Smith & Wesson thirty-eight caliber. We need to know if you'd like it returned."

Did you really just ask me that?

I want to hang up. I'm still raw from the suicide. Of all things, the absolute last I want to deal with is the gun that Tom Terrific used to kill himself.

Somehow, I stay on the line.

The detective explains that department policy requires offering the gun back to the family. I think, *How crazy is this?*

"What happens if I don't want it?" I want to make sure they won't sell it at some macabre police garage sale.

"We destroy it," he says coldly.

My response can't come fast enough. "Yes, please destroy it. My family wants nothing more to do with that gun."

I find a manila envelope with a Dallas Police Department return address on my desk when I get back from court. I close my office door and sit down.

With the envelope in hand, I pause. A moment later, I tear at the flap.

I pull out a two-page police report, a form with checked boxes and filled lines. The phrase "subject decedent" stands out. The report details arriving at my parents' townhouse, an interview with my distraught mother, and the conclusion that this was a suicide, not foul play. No surprises there.

The next document is a photocopied autopsy report. I'm interested in whether, just maybe, my father had a fatal disease; the *real* reason. I bypass the actual autopsy examination and skip to the summary. I read that Dad appeared to be healthy, at least physically.

The report concludes, "Cause of death: gunshot wound to oral cavity, catastrophic brain trauma, blood loss."

There's one more photocopy: the suicide note. It's dated "1/31/90." I recognize my father's handwriting on two sheets of unlined paper. I force myself to read it. After all, I've come this far.

Satch:

OK, I've laid enough guilt on you. Too much really. I am not guiltless in this. My world is as shattered as yours. When I was young, I had so many dreams, hopes, aspirations! I wanted to be a sportscaster (Mel Allen was the best), a pilot, I wanted to drive in an Indy 500.

When we got married, there was no doubt in my mind that ours would be the best there ever was. Well, it really wasn't that bad. We have the three greatest kids in the world. Somehow, somewhere, we did something right.

Why can't I recall more than that?

I just checked with the benefits (life insurance) people and they said that there is no "suicide clause." So, get Ed—no, don't get Ed!! Get a smart lawyer to handle this and you should be a rich lady.

Most of my clothes will fit Ed and Mark. Go to Cedar Rapids. Do whatever with my jewelry. Burn me!!

Tom

p.s. I hope I didn't fuck up the tub.

My body suddenly hurts. I want to puke; I can't. I want to cry. I can't do that, either. I sit and stare, numbed beyond anything else I've ever experienced.

Get Ed—no, don't get Ed!! Get a smart lawyer.

Whack.

Did he have to use *two* exclamation marks? In the final moments of his life—his very last words, his *coup de grâce*—did he need to diminish me one last time?

Oh, Dad. Why?

Later, when the numbness wears off, I've got another thousand questions. Was it about him seeing me as stupid? That I couldn't handle finances? Or worse, that I would cheat Mom? That I would take money from my own mother?

Didn't he understand what Uncle Ed had taught me?

Or was it that he didn't want me to discover how bad things had gotten? That he didn't want me to judge him? As if I was some kind of final arbiter on his life?

Dad, don't you understand it was the other way around? That you arbitrated my life?

I stuff the papers back in the envelope. I push the envelope to the bottom of my bottom desk drawer.

I'm done with all of this, I say to myself.

I know.

I lie.

SEVENTEEN: *Swimming Upstream*

I nearly lost the law firm to a flood.

Iowa's 2008 spring was soaking wet. Much of the state was underwater by the second week of June.

I was in Des Moines for business on a Monday. From there, I headed to the condo in Minneapolis with a plan to make the rest of the week a working vacation.

Sasha called as I got to the Iowa-Minnesota border.

"I just heard that the Cedar River is going to flood the entire downtown. I think we should get the files out of the basement."

The sky was cloudless; the day, gorgeous.

"What are you talking about? It's picture perfect here. Is the weather there that much different?"

"Remember all the rain we got last week? And the week before? That water has to go somewhere. They say this could be a 500-year flood."

That could be a problem. Our office was on the third floor of the Hach Building, which in turn was barely a hundred feet from the Cedar River.

Sasha pressed. "Really, Ed. We need to do something."

It was late afternoon. I was closer to Minneapolis than to Cedar Rapids. Sasha organized the office into a carry party for files in the basement. They got half the files moved before shelving collapsed, making things unsafe.

I Googled "Iowa floods" when I reached Minneapolis and quickly understood that Sasha wasn't overreacting. There was flooding of biblical proportions in Waterloo and Cedar Falls, where the surge had destroyed bridges and flooded thousands of acres. Cedar Rapids was a mere fifty miles downstream.

Crap.

I went to bed uncertain about what to do. I woke up at three with the realization that I had to get back to Cedar Rapids. Six hours later, I was in stop-and-go traffic that snaked through downtown Waterloo because flood waters had submerged the interstate. It took forever to get back to the office.

A chamber of commerce bulletin was on my chair. It contained a map of the 500-year flood zone; a big red bull's-eye covered the entire downtown.

You've got to be kidding me.

I couldn't imagine a flood of that magnitude. Many times, the Cedar had gotten tippy-toe high, but it never actually flooded.

On Wednesday, most downtown businesses closed early. I had the bookkeeper run everyone's paycheck. We locked the office at noon and I walked out of the building with Sasha.

"If we get hit," I said, "I'm sure it won't be that bad." I bent down and held my hand a foot above the sidewalk—my estimate of water height. "At worst, we'll lose the rest of the files in the basement. That wouldn't be so bad. I'll see you on Monday at the latest."

It started to rain as I drove home. The rain intensified and continued unabated for two entire days. At Durango, far removed from any waterway, I watched television images of the Cedar as it lapped at building foundations. Soon, rushing water covered all six downtown bridges. A railroad bridge, weighted down with twenty railroad cars, was no match for the torrent. It collapsed into a twisted mess of steel girders and aluminum coal cars. By the end, the Cedar lost all resemblance to a river; instead, it was a thrashing lake covering 1,300 city blocks.

Just as predicted: a 500-year flood.

The *Gazette* front page had an aerial shot of downtown. The Hach Building was photo center. Brackish water completely covered the building entrance.

Yeah, Ed. Good guess. Maybe a foot of water at most.

It was a week before the Cedar receded enough that I could get into the Hach Building. The police gave me twenty minutes to retrieve the accounting computer. The building, along with the rest of downtown, had no electric service. It wouldn't have mattered if my office was ten stories higher. Either way, the Krug Law Firm was out of commission. There was a chance it might be permanent, too; at least one staff person was already looking for other work even though I had promised to continue paying salaries.

I carried an industrial-sized flashlight as I worked my way up a totally dark stairwell filled with putrid air. The blackness was suffocating. Without that beam of light, I wouldn't have been able to tell right from left, front from back.

I got to the third-floor landing and opened the door to a windowless hallway. Twenty steps later, I unlocked the office door and looked down to see the crisscross prints of my boots; I tracked river muck wherever I walked.

Grabbing the computer and a banker's box with office supplies, I returned to the stairwell door and put the computer and flashlight on the landing. I turned around for the box. Absentmindedly, I let the stairwell door close behind me, separating me from the flashlight. I was instantly disoriented in the jet-black hallway. I panicked, which only made me more lost.

I swore at myself for being so stupid—how could I have become separated from the flashlight, my lifeline and the one thing I needed to make my way out? I felt along one wall, then another, and yet another, trying to find a landmark of some kind. I became frantic and wondered how I'd escape that dead building.

After ten hellish minutes, I stopped and calmed myself. *You're not lost,* I thought. *Pace yourself and eventually, you'll find the way out.*

It worked. A few minutes later, I touched the frame of the stairwell door and felt my way to the handle. I turned the handle and pushed; a spotlight against the stairwell wall greeted me.

I made it, I said to myself. *That scared the crap out of me.*

Downtown Cedar Rapids would be closed for months, creating a scramble for temporary office space. Thankfully, Sasha found a very marginal office in North Liberty—twenty miles away.

After a lot of cajoling, authorities briefly let us back into the building two weeks later. Everyone from the office, plus Lily and my private investigator-friend Jerry Smithey, helped move basic necessities. Boots, gloves, and paper masks were mandatory attire. In fire-brigade style, computers, printers, a postage meter, and box upon box were handed from person to person, floor to floor. Three weeks after the flood, it was enough to get us restarted.

We stayed in North Liberty even after the Hach Building reopened in late 2008; the risk of another flood was too great.

My personal plans went on hold. It was the same old tired Krug line dance—two steps forward, one step back, and a shuffle to the side. I had no idea when I'd make it to Minneapolis again. Most of all, the financial costs were huge. Our income dried up, and I paid the staff out of my savings.

That's money I need for my new life.

Somewhere in the unfolding flood drama, my cell phone rang.

"Is this Ed Krug?" a voice asked.

"Yes, this is Ed. Who's calling?"

"Krug, it's Morse, Joshua Morse. Did the flood affect you?"

We had lost touch after Boston. He had finished his psychiatry residency and now lived in Kansas City, where he headed the psychiatric unit at a local hospital. The Coe College alumni office had given him my number.

I summarized the flood and its impact. By pure coincidence, I was on a bridge over the Cedar River at that very moment.

"I'm sorry you and your firm have to go through all of that," he said.

Joshua related that he was married and the father of three daughters, all under six.

"Holy cow!"

"How is Lydia? Do you have a family?"

I hated telling him I was divorced.

"I'm so sorry, Krug. I thought the two of you would be married forever." He paused and then asked, "Was it someone else?" Maybe he wanted to know because he was a psychiatrist.

"Ah, sort of, but not exactly."

I thought, *What the heck. Tell him.*

"It ended because of me. Remember when you said that thing about people who gay-bash? That those people most likely have gay tendencies themselves? Well, you were right. I'm queer."

There was silence until I heard, "I don't know what to say. Frankly, I'm shocked."

I explained how I had tried therapy for many years, something that he, of all people, should have appreciated. "I didn't want to leave Lydia," I said. "But I need to live life as myself."

The phone pulsed with an unexpected reaction.

"I don't know, Krug. Gay? I never expected this from you."

Instantly, I decided to tell him the whole story. With his training, surely he would understand.

"Actually, it's more than that, Josh. I'm transgender. There's this woman inside me who needs to come out."

The phone went dead again. Before I could inquire, Joshua asked, "Are you thinking of surgery?"

"I don't know," I answered. "Maybe. Probably."

More silence. Finally, a diagnosis.

"That's plain wrong, Ed," he said. "God gave you a body and you shouldn't tinker with it. Surgery to change your gender violates something sacred."

It made me wonder if he was holding a bible.

Joshua went on. "You know, the science built up around gender identity disorder is very questionable. I don't believe people can really be stuck in the wrong bodies."

I felt the cold, hard vise of judgment squeezing.

"Ah, I've got to go," I said. "There's another call coming in. Take care."

I didn't wait for a response. I threw the phone on the passenger seat and turned up the volume on a Pat Benatar song, "Fire and Ice."

A few months after the flood, I traveled to Philadelphia to meet with Big Insurance Company, the insurer for DEF Trucking. We needed to prepare for a pre-trial mediation in Mr. Ford's (the jaywalking jogger) case. His attorneys wanted $35 million.

I had met John, the insurance company claims manager, once before. He waited in the main lobby of Big Insurance as my escort. He took one look at me, and without even a "Hello," said, "What have you done with your hair?"

It was more exclamation than question.

Maybe I should have expected this; by then, my hair was just touching my shirt collar. I answered, "It's a midlife crisis thing." It was the best I could do under pressure.

He frowned but let it pass. We went upstairs to a conference room where three other people waited. After two hours of strategizing on the Ford case, I thought I had their confidence, even if I looked odd.

In January, 2009, Sasha accompanied me to the mediation at the Marriott Hotel in Des Moines. We sat on one side of a large conference room with John and David from DEF Trucking. Sitting across from us were Mr. Ford's lawyers, a high-powered group from St. Louis.

Mr. Ford soon rolled into the conference room, followed by his wife and six-year-old daughter. I saw a wheelchair full of gritted teeth, angry eyes, and unavoidable tattoo.

The mediator opened the proceedings with a short speech. It was my turn next.

I talked for twenty minutes, much of it in eye-to-eye contact with Mr. Ford. My job, as always, was to convince him and his attorneys that they had a losing case, and that DEF Trucking would win, if we ever proceeded to trial.

At that precise moment, Ed Krug was a strange confluence of obvious man and hidden woman. The man defaulted to an old habit of brandishing voice as a weapon. The woman, soft and gentle, would never imagine attacking anyone — especially this poor soul, Mr. Ford, a victim of horrible circumstances.

I vocalized many well-honed attack phrases: "your fault," "you'll lose," "we'll fight the whole way," but my passion seeped. Something tore at my spirit, something that no one in the room would be able to fathom.

This isn't who I am, I said to myself midway through the word assault.

Killer Krug was fading, losing resolve and vigor.

I ended the onslaught and folded my notes. Mr. Ford appeared entirely unfazed by my presentation.

The two sides separated and the mediator shuttled between camps. When it was lunchtime, our group recessed to the hotel restaurant. Over soup and salad, John speculated about how the negotiations would turn out. Midway through the discussion, I excused myself to find the mediator to discuss a new issue.

I was back in the conference room when John, David, and Sasha returned from the restaurant. By mid-afternoon, the mediator reported that Mr. Ford was unwilling to accept our figure to settle the case.

This didn't make John happy. "You assured us in Philadelphia that Ford would take our offer," he said.

I had made strategic assumptions about settlement, as lawyers sometimes do, that had been proven wrong. I was good, but not perfect.

Sasha and I left to drive back to North Liberty. We were barely out of the Marriott parking garage when Sasha reported on a discussion that occurred after I left the lunch table to talk to the mediator.

"You won't believe what John said after you got up from lunch." She twisted to face me.

"Okay, I give. What did he say?"

"I kid you not. Out of the blue, in the middle of talking about settlement negotiations, he goes, 'Wouldn't it be weird to be transgender? How could someone really have surgery to change their sex?'"

My right foot shifted to the brake pedal. I caught myself before I slammed to a stop. I yelled, "Are you shitting me?"

"No, I'm being totally honest. It was so unbelievably strange."

"Did anyone say anything in response?"

"No, David and I were speechless. After a few seconds of awkward silence, David changed the subject," she said.

I was stunned. In 2009, transgender people weren't a customary business lunch topic. It couldn't be something random.

"Do you think he knows?" I asked.

"I don't know, Ed." Sasha cracked her window so that she could smoke. "It was way too odd, as if he was trying to get me to say something."

"Well, did you?"

"Of course not! Do you think I'm an idiot?"

A loop played in my head for the rest of the drive. I tried to convince myself John's comment was the biggest coincidence ever, that there was nothing to it, and that he hadn't figured me out.

I suspected this wasn't the end of it.

John called two weeks later. "I'm pulling the Ford case from you," he said. He was giving it to some guy named Sweeney in Philadelphia. I thought I heard actual joy in his voice.

Instead of angst, I felt relief. I had dreaded cross-examining Mr. Ford and his big tattoo at the trial. I didn't have the heart to blame Mr. Ford as the reason why his legs were missing or his life destroyed.

I had another session with Sam the Hammer where I reported on Emily (distant but still communicative), Lily (supportive but temperamental), and Lydia (colder now that Stephen was back). I had resumed my weekend trips to Minneapolis. "I'm still determined to build a new life there as Ellen," I said.

"I'm glad to hear that," Sam answered.

We discussed the Ford case, and how from nowhere, John had made the transgender comment at lunch.

"Do you think he knows, Sam? It's such a leap."

Sam thought for a second. "I don't know. Some people are intuitive, they can feel things. Maybe this John guy is one of those people."

"I was okay with transferring out that case," I confessed. "I didn't want to attack Mr. Ford. It's not who I am anymore."

I told Sam that the Ford case was easily worth four or five hundred thousand dollars in legal fees. "I don't care that I lost the fees," I said.

Sam looked up from her clipboard and smiled. "You're getting away from the money, away from the greed. That's good," she said. "More importantly, you're so much gentler than when we started a year and a half ago. You've lost that hard edge. When I see you now, Ellen, I see a woman, not a man."

Her words melted into me, like butter on warm French bread.

"Thank you, Sam, that's the best thing you could ever say to me."

She moved her clipboard to the floor. "That's good because I mean it."

I relaxed and snuggled into the chair. There was something I wanted to explain.

"Sometimes, I feel like I'm driving down this road in Lincoln, back in Massachusetts, near Walden Pond," I said. "It was one of those classic New England country roads—narrow roadway, stone wall borders, and huge oaks, almost a tunnel of trees. On a sunny day, Lydia and I would drive back from swimming at Walden and see sun bursts on the windshield. They'd be there for a second, and then be gone, blocked by oak leaves. I'd speed along, accumulating sun bursts, wanting more and more of the sun. That's what my life is like now—spots of sun popping from leaves, briefly illuminating what life could be like if I ever got the guts to completely be Ellen."

I sat up. "I want more than sun spots on the windshield," I said. "I want the full sun, a bright summer day without a single tree in sight."

Sam's smile widened. "I hear you, Ellen," she said. "But remember, little in life is pure sunlight. Most of the time, the best we can do are sun spots. There's always something, some shadow, mixing with sunlight. The key is appreciating the sun burst, the moment when light shines into our lives amidst the shadows."

"I'm going to try for pure sunlight," I answered.

"You'll figure it out," she replied.

Time was up. I put on my coat and started for the door.

"Wait a second." Sam took half a dozen steps and got next to me. "You're ready for this."

She parted her arms and wrapped them around me in a good, tight hug.

I got past the surprise and hugged back, just as my eyes became wet.

"Remember," Sam whispered, "I only hug women."

———

Gerard's hair-growing plan was succeeding. By early 2009, my hair was beyond my shirt collar and just enough for a small ponytail. I tried a case for DEF Trucking and looked like a shaggy dog in pinstripes. No one said a word about my appearance. When the jury came back in our favor, I figured I was safe for a while.

I had lunch with Drew Bloom two weeks later. Midway through burgers, the conversation shifted to how I had changed.

Drew asked, "Why do you have to do that?" He pointed to my hair. "Wasn't it enough to be gay?"

"We've talked about this, Drew," I said as I shifted in my chair. "I'm transgender. This is really who I am."

Drew shook his head. "Every time we get together, there's something new about you. I feel like I've lost the Ed Krug I knew. When I look at you now, I see a ghost."

The words were bittersweet. I so wanted to move from boy to girl, and now Drew confirmed I was progressing. I wondered who was losing whom.

I tried to explain it, again.

"I don't know what I am sexually, but for my gender, I'm a girl."

"Are you sure?" he asked.

How could he not understand? Hadn't we talked about how I was happier? Couldn't he see that?

"Yes, Drew, I'm sure."

Drew sank in his chair.

"When I go to Minneapolis, I feel so alive there. Alive as a woman."

I watched Drew flinch.

"I don't mean to make you uncomfortable," I said.

"I'm trying not to be uncomfortable, but it's not working," Drew said. "I don't know why this is so difficult for me. I've always been open to people. When you said you were gay, that was easy. Now, though, there's a loss. The person I knew is leaving; hell, he may already be gone. I can't get my head around it."

Loss. The word hurt.

"I understand, Drew." My brain fumbled for something more concrete. "You've got a great heart. It may take you some time, but you'll come around. I'm certain of that."

Drew took a breath, an acknowledgment, and—I hoped—a sign that he would keep trying.

A second later, I saw him half-smile, half-grin, with eyes that I couldn't interpret.

———————

Winter, 2008 blurred into spring, 2009.

Each weekend escape to Minneapolis was another step in my gender journey. I got better at makeup and clothing. Softer cover and blush replaced pancake-thick foundation. I gave up fishnet stockings and heels for tights and flats. I stopped inflicting third-degree burns with the curling iron.

As my confidence grew, so, too, did the split between Ed and Ellen. Before I knew it, I stopped cooperating with myself. The resistance first masqueraded as laziness — *I'm too tired to take off my makeup. I'll do it after I get to Durango.*

Things quickly turned into outright revolt. In no time, Ellen was at the wheel in both directions for the 280-mile drive between Cedar Rapids and Minneapolis. Each trip was a probe, an envelope push, an extra women's restroom stop, one more convenience store purchase. The height of the insurrection: a skirt-wearing Ellen popped into the Cedar Rapids Target on the way home from Minneapolis. *I just need a few things,* I told myself. It was twenty minutes of white-knuckle shopping as I pushed a cart from aisle to aisle, part excited for the freedom and part scared to death of being spotted by someone I knew.

Yes, Ed had lost control.

The problem with Ellen running the show? She was a total amateur and completely unprepared for the arduous task of womanhood.

Take my voice, for instance. At my best, I looked like an average middle-aged woman. The illusion fell apart once I opened my mouth.

On one weekend commute, I stood unnoticed in line at a fast food place, the den of one of my addictions. At the counter, an acne-adorned youth smiled and asked, "Can I take your order, ma'am?"

With a voice pitch that risked an aneurysm, I said, "I'll take a fish sandwich and medium Diet Coke, please."

Instinctively, the teen punched the register, only to pause once she processed the disconnect between eyes and ears. Next, what I came to call the "Look" appeared: a smile of sorts, but not one of those you're-a-nice-person smiles. Instead, it was a ha-ha-look-at-the-freak-in-front-of-me grin. A lightning-speed glance to a sixteen-year-old co-worker followed. With the kind of shrug that only teenagers understand, she directed the co-worker my way. When I walked out the door with my fish sandwich and Diet Coke in hand, I glanced back.

There they were: a pack of blue-shirted teens, pointing and giggling.

Some people just plain ignored my appearance entirely, like the Minneapolis garage attendant who said, "Thank you, sir," as I handed him a tip. I was dolled up with curled hair, a skirt, tights, and boots.

Clearly, I had to do something with my voice.

Ann Fennell, a speech therapist at the University of Iowa's speech clinic, had a gorgeous voice, the kind that I'd die for. Elizabeth had given me her name.

"We can help you," she advised when I called about an appointment. "But you need to come dressed as a woman. It's very difficult to feminize someone's voice when they present as male."

Oh, crap.

Revolt or not, the office was off-limits to Ellen. I received clients there and often needed to attend court or depositions. Only Sasha knew the whole story. Surely, the staff thought something weird was up because of my ever-lengthening hair. Still, it's one thing to let people guess; it's entirely another to walk in the front door of the Krug Law Firm wearing a dress and heels and announce, "I'm really a woman!"

On the day of my first speech appointment, I left the office and drove to a hotel down the street. I took a back door to the main floor men's restroom, a one-toilet bathroom with a locked door. In record time, I stripped out of a pinstriped suit and threw on a pink top and black skirt. I slapped on mascara and eye shadow, and pulled my hair into a pony-tail. I opened the bathroom door to find a female cleaning person with a what-the-hell look.

"Have a nice day," I said as I bolted out the back door.

The speech clinic was situated in a building frozen in the year 1965. Ann's appearance matched her voice; in her late thirties, she was striking with short black hair and a pencil-thin waist. She addressed me as "Ellen" from the start. In the year that I attended the clinic, I never once heard "Ed."

Two very eager female grad students accompanied Ann. I was their first transgender.

We started out with my baseline metrics. Women have a voice pitch in the range of 190 to 220 hertz. Most men average 120 to 140 hertz. I spoke from a printed script into a microphone and looked at a computer screen. The screen displayed an irregular line of peaks and valleys—highs and lows of inflection.

Ann pressed a button to calculate my pitch. The verdict? I was in the sub-basement at 90 to 115 hertz.

Ann's mouth crooked. "We've got a lot of work to do."

In weekly hour-long speech therapy sessions, I learned about vocal folds that regulate the amount of air that passes from throat to mouth. I needed to relax the folds. I did silly voice exercises, "Meet me, Peter, meet me."

I brought along a tape recorder so I could remember how my voice sounded when the computer showed higher pitch. I practiced during the drives between Cedar Rapids and Minneapolis.

There was more. On my third session, Ann said, "For this to really work, you'll need to talk like a woman."

She explained feminine speech patterns, and the difference between masculine and feminine words. Asked about his girlfriend's new department store purchase, a man might say, "That's a nice-looking shirt." A woman, on the other hand, would gush, "Your top is adorable," or "What a lovely blouse!"

Some of this was easy since "lovely," "wonderful," and "adorable" were already part of my daily vocabulary. What wasn't easy: learning deferential speech patterns. Ann saw my nose turn up.

"Ellen, think about it," she instructed. "If a woman at a restaurant says, 'Waiter, bring me a glass of water,' she'd be perceived as *aggressive*. Most women want to avoid that."

I knew Ann actually meant "bitch," but she was far too proper to say it.

"More likely," Ann continued, "a woman will ask, 'Sir, would it be possible to get a glass of water when you have a chance?' That's far more feminine."

Ann might have called this a "feminine speech pattern," but I had other labels for it: submissive, subservient, and second class. It didn't sit well with me, someone used to ordering others around.

Still, I started to pay attention to how men and women speak. I quickly realized Ann was right. If I was going to offset my voice, I needed every tool I could muster—even female deference.

Ann's requirement that I attend weekly speech therapy in full-woman mode forced a decision. I would tell the office staff I was transgender so that on the days of my therapy, I could dress in the office bathroom. Yes, this was scary, but the alternative was to risk running into some guy in the hotel restroom. Sooner or later, there would be a problem. I didn't want to be the lead story—as either the victim or culprit—on the six o'clock news.

I asked everyone to assemble in the conference room.

"I have an announcement," I said. I saw four attentive faces. "You've seen my hair grow for almost a year. Let me tell you why. I'm transgender; I'm really a woman inside."

I kept eye contact. Some pupils faded, the lost-in-space look. Sasha played coy. I went on.

"I know this is really weird. The last time we had one of these meetings, I said I was gay, that I had left Lydia to date men. I thought I might be gay, but I was also secretly dressing as a woman. Lydia and I didn't know where it would go. Now I have a pretty good idea."

Concern replaced shock.

Mary, the bookkeeper, asked, "Does this mean you're going to have surgery?"

"I never thought I'd get this far," I answered, "so anything's possible. It's scary to think of actually having surgery, but who knows. It could happen."

Someone asked, "So what's next?" The unstated elephant-in-the-room concern was about the law firm's future. They were justifiably worried about their jobs.

I didn't want people to run out the door, at least not before I was ready to run myself, so I tried to minimize the impact. "I'm telling you this because I've started speech therapy lessons where I have to present as female. On the days I have therapy, I'll change in the office bathroom. For the rest of the week, I'll be dressed as I am now. It's actually androgynous women's clothing."

Mary grinned and looked at Sharon, the paralegal. "We've wondered about some of your clothes," Mary said.

Okay, then again, maybe the clothing wasn't as androgynous as I had thought.

"As far as our clients go, I don't plan on telling them," I said. "I hope that it'll be enough to spend more time in Minneapolis. If I can get to the point where I'm here only three days a week, maybe that'll be all I need."

Did I really believe this? Not really. Yet, how could I be sure? Nothing was certain anymore.

Sharon asked, "Do you have a female name?"

"Yes," I answered. "It's Ellen."

The secretary, Julie, spoke. "This must have been very hard for you, living in a body different from who you really are." It was nice to hear empathy. Even better was not hiding the real me from the people I worked with.

The meeting broke up. Julie paused at the door and said, "Ellen, I think you're brave."

"Thank you," I answered. "This isn't anything but self-preservation. Bravery is when the soldier in a crowded Humvee jumps on a hand grenade to save his or her buddies."

"Still, Ellen, this takes a lot of courage."

I hoped my clients would feel the same way when word got out, as I knew it would. It was just a matter of time.

I called Mark on my way to Minneapolis. "Hey, meet me for coffee tomorrow morning at nine."

"Okay, I'll be there."

Mark was the unsung hero of my gender journey. I talked to him far less than I spoke to Thap, but that didn't mean I was unappreciative of Mark's support. He often said, "I'm here for you regardless."

Our sister, Jacki, had been supportive too. I sensed this would wane if I ever told her I was transgender.

The next day, I walked around a corner to an outdoor café where Mark waited. It was the first time he would see me dressed as a woman. I wore an auburn wig—I didn't have time to style my hair that morning. I had on a black skirt and white top; in my bra were breast forms I had bought at a lingerie store.

Mark stood up. "Hi," he said. He gave me the once-over. "You look great."

A smile replaced my apprehension. It was good to cross the gender divide with yet another person I loved.

I sat down and the server came for our orders. "She's my sister," he told the server.

A few minutes later, Mark blurted, "You look like Mom."

Our mother? Satch? Oh, Mark, I thought.

He saw my reaction and tried to recover. "It's the wig, that's what I'm talking about. It's the same color as her hair, at least until she got it frosted."

I never wore that or any other wig again.

———————

Thanks to Nora, I understood I needed a therapist familiar with the Harry Benjamin Standards. I found a Minneapolis psychologist who specialized in gender identity issues. Sam gave her blessing. "I'll be interested to hear what she thinks."

The psychologist, Renee, was square-shaped and quiet with little warmth.

To begin, I completed several tests and questionnaires. This included the MMPI—the Minnesota Multiphasic Personality Inventory—a three-hour ordeal. I knew I was in trouble when I got to the question, "True or False: I don't like myself."

For a genetic male struggling with a female identity, there was no right answer.

The first couple sessions with Renee went relatively well. She asked, "When you were in first grade gym class and the teacher instructed, 'All boys on this side of the gym and all girls on that side,' which side of the gym did you think you should be on?"

In fifteen years of therapy with four different therapists, no one had ever asked such an insightful question. I answered, "The boy side."

I was being honest. As a first grader, I had no clue about my need for clean lines. Besides, just as Steven, Therapist No. 2, had said, a lot of my self-discovery time was taken up at the Kendall Drive living room window waiting for my father.

At the next session, Renee smiled for the first time. "Do you want my diagnosis?" She sat cross-legged on a big brown chair.

"Sure." I figured, *Why not?*

Renee flipped a couple pages in her file, and adjusted her glasses. She held up a single sheet to the light and read, "Based on MMPI results and other diagnostic tools, as well as sessions with the patient, my preliminary diagnosis under the Diagnostic and Statistical Manual, Fourth Edition, is yada yada yada yada Transvestite yada yada yada."

I had never been very good at deciphering medical-psychological mumbo jumbo. Still, "transvestite" registered like a cancer report.

Transvestite.

That word. That horrible awful word.

To me, a transvestite was nothing more than a weekend warrior, some dude who dressed as a woman on Saturday night, and after a masturbation spree, went back to man mode in time for Sunday church. Transvestites weren't real girls. They were guys with hairy chests who got turned on by women's bikini panties three sizes too small.

A transvestite sure wasn't *me*.

I wanted to fold into a human plane and fly out of Renee's office.

"This surprises me," I said. "A *transvestite?* Really? With all that I've gone through?" My voice echoed devastation.

In her own austere way, Renee tried to make me feel better.

"Ellen, this is just a preliminary diagnosis." She switched positions on her chair. "It's not final. It doesn't mean you can't get on hormones or have reassignment surgery someday. It simply means we need to talk more. We can do that during the year you live full time as a woman."

My neck got rubber band tight. I didn't want to spend a year of my life trying to convince Renee I wasn't a transvestite.

Renee wrangled a promise that I wouldn't do anything to hurt myself. I left her office weak in the knees. I got in my car and looked in the rear-view mirror, only to see reeling hurt and anger. I completely forgot about Buddhist grasping and suffering.

By the time I got to the condo, things had gotten worse.

Panic flooded in. *What if Renee's right? What if I've deluded myself, and I'm really not a woman at all?*

That was nothing compared to the super-duper, don't-ever-go-there thought: *What if I left Lydia just because I'm a stupid transvestite?*

If that was true, how could I ever live with myself?

I spent that Friday night and most of Saturday drowning in Heineken and chardonnay. On Saturday night, drunk and seeking an escape, I visited the Gay 90's, the oldest gay bar in Minneapolis. By night's end, I sat at the bar making out with a tall transgender brunette in fishnet stockings, a total stranger.

On Sunday morning, weighed down with a headache and dressed as Ed, I got in the car for the drive back to Iowa.

My gut began to wrench. It had been silent ever since Gay Lite ended. This time, the gut pulls were intellectual. I approached Renee and her diagnosis like the trial attorney I was.

I machine-gunned myself with questions.

How many full-of-crap scientific experts have you cross-examined? How many times have they gotten it wrong? What about your winning closing argument that science isn't black-and-white? That often, it's nothing more than speculation? That there's a real reason why they call it "junk science"?

Ellen, haven't you learned anything in twenty-seven years?

I remembered how much better I felt when I moved into Durango for my own life. *Isn't that proof there's way more to this than simply being turned on by women's clothing?*

By the time I got to the Iowa border, I had cried, laughed, and cried some more. For a respite, I called Thap. I needed to hear his voice.

"Tell me you love me, please, Thapper."

"Ellen, of course, I love you." Obviously, he sensed something was up. "What's going on? What's wrong?"

I told him about Renee's verdict. I didn't get into kissing at the Gay 90's since it only would have worried him more.

"What the hell does this Renee know?" Thap said. "I know you better than anyone in this world. You're a woman. You're so much better as Ellen than you ever were as Ed. Trust your instincts and be yourself. You aren't making a mistake."

I gripped the steering wheel. Blood flowed back into my heart. Thap was right.

I saw Renee three more times. By the last visit, she realized she had screwed up. "We can talk about getting you on hormones," she offered.

"We have to run it by the treatment committee first. It won't meet for a couple months. You'll also need to take another MMPI."

I didn't want any more delays. I resented that this woman was my gatekeeper, the final authority on whether I went forward as Ellen. I hated that there was even a system where doctors wouldn't prescribe hormones unless someone like Renee gave the okay.

I walked out of Renee's office for the last time. *I'm done with you.*

Someone told me about Roberta Livingston, another private practice psychologist who worked with transgender people. I explained my experience with Renee.

"Sometimes, even therapists get it wrong," she said.

No kidding.

Once more, I went through my life story: my parents, Tom Terrific's alcoholism, growing up afraid, Lydia, and fighting myself for decades. Roberta asked how I had stayed with Lydia for so long.

"I didn't want to lose her, so I hid it from her," I admitted. "She was the best in the world and I still love her with all my heart. But now, I understand this is who I am, even if it meant hurting Lydia and everyone else."

"You have to love yourself before anyone else," Roberta said. The words rolled across the floor. "Nothing works without that."

Roberta gave her pronouncement as I wrote out my check.

"You have your act together and understand many things about yourself. I don't see a problem with giving you a letter to start hormones."

Validation tasted exceedingly sweet, Dairy Queen-like.

I found two letters from Roberta in my condo mailbox the next weekend. One was directed to a local gynecologist, Deb Thorp, recommending me for hormone therapy.

The other was a get-out-of-jail-free letter addressed, "To whom it may concern."

Every transgender person in transition must use public restrooms. I feared an ordeal like Elizabeth's at that hotel-bar in Ohio. The letter explained that Roberta was treating me for gender identity disorder. I was actually a woman with a man's body. The reader was to call Roberta if there were any problems.

I carried the letter, my gender lifeline, at all times.

Getting to Ellen was way more complicated than what I had imagined. There was no transgender owner's manual, no how-to guide, that laid everything out. Electrolysis, voice, speech patterns, mannerisms, language, hormones, surgery—the whole package—overwhelmed me. I would have been lost without people like Elizabeth, Nora, or my speech therapist Ann, and the ultimate, Sam the Hammer. In their own ways, each pushed me to take another stroke upstream.

At times of doubt, my spirit resonated with Elizabeth's pronouncement, "You'll be a beautiful woman." I remembered the comfort of Sam's newly found hugs. They were enough to get me to swim on. Just when everything looked midnight black, someone or something showed up and telegraphed, *Ellen, you can do this.*

Thap in particular went the distance for me. He was an avid hunter who believed that God created the sporting goods store Cabela's solely for his personal enjoyment. As young men, we camped and rode motorcycles along mountain trails. We reminisced about our high school days over beers and beans, staying warm with a crackling fire in the Colorado night. "How did we ever make it through those two-a-day football practices?"

For four decades, we remained confidants, blood brother-like. Still, I never took for granted that he'd accept me in whatever body I appeared.

"I'm coming to Minneapolis, Ellie," Thap announced with my new nickname. "I want to see this place you call your real home."

I would meet him at the airport.

I decided to conduct an experiment to see just how far I had progressed. Thap hadn't seen me in months; certainly not since my hair had gotten shoulder length. Wearing a skirt and boots, I planted myself in a chair at the baggage claim area. Ordinarily, I'd wave as soon as he got past security. This time, I decided to look straight ahead, as if waiting for luggage on the carousel.

Thap came through the security doorway. I fixed my eyes on the baggage carousel, and he walked right past me. My phone beeped with a text message, "Where r u?" He was ten feet away. I texted back, "Right next 2 u."

I turned toward Thap and smiled. I saw a toothy grin in return, Thap's way of signaling acceptance and decades of loving me as another human. We hugged as Thap said, "You're looking good, girl."

The next day, I asked for help in hanging a large picture. Thap took over. In no time, with a tape measure, hammer, and hooks, he had the picture perfectly centered on the wall. As he went to work, I felt a surge of relief. Never before had someone taken charge like that, where a *man* did something for me *because I was a woman.* It was another glimpse of how things could be.

Later that night, Thap and I walked to a restaurant. It was close to midnight when we started back to the condo. I grabbed his crooked arm, as any woman might do. He didn't shirk or hesitate. It was as if we had been touching like this all our lives.

Up ahead, two blocks away, a man walked toward us. He weaved, obviously drunk. As the stranger closed in, Thap got a foot ahead of me. We stopped when the man blocked the sidewalk, with me behind Thap.

The stranger raised his hand to chest height and reached for Thap, as if to ask for something.

"No touch! No touch!" Thap yelled. His neck veins bulged.

The man was Native American. A chill went through me because of the stereotype. The man continued forward. Thap pushed me back behind him further, the quarterback now protecting the guard. Thap's hand was out, fisted, an unmistakable statement of intention.

"I said no touch, goddamn it!"

Thankfully, the man stopped. He dropped his hand. Thap quickly pulled me over to the grass and then back onto the sidewalk.

As we put distance between us, I looked back. In the glow of the streetlight, I saw the man, motionless, staring our way.

He had a look that I knew well. It was the same face I got from swimming against the current, like when I encountered blue-shirted teenagers at fast food joints.

EIGHTEEN: *Getting My Groove On*

It got to the point that I so loved mascara.

Slow stroke after slow stroke, lash by lash, mascara transformed a multitude of fine hairs into a chorus line of kicking dancers chanting, *Ellen! Ellen! Ellen!*

Mascara soon became impossible to go without. I incorporated it into my workweek morning routine of showering, flossing, teeth brushing, and face shaving. There you had me: white dress shirt, gray pinstriped suit, Jerry Garcia tie, and shimmering mascara-illuminated eyes.

In the end, mascara helped change my life.

On the first Thursday in May, 2009, I sat in my office parking lot with Rick, a goateed, stressed-out litigation coordinator for the Midwest Railway Company, my client dating to 1988. He had finally bought his long-dreamed-of "baby," a cherry red Mustang, and wanted to show it off.

We talked about his cool new car, the cases I was working for him, our teenaged children, and life in general. He had been with me through twenty years' worth of MRC depositions and trials. He was as much friend as client representative.

The conversation shifted. Rick looked away and then back. I didn't see the question coming.

"Tell me, Ed. Are you wearing women's eye makeup?"

The words echoed through my brain.

What did you just ask? Oh no! Of course I'm wearing makeup: L'Oréal Clean Definition black noir mascara.

Reality had finally arrived. In a split second, I answered.

"Heck yes, I *am* wearing eye makeup." I stepped out of the car to escape. As I shut the door, I said, "And I think I look pretty good with it."

I ran to the office.

I found Sasha at her desk, laptop open, working away.

"Sash," I said. "Rick just asked if I was wearing eye makeup."

Sasha looked up from her computer. I saw shock on her face.

"Are you kidding me? Why would he ask that?"

"Ah, maybe because I've got mascara on?"

She had seen the mascara before and acted as if she didn't care. Maybe that was because I was her boss.

With pursed lips, she asked, "What are you going to do?"

I shrugged. "I don't know."

Clearly, I needed to do *something*. My clients—railroads and trucking companies—were nepotistic rumor mills. The management of one company routinely talked to the management of another. Unless I dealt with this quickly, someone else would spin my story.

I spent the rest of that day and evening alternating between utter fear and soaring excitement. It had taken a lot of time and money to recover from the flood. Now everything was at risk again. If things fell apart over my gender issue, people I cared about would pay the price with lost jobs. I'd be on the street, too, with bills to pay and tuitions to cover.

On the other hand, years could have passed before I would have felt ready to tell the world I was a woman. Maybe I would never have worked up the courage.

Rick's bold question took care of everything.

The idea of finally being whole, a complete person as a *woman*, made me feel like I had won at Powerball. This was my chance to unlock every closet door that limited *me*.

Overnight, new blood surged through my veins. It was "Type E" blood. "E" for exhilaration about living without hidden compartments. "E" for expressing the real me.

"E" for Ellen.

People often write letters to family and co-workers as part of their coming-out process. I decided to write to my clients and friends to announce Ellen's arrival, but I couldn't do it overnight. I needed Rick to keep my secret quiet until I could get a letter out to MRC's Chicago headquarters.

On the day after our Mustang ride, I sat with Rick in a conference room. We had a half hour wait before the deposition of a witness in one of our cases.

I came clean and told him the whole story. Then I tried to bargain.

"I'm going to write to headquarters about being transgender. I need you to keep this quiet for a couple weeks until I can get the letter out. Can you do that for me?"

Rick shook his head.

"It's too late, Ed. It was headquarters who told me to investigate in the first place. Somebody asked why our lawyer wore women's makeup."

Oh.

I remembered that the month before, I had been at the deposition of a middle manager, someone new to the company. I sat next to him where he would have gotten a good look at my eyes.

"Okay," I sighed. "What do you think I should do?"

Rick was expressionless. I had lost him. Even with twenty years between us, this was too much.

"I don't know," he answered. "If I were you, I'd get that letter out to Chicago as soon as possible."

I spent the weekend working on a letter. With Thap and Sasha's help, I had a final draft by Sunday night.

The letter wasn't brilliant, but it did the trick:

Dear Midwest Railway Company:

This is a very difficult letter to write.

In twenty-seven years of practicing law, I have built my reputation on being a tough, aggressive lawyer who does extremely well in front of juries for several reasons: I'm prepared, I'm personable, and jurors believe what I say.

My success has been fueled by an energy that I purposely directed to my legal career. I worked to be the best I could achieve.

In the process, an important thing went missing: me. I know that sounds simplistic, and perhaps it doesn't adequately convey what happened. In essence, unlike most people, for a variety of reasons, I did not get the luxury of figuring out myself when I was in my twenties and thirties.

I often tell the story that but for 9/11 and realizing that I could die without being Me, my true self, I likely would have continued with a life of depression and low self-esteem. However, with 9/11, I realized I needed to be Me regardless of the consequences. Those consequences have been quite severe, resulting in a divorce and many broken relationships. In the end, being Me, being honest as Me, takes precedence. For people who have never questioned their identity, this sounds foreign and selfish. For people like Me, it rings very true.

Who is the real Me? I am, in fact, transgender. This means that I have long known I am female inside my head, inside my soul, but I present with this deep voice in a male body. I was aggressive in my career because that compensated for the fight inside me where I resisted an inner voice telling me to be true to myself. Only now, after years of therapy, can I see and understand this. And, after all of that therapy, I can be forthright with my clients and tell them this story, "the whole story," as my ex-wife and I used to call it.

What does this mean for my clients? First, within the next 60 days, I will present only as a woman. I have spent much of my free time presenting as a woman and in many respects, I have already transitioned.

Additionally, I will soon legally change my name to "Ellen Jean Krug."

I understand you hired a lawyer who presents as a man. Certainly, I know that the work of a trial lawyer is unique. Likewise, I understand my clients can be penalized if a jury does not like me. Hence, this also means that my clients can choose to utilize another lawyer.

I hope that my clients will recognize that I have the same brain and skill set that existed before this self-disclosure. It is not realistic to expect clients not to be afraid or troubled about all of this. Still, I hope that in 2009, attitudes may change and that people will be open to the diversity this encompasses.

Finally, another question may be, "why now?" For approximately a year, I have had one foot firmly planted in my life as a woman and the other foot in the world of presenting as a man. Every time I go back to being a man, there is a bigger and bigger disconnect. I can no longer sustain the dichotomy, the division of my life. At age 52, I have to be whole, at last. Please believe me when I say that I really would prefer for all of this not to be happening. But, this is reality and I need to continue to be healthy mentally.

I hope the shock value of this letter wears off after a couple readings. It has been a privilege to be of service. Thank you for your consideration.

Very truly yours,
Ellen Krug

This letter, and variations, went out by email on Monday afternoon, barely four days after Rick's bold question, to MRC and other clients, and to lawyers, friends, and judges.

DEF Trucking, my largest client, was far too important to get the news in a letter. I needed to talk to David, the company president, in person.

On Monday noon, Sasha and I met David at Applebee's. David was a classic bootstrapper, who started out as a green driver. Thirty years later, he had worked his way to the top. He was balding with sour eyes and a dry wit that surfaced with uncanny timing.

I had always imagined that a day like this would come; one where I'd be able to open the closet door and talk to a client about the real *me*, where there would be no more pretense, no more posturing as Killer Krug. Now that moment was here, and I was scared to death. What if David rejected me? I feared my professional life would crash down—and then what? I would have lost one identity before I cemented another. It all seemed like quicksand. Still, I pushed on.

I had no choice.

I waited until the food came. I didn't want to be interrupted by the server asking for our orders.

My opening came over a half order of grilled chicken Caesar salad.

"I know it was a pretty sudden request that we meet for lunch," I began. "It's because I need to talk to you about something going on in my life. I wanted you to hear this in person."

Looking attentive, David stabbed a French fry. He wasn't a salad eater.

"I'm sure you've noticed my hair. The fact is, I'm getting the outside of my body to match my inside."

David went for another fry. It compelled me to talk more.

"It's called being 'transgender.' I know, it's not something that you may know anything about. I've been in therapy for years, and trust me, talking about it is the last thing in the world that I want to do. But I have to. I need to live as who I really am: a woman."

The word, "woman," got David's attention. He put down his fork and clasped his hands with a Buddha-like look. For a second, I wondered whether he'd get up and walk out.

Finally, David spoke. "Nothing surprises me anymore," he said. He looked at me squarely and then promptly went back to his lunch.

I was emboldened. "I want to stay your lawyer," I said. "Yes, this is out of the ordinary, but it hasn't affected my brain. I'm still a good attorney."

David continued to eat his fries and burger. Five minutes later, he answered, "It's all right. I can't say that I understand, but I've always had confidence in you. This doesn't shake that. Don't worry, we'll keep you."

I breathed out. It was what I needed. Half giddy and half exhausted, I started in on my salad.

In the car on the way back to the office, Sasha and I rehashed the lunch. "I can't believe how accepting David was," I said, beaming.

"Yeah, it went way better than I expected." As usual, she cracked the window for a cigarette.

"Do you think he'll backtrack and decide to find another lawyer?"

"No," Sasha answered. "I think David is his own person. You can trust what he says."

The next day, Matthew, the chief lawyer for MRC, which had started all of this, telephoned from Chicago.

"Your letter took us by surprise," he said. "I need to know more so that I can explain this to my boss."

That was fair. For the next hour, Matthew asked questions across the board, from how my appearance would change to, "How do you plan to handle a jury if someone questions your gender?"

Near the end of the conversation, he said, "I think I get everything, Ellen, but my primary concern is your aggressiveness in the courtroom. A big reason why you're our attorney is that you're very tough. That's fine for a man, but an aggressive woman? I'm worried a jury will think you're, excuse the phrase, a 'bitch.' How do we handle that?"

We're back to stereotypes, I thought.

"My speech therapist is working with me on feminine voice patterns," I answered. "This should take some of the edge off my style." I went on. "There's another thing at play here too. With finally getting to be myself, I'm not frustrated anymore. The frustration translated into anger, which showed up in the courtroom, I guess, with good results."

For that matter, the frustration made me an angry person outside the courtroom as well, something I better understood now.

"Ellen, we don't want you to lose too much of that anger," Matthew said. "We still want you tough. You'll need to find the right mix."

We got to the last subject. "What about your voice?" Matthew asked. "No offense, but it's not very feminine. How do you think a jury will react? Will it detract from what you're trying to do in the courtroom?"

I had made some progress with Ann, but it wasn't good enough. Still, with hard work, I thought I could get it into the woman-who's-smoked-two-packs-a-day-for-thirty-years range.

"I know, Matthew, the voice. I'm working on it. My speech therapist believes I'll be able to soften it quite a bit."

"Okay, we'll just have to see on the voice. As far as I'm concerned, you don't have anything to worry about with us. We're still your client."

How wonderful! I would remember Matthew's decency forever.

Suddenly, I was on a roll. My two biggest clients would stick it out. The firm would survive.

By the end of the first week, at least forty people had responded to my letters with supportive emails or phone calls. I found that Iowans were egalitarian, willing to bend and understand. "We support you and hope for the best," one email read. A judge wrote: "Thank you for your courageous letter. I have nothing but the utmost respect for your decision and the way in which you are handling it."

Two Cedar Rapids attorneys, a man and a woman, called from that twenty-six-lawyer firm I often tangled with. "Ellen, we accept you. What can we do to help?"

Susan, another Cedar Rapids lawyer, emailed, "Ellen, I got your letter from Bill West in Waterloo. It's being passed around our office here. I think you're brave."

Nice, but Susan hadn't been on the list to get my letter. Nor, for that matter, was Bill West, or anyone else she talked about. Obviously, my letter was floating across the Iowa legal community as part of some unofficial "can you believe this" communique.

It didn't matter.

Most important was an email from Sasha, who understood that her job would evaporate if things didn't go well. She wrote, "I love you for who you are and believe you should express yourself. I am here for you through whatever."

Wow. Kindness. Understanding. Grace. Peace. I never expected any of this as Ellen in real life. They were the rewards for finally speaking the truth—to myself and the world.

I filed papers to legally change my name to "Ellen Jean Krug." Judge Marsha signed the court order that confirmed the name change.

"There you go, Ellen. I'm very happy for you," she said.

I looked at the order and smiled.

It's another step on the journey.

A few days after my coming-out letters, Lydia called.

"I would have appreciated a heads-up about your letter. Why did I have to learn about it from one of my friends?"

Uh-oh.

Given our on-again, off-again relationship, I didn't think it would do any good to consult Lydia about the letter.

"I'm sorry about that," I said. "I didn't think it would matter given how your life has gotten so much better."

I couldn't help the dig. At this point, she and Stephen had been together for three years. Every once in a while, during a co-parenting telephone call, she'd let slip that the two of them had been out biking—that had been *our* thing—or that they planned a trip to South America. These innocent disclosures pounded on my heart like some errant drummer.

Try as I might, I couldn't stop loving Lydia. Sure, Janelle had been important for separate reasons, but Lydia was my one true love. For three decades, we had been best friends and gigglers in consort. I didn't leave because I had fallen out of love with her.

I left because I needed to fall in love with *me*.

I also missed my home, the place in the dappled sunlight picture. I *belonged* with the girls of Knollwood. Even with the newfound freedom of living as me, I still grappled with what I had given up—no, make that *sacrificed*—to get to Ellen.

Worse yet, coming out as transgender meant I had publicly entered a subset of another subset, another no-man's land. Now I faced the real risk of being alone forever, an old hag, just like Lydia had feared early on.

Welcome to middle-aged single transgender womanhood, Ellen.

As a bisexual, one would think my options for companionship and love would be doubled. It didn't work that way. Gay men weren't interested in a biological male who presented as a woman. Heterosexual men and women also weren't attracted to people like me. As long as my plumbing remained male, lesbians wouldn't have an interest either. Even if I went through with sex reassignment surgery, I wondered whether lesbians or straight men would be happy with a man-made vagina and artificial breasts.

That left other transgender people and men attracted to biological men who dressed as women. Neither was for me. There was the competition factor with another transgender woman. I quickly appreciated that biological women compete for the prettiest-girl-in-the-room award; it was also that way with transgender women. Who was more feminine? Which of us passed as female more easily?

I didn't need that kind of pressure. I was certain that I'd always lose the contest.

Men who like transgender women were regulars at the Town House. They came alone and were always good for free drinks. After a while, the man might be inches from a tall, broad-shouldered blonde in a way-too-short skirt. Soon, the man would whisper in the blonde's ear, provoking a laugh. Later, they would walk out the door together.

Those transgender-preying men weren't for me.

The idea of being alone, possibly for the rest of my life, was scary. It was a root fear that went all the way back to the Kendall Drive living room window.

Now, after finally figuring out who and what I was, the question had become *Will anyone ever love me again?*

I bounced against decades of Lydia's million strong whispers, "I love you, Bo." A deep serrated groove had been worn into my heart; it made me believe that love was the answer for everything—especially for fear. As long as I had someone's love, everything would be okay.

How could I possibly fill that groove?

I didn't know. What I did know: I was going somewhere different, possibly to a safe suburb of Womanville. Maybe I'd even have reassignment surgery and go all the way to downtown Vagina City. In either case, I was headed to a place I never thought possible.

It looked like I'd have to go there alone too.

I soon understood there was no easy way to spin your father or ex-husband turned woman. No matter how many times I said, "I love you," or "I'm sorry for this," or "I know it's weird but I had to do it," I couldn't muscle acceptance from Emily, Lily, or for that matter, Lydia. Each had to get there on her own.

I could only hope for the best.

Lily continued to approach everything in her own unique way. I wondered if she had been ordered up just for me, for this precise moment in my life. My hunch was confirmed a few months after I went full time as Ellen. We were at a mall. I was dressed in a skirt and sandals, a middle-aged female parent with her daughter. We passed a pair of cute short-haired twenty-something men dressed in referee-like shirts who stood in front of an athletic store entrance.

"Good afternoon, *ladies*," one said.

The plural in his hello was loud and clear. My heart soared. I glanced down at Lily. She tilted her head.

"Yeah, Lily," I whispered. "*Ladies*. This happens to me all the time now."

Lily grabbed my hand and squeezed. This was quite remarkable, since Lily's idea of affection was a glancing kiss to the top of her head. I felt it immediately, right there in the middle of that crowded and noisy mall: *acceptance*.

Magically, the shopping bag in my other hand transformed into a hundred pink helium balloons.

It was more difficult for Emily. Yet, there was hope.

One Saturday night, Emily called from her dorm room. It was a wake-up-at-10:30-at-night phone call, the kind that quickens parental pulses.

There were tears in her voice. I asked if she wanted to talk. A very weak, "Yes," answered.

"I'll get in the car now," I said.

I met Emily outside her dorm at close to one in the morning. We found a hotel with a bed and pullout couch, the best I could do that late at night. We sat on the bed and talked. It turned into three hours of extremely needed honesty.

Toward the end, Emily whispered, "It's hard, Dad. I have roommates who would never understand."

"That's okay," I offered. "You don't need to tell them. I don't want to crash your world any more than I already have."

"I miss our old family," she said with tissue in hand. "Why can't we have our old family?"

The question tore at me. I put my arm around her. "I miss our family too," I said. "Every day."

I thought about New Orleans and how I had wanted to run back home to Emily. Now, things were different. I finally had me. I so wished she understood.

We were quiet until I said, "You know I love you, right?"

"Yes, Daddy, I know. I love you too. I always will."

By then it was 4:30 a.m. Darkness was giving way to morning light. I better understood her pain and hoped she understood that I needed to be true to myself, even with all the hurt it caused.

Afterward, Emily and I entered into an unspoken pact—one grounded on survivorship and love. I became "Telephone Dad." Every Sunday, we talked by phone where my voice remained a comforting reminder of happier days and the man she loved as Dad. In return, I remembered that Emily needed time—maybe a lot, maybe a decade— before she could process the reality of my gender change. Until then, seeing me in person as Ellen was too much to ask.

I accepted our pact because I *knew* Emily would never give up on me. I would be patient.

Lydia was different. Not long after my coming-out letter, she met me at a hospital emergency room for a brief health issue that affected Lily. Lydia hadn't seen me—or my developing womanhood—for months. She paused at the examining room doorway and barely acknowledged me as we talked to the doctor.

On the way out of the hospital, Lydia and I stopped to talk. She refused to look at me and walked away in my mid-sentence.

I hated the canyon between us, a gray void of lost love, substituted lovers, and raw honesty.

The denial persisted as Lydia continued to call me "Ed," with no apparent intent to adopt my new name. One day, this changed too.

It was Lily's birthday celebration. Lily sat down to open gifts and Lydia asked, "*Ellen*, would you please hand me that gift bag over there?" Her use of "Ellen" resounded in my heart, but I didn't say a word.

I wasn't about to jinx whatever had just happened.

A couple days later, I recounted this to Bill, a good friend who along with his wife Jillian, still socialized with Lydia.

"I'll tell you how it happened that she called you 'Ellen,'" Bill said. "Jillian and I had dinner with Lydia and Stephen the other night, before Lily's birthday. We got around to all that was happening with you. Lydia said that Lily had become upset because Lydia still called you 'Ed.' Lily told Lydia that she should use 'Ellen' because that's who you are now; it was disrespectful to refer to you as 'Ed.' She even made Lydia promise to use your new name."

The story shook me. I knew that Lily supported me, but to take a stand like that with her mother? Incredible.

And she's barely eighteen.

Eventually, Lydia and I talked again, human to human.

"Let's meet for a drink," I said in an earnest voicemail. When she walked into the bar, we hugged. It was a clear signal that we'd be able to find our old footing, albeit in new shoes.

We talked about the girls, my plans for shifting to Minneapolis, and the thrill of finding inexpensive clothes at Target. I complained about the everyday headaches of operating a business. Lydia shared about her job as an insurance company manager, where she was well respected and rising.

I lamented that I took twice as long to put on makeup as she did. She said, "You'll get the hang of it." We laughed.

I loved seeing her smile again, although I didn't tell her that. Sentimental as usual, I confessed, "I miss our family—everything about it." Lydia's smile evaporated. She looked away and then back with wet eyes.

I changed the subject.

We went on for an hour. Just as the check arrived, Lydia looked up from her almost-finished cosmo. She said, "You know, we're both better people than we were."

Her honesty caught me off guard. It shouldn't have; we had formerly excelled at diving to the deep water of each other's heart.

I answered, "For sure. It's as if we're entirely different people now."

We walked to our cars. "Thank you for being so kind," I said, as I leaned in.

It felt so incredibly wonderful to have her arms around me again.

Any passerby would have seen two women embracing, apparent friends for life.

———————

Not all of it was good.

In the category of silence-speaks-volumes, a neighbor on Knollwood never again talked to me after my coming-out letter. I wrote a note across the top of the letter, "I know this disappoints you, but it's absolutely necessary for me." We had been close for years.

Jacki had embraced me when I came out as gay. That changed with my transgender disclosure.

"You were my big brother, and now I don't have that security," she said uneasily. I missed her, but I understood. Over time, the freeze would thaw, thankfully, but the relationship never returned to what it had been.

Then there was Drew Bloom, my best friend in Cedar Rapids.

I had a brief court appearance one afternoon. Drew's office was a block from the courthouse, and I did something that I almost never do: I simply dropped in.

A secretary rang Drew. "Ellen Krug is here to see you."

I waited in the reception area. Drew's nonprofit funded civic and arts projects in Cedar Rapids. The agency was housed in a preformed concrete building with high ceilings. The place was cold and austere, prison-like.

Drew walked into the waiting area. He greeted me tersely. I immediately understood my visit wasn't what he particularly wanted.

In his office, Drew planted himself behind a file-filled desk. I took a chair in front, the two of us separated by wood, paper, and gender.

"I won't stay for long," I said. "I wanted to see how you're doing."

"I'm fine," he clicked. "Work is good, but busy, as you can see." He motioned to the papers on his desk.

I pushed a conversation. I asked about his son and daughter and talked about Lily's college plans in Minneapolis. I knew this would be the last time we'd talk, at least until he stopped seeing the ghost of Ed Krug.

I got up to leave. Drew walked me to the hallway.

"Well, take care of yourself," he said. He put out his hand. I half-smiled, and returned my hand for a limp shake.

"Goodbye, Drew." I turned and walked a couple steps.

I stopped. *A good Buddhist stays open,* I told myself. I backtracked to an expressionless Drew, where I hugged him and held.

"I'll wait for you," I whispered.

"I'm sorry." His voice was blacktop flat.

I let go and headed down the hall, quickly putting distance between us. I didn't want Drew to see me cry.

———

Almost everything I knew as a man changed when I transitioned to live as a woman.

I quit my gym because they knew me only as Ed. I scouted out a new athletic club and went there dressed as Ellen. I put on the best performance of my life, and used every ounce of feminine voice I could muster, enough to even make Ann proud. I knew I had pulled it off when the club assistant let me inspect the women's locker room.

"I'll wait for you out here," he said.

It took all I had not to shout for joy in the middle of the women's lockers.

I started at the new club the next day. I quickly learned how to conceal my male plumbing through the art of "tuck and hold" and the adroit use of towels. I had silicone breast forms in my bra; from a distance, my bra line appeared natural. With my longer hair, cosmetic bags, curling iron, and blow dryer, I looked like any other woman readying for work.

The court order for my name change got me a new driver's license. The DMV kept me "male" because I hadn't had reassignment surgery. Without a doctor's letter attesting to a new vagina, they weren't about to change the gender marker.

A new Social Security card worked out better. I found an extremely friendly Social Security clerk, a tattooed woman with sparkly glasses. I gave her the court order, my new driver's license, and my get-out-of-jail-free letter from Roberta Livingston.

I thought, *Why not try?*

After a couple dozen clicks, the clerk was done. She handed back the papers and said, "Okay, hon, here you go. You'll get a card with your new name in about four weeks." She added, "I changed your gender too. You're now female as far as the Social Security Administration is concerned."

I gushed "Thank you" way too many times.

I made other changes: business cards, automobile registration, car and life insurance, and utility bills. Some vendors required a copy of the name-change court order, which contained intimate details of my life. I felt violated each time I sent it off. I imagined a perfect person reading the court order and busting a gut.

He'd announce to other cubicle dwellers, "Hey everyone, look at what I just got from this freak in Cedar Rapids. Can you believe it?"

Still, I always sent off the court order.

It took three months before I could get in to see my new gynecologist, Deb Thorp. Remarkably, Dr. Deb had convinced a large hospital health-care organization to let her host a once-a-week clinic for male- and female-born transgender people. This meant that genetic women sat alongside transgender folks in a busy waiting room. It also required training staff to use proper female pronouns when patients like me presented with distinct male voices.

In other words, this was no small feat.

Dr. Deb's frontline nurse was a tall, curly haired woman named Mary. "I just love Tuesdays when we see our trans people," she said as she slipped a blood pressure cuff over my arm. "They're so real, just struggling to be themselves."

A few minutes later, I heard a knock. A cute short-haired blonde appeared. I guessed that Dr. Deb was in her mid-forties. She reminded me of a field hockey player with heart, built solid and unwilling to let anything stand in her way, yet intent on having fun.

"So, you're here for hormones," she said. "Tell me why you want them."

"Uh, I've been dressing full time for a few months, and it feels so right," I answered. "I don't have any doubt this is who I am."

Dr. Deb tapped at a keyboard. "You understand your body is going to change, right?"

"Oh yeah. Isn't that the whole idea?"

"It sure is. I wanted to make sure you knew too."

"Will the estrogen make my voice any softer?" I hoped for a quick fix.

"No, sorry. It won't do a thing for that voice of yours."

Drat.

She went over the changes estrogen would bring, like softer skin and redistributed fat, maybe even real hips. Most importantly, there would be breast growth.

"All males have some amount of estrogen, so we're just supplementing what nature's given you," she explained. "I've had some male-to-females develop B cups, even close to C cups. It'll take six months to know where you'll end up in terms of growth."

The thought of growing my own real breasts was just plain exciting. Oh yeah, I was all for it.

Dr. Deb also prescribed Spironolactone to block my testosterone production. Eventually, it would eliminate sperm altogether. "The pill is a diuretic, so don't take it when you go to bed or you'll be up all night peeing," Dr. Deb cautioned.

There were also risks—some real big ones. "The most significant risk is stroke," she said. "If you have dizziness or a balance problem, get to a hospital immediately. Some people have a higher risk of heart attack. And, of course, there's the literature about a greater chance of breast cancer."

All of a sudden, my legs wanted to run out of the room. I channeled *Stay, girl.*

Dr. Deb bent forward as if to make a point. "You understand this isn't an exact science, right? I'm confident everything will be fine, but sometimes I get surprised."

Hmmm. Stroke, heart attack, cancer. Is there anything I'm not willing to risk?

A clinic technician drew blood to get a baseline reading of my testosterone and natural estrogen levels. I walked out of the clinic with a prescription for estrogen patches and Spironolactone. None of this—the visit with Dr. Deb, the blood test, or the drugs—was covered by insurance.

Things went well for a couple weeks. At first, the only noticeable effect was weight loss; I dropped ten pounds almost overnight. With that kind of result, I wondered if I could stay on Spironolactone forever. It sure beat exercising.

I woke up one morning intending to drive to Minneapolis for the weekend. My feet itched. I noticed red welts and blisters around my groin; they itched too. I yanked off the estrogen patch and decided against a Spironolactone pill that morning.

Thinking this would go away, I headed to Minneapolis. I wasn't ten miles from Durango when my feet itched so bad that I had to pull over. I found a drugstore and bought Benadryl, which got me to Minneapolis. Things settled down over the weekend.

I understood this was an allergic reaction, but I didn't know which drug—the estrogen or the Spironolactone—was the culprit. A fear shot through me. *What if it's the estrogen? How will I ever get to real womanhood without it?*

I couldn't imagine getting this far only to have my body go on strike.

I talked to Mary from Dr. Deb's office. The Spironolactone, not the estrogen, was the cause. I breathed relief. The phone call turned serious. "You need to see your primary care physician immediately," Mary ordered.

"Why? It's going away," I responded.

"There could be neurological damage to your feet from the blisters," she answered.

By then, I was back in Iowa. I didn't want to see my local doctor. He only knew me as Ed. No way was I going to show up in a skirt and get into the whole story.

Hesitantly, Mary agreed that I could hold off for one more day. If the symptoms continued to abate, we'd wait until I returned to Minneapolis to see Dr. Deb. Things kept improving. Dr. Deb later prescribed an alternate testosterone blocker, which worked fine. To my chagrin, it had no diuretic effect. I put the weight back on.

If I wanted an attractive body, I'd have to exercise, just like a hundred million other women.

———————

I noticed body changes a couple months into hormone therapy. Curves appeared on my formerly straight-boy hips. Suddenly, women's jeans fit way better.

My breasts changed too. At first, they were exceedingly tender; simply rubbing up against something gave me a big *ouch!* Next, little breast buds appeared, hints of womanhood. Soon I had more mass, real breasts, something to actually fill the two dozen bras I owned.

On many mornings, I stood in front of the bathroom mirror in awe of new curves and bumps. My nipples and areolas did not enlarge, which lent to my chest appearing pubescent. It was as if I was coming of age, giving notice to all parts male that things were going to be different from here on out.

My beard growth thinned, although not nearly enough to forgo weekly electrolysis sessions. My skin also became shiny, almost glowing.

A profound change in my brain accompanied all of this. My sex drive slowed, and then left entirely. Surprisingly, that didn't bother me. I had never fully understood how, as a man, testosterone controlled me, like some hormonal dictator. In the process of changing, I realized that many men have an instinctual need to survey any physical environment in which they find themselves. Many have one innate goal—to find sex partners for fleshy places to deposit DNA. For all my mature life, it was automatic: I'd walk into a restaurant and within a minute, if even that, I'd identify every woman (or later, every man, too) whom I found sexually compatible. It didn't matter if I entered the restaurant with Lydia or some other partner.

Most women don't understand this. I certainly didn't appreciate it until my sex drive was replaced by something else.

In changing genders, I lost one perspective and gained another.

As Ellen, I entered a restaurant with a different agenda. I still looked at women—that habit remained—but now focused on their clothes, shoes, hair, and even their cute purse. I no longer imagined having sex with them; I wanted to *be* them. I became jealous of their beauty, and the ease with which they seemed to make their way. I constantly compared myself; in an instant, I could tick off a dozen reasons why I wasn't pretty or desirable enough.

I told Sasha about the interplanetary shift in my head. "Don't you know, this is how *all* women think?" she answered. "I always wonder why some other woman has bigger boobs or a smaller butt than me."

If Sasha, with her *Vogue*-model beauty, felt that way, womanhood sounded like a real battlefield. What was I getting myself into?

My brain changed in another way, this one far more important: I found real peace of mind. For the first time in my life, I felt an odd but lovely serenity, the ability to simply sit and enjoy, to no longer *want*. For someone consistently described as "too driven" or "too intense" or "way too aggressive," this seemed impossible.

Killer Krug had left the building, courtesy of Dr. Deb.

People around me noticed. "Ellen, you're so much more relaxed than you used to be," Rita, my aunt, said one bright afternoon when I visited Connecticut. "I've known you your entire life, and I've never seen you like this."

The fact that my sixty-two-year-old aunt could embrace Ellen was, in itself, remarkable. Her confirmation of how much I had changed was icing on the cake.

On visits to a half dozen friends who didn't know each other, I heard the same word—*relaxed*—to describe my transformation. I was amazed.

Even my former adversaries noticed something different about me. Six months after coming out as Ellen, I lunched with Jake Collins, an attorney who had been on the opposite side of a contentious car accident case a few years before. We had argued back and forth over various issues. Later, we became friends. Lunch was a way of catching up.

Twenty minutes into our conversation, Jake raised a hand to his chest.

"I'm sorry Ellen, but I've got to tell you something."

"What?" I wondered if I had shared too much.

"I don't know how to put this, so I'll just say it. You were a real asshole as a man. It was your disposition: angry and aggressive. Now I see you as a woman, and you're so nice, sweet actually. I like Ellen a hell of a lot more than I ever did Ed."

He went back to his sandwich.

"*Sweet*"? "*Nice*"? I would have used something else to describe my new persona: *loving-kindness*. No longer frustrated and angry, my true disposition, grounded in the freedom to live as myself—and influenced by Buddhism—showed through.

It turned out that the real me was a kind person, quite the opposite of a killer.

———————

I stopped at Hy-Vee. With items in a cart, I got in line at the check-out. Ahead of me, a woman looked at *People* as she waited. Something registered. Without thinking, I said, "Leslie, how are you?"

She and her husband had socialized with Lydia and me for several years. They also were good friends with Drew Bloom and his wife. I hadn't seen Leslie for nearly three years.

Leslie looked up from the magazine. She gave one of those I-don't-know-who-you-are-but-I'll-act-like-I-do-anyway smiles.

"Hi," she said.

I got closer and whispered. "It's Ed, Ed Krug."

Her faced changed from bewilderment to amazement. "Oh my god!" I saw a genuine smile. She grabbed my arm. "How are you?"

"I'm doing great," I said.

The conveyor moved. We chatted quickly for the couple minutes it took to ring up her items.

"So long," she said. She started for the door with a bag in hand.

I watched her stop just as the automatic door opened. She did an about-face and came back.

"Let me give you this," she said, as she reached up and hugged me. Emotion flooded in. "I've lost so much," I said. It came from nowhere.

"Yes, but you've gained a lot too," she answered.

It was only a few seconds. Leslie's kindness resonated with me for weeks.

––––––––––––

Lily and I had Joe Joe—my very last boyfriend, turned friend forever—over to Durango for dinner. Lily and Joe Joe were also close; he had taken her on "junking" excursions for 1960s furniture to fill his immaculate home. Lily enjoyed having an adult friend who respected her extremely liberal political and social opinions. It was a delightful meal of grilled steak and baked potatoes, not gourmet, but not abysmal, either.

A few days later, I received a thank you from Joe Joe:

You have really grown, Ellen. I am so happy to see the real you. You are more relaxed, more natural and very focused on the near future—girl, you've got your groove! I'm so happy for you!

Love,

Joe Joe

I left the note on the kitchen counter, where I went back to it again and again.

It was more proof. How could I have ever doubted my course?

More importantly, how could I have been so ignorant? I blindly ran in circles as Ed.

Now as Ellen, I sprinted fast and far. I did it with my eyes wide open.

NINETEEN: *Letting Go*

My cell rang.

I heard Thap's voice: "How are you doing, Ellie?"

"I'm well, Thapper," I answered. "Life and business are good. Amazingly, my clients have stuck with me. I'm crossing my fingers it will stay that way."

"That's great," Thap said, only to shift a split second later. "Watch out. I predict some will get nervous the more they think about what it means long-term. You're a good lawyer, yes, but people get afraid."

"I hope not. I'd hate to lose anyone now that I've got things figured out."

"Don't you have a trial coming up?"

"Yeah, I do. One of my cases goes to trial later this month." Instinctively, my mind raced down a mental checklist.

It was early July, 2009. In three weeks, my clients Fred and Jane Allen would go to trial over the sale of their high-end house. The buyers claimed Fred and Jane intentionally didn't disclose that a number of windows in the house had rotted sills. In their defense, Fred and Jane never opened windows where they could even see the sills; they were air conditioner people.

The buyers wanted every window replaced—$100,000 worth—in the 5,000-square-foot house.

Thap pressed. "How are you going to pull the trial off now that you're full-time female? What do your clients think?"

Good questions. Fred and Jane had hired Ed two years before. They hadn't yet responded to Ellen's coming-out letter.

"I've got to talk to my clients," I said. "I don't know what they want."

Thap and I shifted to something else on the shared menu of our lives. We ended with the usual goodbye, "Miss you, love you."

I met with Fred and Jane a few days later. Fred was outgoing and worked in sales. Jane, a wisecracking nurse, bordered on cynic. They'd been married forty years and the lawsuit threatened their retirement plans.

I waved a hand in front of my face and said, "I know you didn't sign up for this. I'm sorry things have changed so dramatically. Trust me, I couldn't avoid it."

Fred looked at Jane and then at me.

"Ellen, it's all right. We understand. We still believe in you," he said.

"Thank you, but the problem is that we don't know what a jury will think. We're talking about Cedar Rapids, after all."

I wasn't about to force a decision on them. Certainly, I didn't want to hurt their case. If Fred and Jane elected, we could postpone the trial for them to get a new lawyer. Alternately, I could show up at the trial as a man.

"I'm not that far along on hormones that I can't wear a man's suit with a ponytail," I said. "I'll do that if it'd make you more comfortable. This is your case, after all—your money."

Fred nodded. "Jane and I have already talked about this. While we appreciate your offer, Ellen, the real question is what will make *you* most comfortable. We don't want you at less than your best. If you won't be at ease trying the case as a man, we don't want that."

I had traveled so far by then. It *would* be hard to masquerade as a man in a suit and tie. "If you want the truth," I answered, "no, I wouldn't be comfortable presenting as a man. It's not who I am."

Once more, Fred looked at Jane. This time, Jane spoke. "That settles it. You'll go as Ellen."

I fought the urge to jump across the table and kiss them. Ellen Krug would get to try her first case.

———————

Courtroom decorum requires a certain class of attire. Skirts and sandals just don't cut it.

I poked my head into Sasha's office and announced, "We're going shopping!"

At a mall down the road, we looked for suits. Sasha's taste tended to Calvin Klein; that was far too flashy for me. I was happy with the discount rack.

We took several options into a large dressing room. Like any good girlfriend, Sasha stayed to offer her opinions. I undressed to bra and panties; neither of us gave it a second thought.

Sasha rendered verdicts as I tried on skirts and blazers: "Too loose." "Too tight." "Your butt looks big in that one." "Not a great color."

Two hours later, I had three suits—two variations of gray and the third a soft brown with wonderful buttons.

Shoes were next. With a size 10½ to 11 foot, finding stylish, non-garish shoes was near-impossible. I always feared that my large feet would give clerks a reason to make me as male too.

The shoe department clerk, a friendly university student, was nice. She put me at ease and I quickly found several pairs of heels to match the suits.

"Now you need hose and blouses," Sasha instructed.

She laid out the rules. On shades of pantyhose, "Keep it lighter in the summer, almost nude. You don't want your legs to appear too dark; it's distracting."

Blouses shouldn't be sheer, and they need some—but not too much—V at the neck, so that they're still feminine.

"And make sure to tuck your blouse into your pantyhose," she ordered. "You don't want it sticking out the back of your suit."

On the last point, Sasha dropped her chin and gave me the eye to make sure I got it.

———

Our trial judge was Douglas Russell, a smart, glasses-and-mustached man who had written a book about Winston Churchill. He was a good draw—I was certain he'd be fair and open-minded.

The people who initiated the lawsuit, Jeremy and Alice Compton, were beautiful high fliers, both architects. Buying Fred and Jane's expensive house at their thirty-something ages just didn't seem fair. Jeremy Compton was tall, dark, and personable enough to have a beer with. Alice, the smarter of the two, ran the show. She was a numbers person, so much so that I wondered if she counted strokes while brushing her oh-no-way-that's-natural-blonde hair at night.

Bill Hughes, the Comptons' attorney, was my age. We had been on the opposite sides of other cases when I was still Killer Krug. Now, as he adjusted to Ellen, like almost everyone else, he tripped over pronouns. I heard "him" followed by "Sorry, Ellen, I mean, 'her.'"

It was an inevitable part of gender-flipping. I appreciated that he tried.

Our court reporter, Wilma Porter, was a well-dressed veteran of a thousand trials who had no fear. She'd interrupt anyone—lawyers, witnesses, or judges—who talked too fast for her hands. "You need to slow down, now!" She once walked out in the middle of a trial after repeatedly warning an errant judge who refused to pace his dictation.

"The hell with him," she blurted, glancing back to the courtroom door.

I was at the defense counsel table unpacking files when the courtroom clerk announced that Judge Russell wanted a short conference. The lawyers paraded down a hallway into an office. Judge Russell sat behind a desk with two tall folders, the papers from our case.

He had received my coming-out letter a couple months before and seemed entirely unfazed by my appearance.

For twenty minutes, the attorneys and Judge Russell discussed various legal issues that would come up as the trial progressed. At the end, Judge Russell asked, "Is there anything else we should address before we pick the jury?"

That was my opening. I needed permission for something that was exceedingly critical.

"Your Honor," I said, "I would like to tell the jury that I'm transgender. The Comptons claim my clients deceived them about the windows. I don't want the jury thinking that I'm also a fraud, a female imposter. If that happened, the jury could sock the Allens with a big verdict."

Because being transgender was something very personal and not the kind of thing attorneys usually talk to juries about, just like attorneys wouldn't ever disclose their religious or political affiliations, Judge Russell and Bill Hughes both needed to agree.

Judge Russell leaned back in his chair, Solomon-like, and glanced at the ceiling. A few seconds later, he pronounced, "I don't have a problem with you doing that."

He turned to Bill Hughes. "Do you care if Ellen tells the jury she's transgender?"

Although Bill didn't realize it, this was a trick question. On the one hand, if Bill thought like a man, he'd immediately seize on the freak factor: that Ellen Krug would be too weird for any jury. In turn, he'd believe that no matter what I said to the jury about being transgender, the jury wouldn't get past the critical fact that I used to be a man.

Under that scenario, Bill would believe that I'd certainly lose the trial. Thus, he'd be more than happy to let me self-disclose to the jury.

On the other hand, if Bill thought like a woman, he would understand that disclosing I was transgender, a real vulnerability for any human, would endear me to many people, particularly women. Vulnerability, I knew, was extremely powerful toward establishing one's credibility; in other words, "You should believe my clients because I've been honest with you jurors about my story."

If Bill had any clue about this vulnerability thing, he'd jump out of his chair and object as if his professional life depended on it.

I was betting Bill didn't think like a woman.

I bet right.

"No," Bill said with a slight smile. "It's fine with me if he, I mean, she, tells the jury she's transgender. I don't have a problem with that at all."

I tried not to grin too much. I had just scored a huge victory, only no one in the judge's chambers, other than Sasha, had any idea.

We returned to the courtroom. It was packed with people, prospective jurors reporting for jury duty. We would start out with sixteen people picked by lottery. The attorneys would talk to the sixteen through a process called "voir dire." It was intended to weed out anyone biased toward one side or the other. Each side would then strike, or disqualify, four jurors, bringing the number down to eight.

The clerk started calling names. "Number 15, Mr. Doe."

Because body language can say a lot, I watched Mr. Doe walk to the jury box. Each juror had filled out a questionnaire beforehand, so I knew Mr. Doe was a thirty-year-old welder with a high school education. He worked with his hands, so he might know something about installing or repairing windows. It was a point to ask about during voir dire.

The process of number and name calling repeated until the jury box contained sixteen people, about half men, half women, ages twenty to eighty-two. Judge Russell talked about the trial process and what to expect. He finished and turned to the attorneys.

"You may proceed, counsel," he said.

Since Bill represented the plaintiffs, he went first. There's an art to questioning jurors: it requires a combination of light humor (so the jury likes you), seriousness (so the jury respects you), and storytelling (so they believe you). Questions to the jury can run the gamut from A to Z—the juror's occupation, prior jury experience, relatives who've had accidents, and whether the juror has ever had their own lawsuit.

Bill was personable, and it showed. I listened intently, made notes, and tried to decide which jurors might be good or bad for our case. Some jurors were forthcoming; others were quiet, even reticent—they gave only "yes" or "no" answers.

When it was our turn, Sasha stood up. It was her first jury trial and she needed the experience. She asked questions for twenty minutes with a legal pad stuck to her perspiring hand.

She then announced, "At this point, Ms. Krug will ask some questions."

It was my introduction into center stage.

I breathed deep and pushed back from the counsel table. I wobbled to the front of the jury box on new heels. I wore one of the gray suits, and as instructed, my blouse was pantyhose-tucked. I had fretted over hair and makeup for much longer than normal that morning. Eventually, I sounded my usual mantra, *It's as good as it's going to get.*

I smiled at the jury and tried for my highest voice pitch. "Good morning everyone," I said. "I have some other questions to ask you. After that, I'll talk about something a bit unusual."

I launched into my standard routine. I asked women if the cans and packaging in their kitchen cabinets were neatly stacked, and inquired if men had garage tools in their rightful places. Yes, it was stereotyping, but it worked. I wanted to know who was neat and tidy—that kind of person didn't like stories with messy gaps or holes. If you're defending against a lawsuit, like I was, you want to hammer at the holes in the other side's case.

I got what I needed. It was time to move onto the real reason why I stood there.

I tried to remember the speech I had rehearsed. I paused and my heart rate went into overdrive. Sweat droplets trickled down my back.

I said to myself, *Let's do it.*

"Okay," I opened. I looked at sixteen faces and thirty-two eyes. "I need to talk about one more thing. I happen to be transgender. Do any of you know someone who's transgender?"

I waited. As expected, no one raised a hand.

I went on. "Does anyone even know what the word 'transgender' means?"

Another pause with no raised hands.

"That's all right," I said, still scanning. "It's not the kind of thing people usually talk about. 'Transgender' means I was born a boy, with a male body. In reality, though, my heart and spirit have always been female. Most of my life, I lived as a man, but now, my outside matches my inside as a woman."

I caught my breath and kept my smile. I wasn't embarrassed about Ellen. Or about being human.

"I tell you this because, as you can hear, my voice doesn't match my appearance. Most importantly, I don't want anyone to hold me, who I am, against my clients, Fred and Jane Allen. I can't be a distraction or a reason for you to decide the case against them."

By then, sweat pooled against my tucked blouse. I focused on the jurors' eyes and looked for fast blinks or glances upward. None of these people expected anything like this.

I continued. "So please excuse me, but I have to ask each of you this question: Do you promise to be fair to the Allens and not hold me, a transgender person, against them? I'm simply looking for the truth. If you're uncomfortable, just say so. It won't hurt my feelings."

Several jurors shifted in their seats.

I started with Juror No. 16 in the back row. Mrs. Lennox was a secretary with two kids in junior high.

"Mrs. Lennox, do you promise to be fair to my clients and not hold me, a transgender person, against them?"

With a hint of smile, Mrs. Lennox answered. "I can be fair, yes."

I looked at Juror No. 15, Mr. Doe, the welder. "Mr. Doe, do you promise not to hold me against my clients?"

Mr. Doe looked at me squarely. "Yes, I promise," he said flatly.

I went person to person asking the same question and getting the same response. It didn't surprise me all that much, since jurors don't like to stand out.

I got to Mr. White, Juror No. 3, a balding seventy-year-old in the first row. He was nicely dressed in a black golf shirt, slacks, and tasseled loafers. A folded Wall Street Journal rested on his lap. I guessed a healthy retirement.

"Mr. White, do you promise to be fair to my clients and not hold me against them?"

He looked at the wall behind me. There was a micro-second hesitation before he vocalized, "Sure. I can be fair."

I made a note. I continued with the last two jurors who gave the same response—without hesitating.

I took one more look at sixteen tired faces. "I'll rely on what you've promised," I said. "Thank you very much."

I hobbled back to my seat and hoped the sweat hadn't migrated down my skirt. I looked over at Fred and Jane and saw nods. Fred mouthed, "Good job."

It was what I needed.

The attorneys began to exchange a clipboard with the jurors' names. Each round involved drawing a line across a juror's name—the rejected juror. The back and forth left nine names; it was time for our last strike.

The remaining list had two jurors that I didn't like. Mr. White, the hesitator, was one of them. I whispered to Sasha, "I think this guy might be prejudiced. We need to get him off."

I took my pen and put a big black line across Mr. White's name.

The clerk handed Judge Russell the clipboard. He announced who would stay, and who would be dismissed.

A short recess followed. During the break, Judge Russell complimented all counsel on their voir dire styles. He added, "Ellen, I think you handled the transgender issue well."

It was nice to hear, especially since there isn't an American Bar

Association course entitled, "How to Try Your First Case in Your New Gender."

The trial progressed as any other lawsuit. Both parties presented and cross-examined witnesses. At one point, Sasha brilliantly cross-examined the Comptons' window expert. I couldn't stop grinning.

On the fourth day, the attorneys presented closing arguments. I made my final point and said, "Thank you for your attention during the trial. I value your respect."

No longer hobbling, I walked seamlessly to my seat. Satisfied, Fred reached for my hand.

Sasha leaned over, I thought to join in the moment.

Instead, I heard, "Ellen, your blouse is sticking out the back of your suit. Fix it."

The jury headed to the deliberations room. As was customary, the attorneys shook hands and wished each other luck. Bill Hughes had consistently avoided male pronouns throughout the trial. I told him that we had made history together—the first jury trial by a transgender lawyer in Iowa.

He laughed. "I wish you only the best," he said. "I know this has to be difficult."

Wilma, the court reporter, stopped me in the hall. "I think you're brave," she said. "I enjoyed watching you try the case." Coming from Wilma, that was quite a compliment; she had yelled at me for talking too fast several times during the trial.

Most important were my clients, Fred and Jane. "You and Sasha did a great job, Ellen," Fred offered as he helped pack files. "We know you gave it your best regardless of what the jury does."

I didn't think Fred and Jane fully appreciated the importance of their faith in me. They had lost sleep over the lawsuit; Fred in particular was a big worrier. They had taken a real chance—in fact, a huge gamble—on Ellen Krug when few would have done so.

For all I knew, estrogen had turned my instincts to crap. I imagined the jurors in a back room giggling about my poor attempt at womanhood. The Allens, and not me, would pay for that.

In Iowa, the practice is for attorneys and clients to leave the courthouse when the jury begins deliberating. Thus, I wasn't present when the jury gave its verdict three hours later. Instead, I was in my car, headed home from the office.

I saw the courthouse number on my cell and picked up. It was Judge Russell. My heart pounded. "Congratulations, Ellen," he said. "The jury voted in favor of your clients."

Oh my god!

I became ecstatic and near yelled, "Bravo!" Instead, I said, "That's wonderful, Judge. It's the best I could hope for."

I called Fred. "We won! It's over! You and Jane can have peace now."

"That's great news, Ellen!"

In the background, Jane cracked, "It appears the jury was smarter than they looked."

There was one more call to make. "Sash, they came back in our favor, we did it! You and me!"

"Hooray!" Sasha yelled. "You did it, Ellen! You won as a woman. I knew you could."

By then, my marrow was porous. I took in the moment, a pinnacle in my career and coming-out process. It was proof that I could succeed without suiting up in the armor of masculinity.

A few days later, Sasha telephoned some of the jurors, something that court rules permitted. She asked about her courtroom performance and whether my being transgender mattered: was it an issue in any way?

Sasha reported back. The jurors thought she did a marvelous job, although they knew she was nervous. As for me, being transgender wasn't a big deal.

"The only time it came up," Sasha related, "was when a male juror referred to you as 'he.' One of the female jurors said, 'No, it's *she*.'"

I laughed. Things couldn't be better.

At a victory dinner with Fred and Jane, Sasha and I toasted our clients and their courage. We told trial stories and shared the relief that comes with jumping life's hurdles. I presented Fred and Jane with a gift—a framed copy of the jury verdict stating, "We find in favor of the defendants."

"Thank you, Ellen," Fred said, as we stood next to our cars. "We'll never forget what you did for us."

Nor would I ever forget what they did for me.

Euphoric from the Allen victory, I emailed every Krug Law Firm client and reported that I still had a winning skill set in my new gender. The timing—late July, 2009—couldn't have been better. Two big trials were coming up, one in mid-September and another in November, both for DEF Trucking. They were huge cases, collectively worth several hundred-thousand dollars in legal fees and millions in liability exposure to DEF.

Several clients congratulated me on the Allen verdict. I felt better about the future and eyed 2010 when Lily would graduate from high school and begin college in Minneapolis. I'd be free to change my life then, and get a fresh start. I would toss aside any residue from Ed and be valued for who I was, a woman named Ellen who happened to be transgender.

I gave Sasha a preliminary partnership agreement to review. The plan: I'd move to Minneapolis and work part-time from there. She would take primary responsibility for daily firm activities and earn way more money. I would handle only a few special clients and forgo most of the headaches of running a small business.

Everything was great until I had a conversation with David from DEF Trucking.

It was an overcast muggy August afternoon, the kind where torna- does jump from the sky to wreck lives forever. I was in my car when David's call came in.

"Ellen," David said softly, "I was at a conference last week, where I had dinner with John from our insurance company."

I bristled at John's name. After his transgender comments at the Ford case mediation, I didn't trust him.

"Well, how is *my friend* John?" I didn't even try to hide the sarcasm.

"He's fine, but you're not going to like why I'm calling. John wants to transfer the two cases coming up for trial to that other attorney, Sweeney in Philadelphia, who he likes so much. He wants the cases shipped out immediately."

I let up on the gas and started for the shoulder. I couldn't believe what I had just heard.

"But David," I yelled, "I just won a trial. *As a woman!* Jurors don't care that I went from Ed to Ellen. Doesn't John understand that?"

"He's pretty set on this. I know it doesn't make you happy, but there's nothing I can do about it. They're our insurance company, and we have to do as they say."

Before I could respond, David added, "I'm the one calling because we felt it best that you get this news from me; we knew it'd be upsetting. I'm sorry."

I felt sucker-punched. It wasn't as if I could object or refuse; I was ethically bound to follow the wishes of my client.

Still, there's common sense. This directive made no sense.

"David, does John understand that one of those cases is set to begin trial in six weeks? The case has been going on for two years. There are thirty or forty witnesses. It's idiotic for some new lawyer to come in so close to trial. Even Clarence Darrow couldn't master the file in such a short time."

"Yes, he understands the short window on that case. Regardless, he wants it transferred."

That was it. While the news wasn't an all-out death blow to the law firm, it meant that I'd have to let go our legal assistant, Sharon. Those files kept her busy.

I told Sasha when I got back to the office.

"What the hell is Big Insurance Company thinking?" she said. "Don't they know you won the Allen trial?"

"It apparently doesn't matter, Sash."

"But you've got a trial next month. How can any attorney step in now?"

"Let them make their own mistakes," I answered. "This is out of our hands."

I told Sharon she needed to box up the cases. "No, this can't be," she said, angry and hurt. Two days later, Fed Ex carted off a dozen banker's boxes.

Sharon's job went out the door with them.

I worried about what this meant for the rest of our business. Was I naive to think my clients would actually stick with me? Maybe Thap was right—clients would become afraid. Was being transgender too much for most clients to accept?

We were down to Sasha, Mary, and Julie. Each depended on me for her livelihood. Would they ultimately be out on the street too? How could I let that happen? Was I really that selfish?

A couple days later, David called again. "Let's go to lunch," he said. I met him and Wayne, another DEF executive, at Applebee's. I wore a blue V-neck dress from Express. It was the first time either had ever seen me dressed as a woman. They seemed okay with it too.

"I know this is hard on you, Ellen," David said. "You still have other cases for us and you won't lose that work. I'm also glad you won that trial. We haven't stopped believing in you."

That was exceedingly generous. I drove away thinking my firm would survive.

Still, I needed to have my say. I emailed John at Big Insurance Company, "Even though my appearance has changed, don't you know that I've still got my original brain?"

I didn't care if it was smart-ass. What did I have to lose?

John never replied to the email. I called and got his voicemail. My terse message: "Why?"

John finally returned my call a week later.

"I don't know what David told you," he started, "but I didn't make the decision to transfer the files on those two cases. *David did.*"

What? "David told me *you* wanted the cases to go to Sweeney."

My stomach got tight and woozy. I was back on the Tilt-A-Whirl at the Iowa State Fair.

"That's not how it came down," John replied matter-of-factly. He didn't care what this meant to or for me.

Obviously, *someone* wasn't giving me the straight story.

Confused and hurt, I hung up the phone. Somehow, I remembered my Buddhist teaching about how life is constantly in flux.

This too will pass, I told myself. *Good things lie ahead.*

Summer turned into autumn. I continued to plan on Minneapolis for my next life. I went online to the Minneapolis Craigslist, and placed a short posting, "Transgender Seeking Long-Term Romance." I hoped to meet someone who would value me as Ellen.

A fifty-seven-year-old married man, Joseph, responded. When I wrote that I didn't date married men, he replied that he needed someone to talk to about his own gender journey. I agreed to meet over lunch in a public place. I felt a duty to help others as they navigated their way.

We sat for an hour and a half at a TGI Friday's. He talked about how he loved women's clothing. Even more, he loved sex with men while dressed as a woman. It enlivened him.

"I've tried to stop," he confessed, "but I can't."

His wife had discovered his secret three years earlier and threatened to leave him. To keep his marriage, he joined Sex Addicts Anonymous. He went "sober," but had recently relapsed.

"Does your wife know?"

"No," he said with a sigh. "If I told her I was doing it again, she'd be devastated."

He was yet another person stuck in no-man's land. Joseph was a living, breathing, reminder of who—or better, *what*—I'd be if I hadn't left Lydia to start on the path to Ellen: a coward.

"You need to do the right thing," I said. "Either stop cheating on your wife or let her know what you're doing now. It's not fair. You could end up killing her or yourself."

Joseph looked at the floor. He knew I was right. Did I believe he'd change his behavior?

Not at all.

I let him pay for lunch.

In early November, 2009, I was at the office, just back from the athletic club. Mary yelled that Wayne from DEF Trucking was on the line. It sounded like an emergency legal matter. I got my pen and legal pad ready.

"Ellen," Wayne said without any pleasantries, "I'm calling to advise that effective immediately, your firm's legal services are terminated. You are instructed to deliver all files in your possession to our office. We want them today."

His words were stilted and forced, as if reading from a script.

I pulled the telephone away and took a deep breath. I didn't know whether to scream or cry or simply hang up. This was totally opposite what David had promised barely three months prior.

I had to ask. "Why? David said I'd keep your business."

"We've noticed some slippage in your work," Wayne answered curtly. He went on. "We need to take it up a notch."

This was news to me. There was never a hint of dissatisfaction with my firm's work. And "take it up a notch"? What was that about? As a woman, wasn't "assertive" just as good as "aggressive"?

I remembered Thap's warning. Was this fear or pure bigotry? Maybe they were one and the same thing.

Once more, boxes went out the door and much money was lost. I let go Julie, the secretary.

Several other clients eventually pulled cases from the office, all without explanation.

Not only was Killer Krug dead—so, too, was his law firm.

I was desperate to talk and emailed Sam, "Do you have any open slots today?"

Twenty minutes later, I had a response. "Yes, can see you at 3:00."

Our therapy sessions had become less frequent since my coming-out letter. Now, I needed help dealing with the losses that had suddenly piled up—being fired by DEF Trucking and other clients; knowing that the firm would close; people I cared about would lose their jobs; and the loss of Drew Bloom's friendship.

Above all else, the same old fear nagged at me—that getting to Ellen meant I might be alone for the rest of my life. Sure, it was one thing to be true to myself and for others to think of me as brave. It was a completely different thing, a cruel enlightenment, to realize that loved ones and clients I had relied on didn't want to march along with me. Translated further, maybe this meant I'd never have someone like Lydia to love again, either.

I was headed back to the Black Hole, the place where I got caught when Lydia started with Stephen. Once more, I asked myself, *Why am I going through all of this?*

This question—more realistically, a huge doubt—dragged like a broken anchor trailing a lost ship.

Sam's clipboard was in its usual place on her lap. As always, we started with how I was doing.

"Not great," I reported. "I'm going to lose my law firm. I've disappointed people who rely on me. Then there are the people I've lost. Sometimes, I feel totally alone."

"I'm sorry to hear that, Ellen."

"Most of all, I miss Lydia and all she gave me," I said. "I'm afraid that I'll never have another love like her."

"You're lucky that you had thirty-some years together. That's a lifetime for many people."

I wasn't in the mood for platitudes. I needed more.

"How long do you think I'll be alone, Sam? Will I ever find anyone like Lydia again?"

Sam glanced at her clipboard. She then looked up and answered head-on; it wasn't in her constitution to sugarcoat.

"I don't know," Sam said. "You might find someone who'll love you, the real you, a woman, in a year; it might be five; or it could be never." It sounded like she pulled the numbers out of thin air.

I felt an electric shock. *Five years! Never! I could die alone!*

Once more, the idea of lying on my deathbed without a love to hold my hand was unfathomable. My mind raced to the edge of the earth.

"I'm strong, but I don't know if I have it in me to hang on for that long," I said. "I miss being loved, and loving someone else, way too much."

Sam shifted the clipboard to the floor. She leaned forward.

"Don't kid yourself, Ellen," she said. "It's not as if you have a choice here. You didn't have a choice in leaving Lydia, and you don't have a choice in being a woman. This is how it is. You're alone for the moment. Moments always change. I've seen your strength and you have it inside you, as Ellen."

I didn't respond. I turned to the wall and the emptiness it offered. I felt wetness at the edges of my eyes. I didn't want to cry, not anymore, not after so many tears already.

I quickly lost that battle. I soon sobbed uncontrollably, my own personal flood. With it came words from some newborn spring in my soul, words that I had never before said to Sam, to anyone, or even to myself.

"But you don't understand, Sam; I've *always* had to be strong. I wouldn't have survived my father's drinking and not coming home without it. I needed strength to endure my mother escaping—where she saved only herself. It never seemed to stop. It was as if they kept kicking me."

I couldn't believe the honesty. I didn't question it and let every word flow.

"And the kicking didn't stop. I had to put up with asshole lawyers in Boston and pricks in Iowa. I had to kick them back and be the tough attack-man-lawyer to get clients and make a life free of my father. Don't you understand, Sam? Can't you see?"

My hands were up to my face, the only hiding place left in the room. Mascara-laced tears streamed and my voice—that horrible man-voice—choked. "I can't take being alone, Sam. I will die."

Suddenly, from out of nowhere, I felt *touch*, a soft gentle hand on my shoulder. Seamlessly, the touch flowed to the center of my back.

I peeked between fingers. Sam the Hammer was on the floor, kneeling in front of me, leaning in.

I collapsed as she put her other arm around me. She pulled me close and held on.

Oh, Sam!

It was the absolute last thing I expected from Sam, the tough one. I fell into her, my savior, and absorbed her kindness. I had forgotten what it was like to be touched so gently—the kind that Lydia routinely served up for most of my life.

I talk-bawled more. I had to.

"The only way to survive was for me to be a *boy*. I would never have made it as a girl. They're too soft, too human. They let things in and can't resist the bad, the horror. Look at my mother—she was scared to death. I had to be a tough boy, Sam! As a girl, I would have died at the living room window on Kendall Drive waiting for my father."

I trembled and wept. I had never cried like this in my life.

Sam didn't let go. It was remarkable.

Between sobs I said, "But for my father, Sam, and how he made me afraid, I might have been able to get to Ellen years ago. If I had done that, I would have been able to live as myself. I'm sure that by now, I would have found someone to love me as me—a woman."

The reality of this insight hit home. I began to shake.

"But here I am, alone. There's no one to love me as Ellen, no one to lie in bed and giggle with. How will I be able to survive this aloneness? I can't turn back into a boy again to find love. And you say I might be alone for five years? Or forever? Will I die alone? I'll never be able to do it!"

I couldn't catch my breath. I desperately wanted to stop, but I also knew it had to play out entirely.

"You don't need to be a boy to survive being alone or to survive anyone or anything else," Sam whispered. "You now have what you need to survive. *You have Ellen.* I hope love comes around again for you. Until it does, Ellen will keep you company. She will keep you strong."

Sam's words made me sob even more. The honesty—by both of us— had me raw. It was cathartic.

In my heart, I knew Sam was right. I had come so far, overcome so many obstacles, that I wasn't even close to being the scared boy or man who lived in the shadow of Tom Terrific.

"And the other losses, Ellen—your clients, your law firm, your friends— you'll survive them too. As Ellen Krug, you can handle anything."

My crying slowed as my soul got its bearings.

I imagined Sam holding a magical broom and dust pan. I watched as she swept around my chair and collected the last remnants of Ed Krug, that angry and afraid boy-man. She tossed everything into a cold blue steel drum and banged the dust pan to be certain nothing remained. In an instant, Sam threw on a black welder's helmet and welded the drum shut. A few minutes later, two mustached men showed up at Sam's door. They loaded the drum onto a flatbed truck and drove away.

All that remained on the stuffed chair in Sam's office was a woman named Ellen.

I pulled back. I felt incredibly better, as if a dark curtain had suddenly been pulled aside. There was something amazing about how Sam put it all together—my fears, my suffering, my strength—that made me realize I had the ability to survive.

I would survive loneliness, the long shadow of Tom Terrific, and everything else.

On that day in late 2009, in a therapist's office above a coffee shop named the Blue Strawberry, I made the final leap from boy to girl.

I walked out of Sam's office repeating, *I am a woman. I will survive— and prosper—as myself.*

As Ellen.

I gave everyone the word that losing DEF Trucking and the other clients was fatal. "We'll shut the firm down in an orderly fashion," I said.

I felt particularly bad about Sasha, my protégé and confidant.

"I'm sorry, Sash," I said. "I wish it could be different. There's just not enough business left for us to go forward with a partnership deal."

She never acted as if it was my fault.

I soon heard from a law firm with an opening. They wanted a reference. "You're crazy if you don't hire her," I exclaimed. "She's the best associate I've ever had."

A couple days before Sasha left for her new job, I leaned into her office doorway. "How about lunch?" This was code; we'd have lunch and drinks.

"Oh yeah, Ellen."

We found a restaurant in Iowa City, a place for salad and wine. "What will you ladies be having?" the server asked. He was tall, gorgeous, and with close-cropped hair, surely a university student.

"We're here to talk," I said. "Bring us wine as needed." Sasha laughed.

We giggle-talked for three hours. We covered it all—fashion, cosmetics, men, and clients who drove us crazy. She offered makeup tips and advice on consignment shopping.

And me? I lectured about the need to listen to NPR and how she should speak up when lunching with clients. She also got the last of my secret trial tips: "Never let a witness escape from being boxed in."

On the fourth wine, I said, "It was so important to have you in my life. I'll never forget how good you've been to me."

Sasha puffed her lips. "Of course. That's what girlfriends are for."

My bracelets jingled. I always wore three slim silver bracelets on one wrist. They bounced as I moved, reminders that I was alive.

Sasha pointed at my wrist. "Can I have one of those?"

I pulled off my favorite. "For you, to remember me."

She slipped on the bracelet and held her wrist in the air. "I love it," she said.

A couple days later, Sasha walked out of the office for the last time.

I promised Mary, the bookkeeper, a bonus if she would stay on to the end. A single mother, she had been with me for five years. Later, I learned that she passed up more than one job offer because of her commitment to stick it out.

In March, 2010, we had an office garage sale. We sold some big items from fourteen years of business—filing cabinets, the reception desk, shelving—but a lot remained. I arranged for several art organizations—music, performing, and visual—to take what they wanted.

That left a large industrial-sized copier that I had bought just two months before the flood. I decided to donate it to the court system; by then, budget problems were hurting the courts.

I called the chief district judge to give him the news.

"Judge, this is Ellen Krug, formerly Ed Krug," I said. I heard a big sigh, as if he next expected grief from Killer Krug.

"Don't worry, Judge," I said. "This is a happy call. Could the Clerk of Court use an almost-brand-new copier?"

Of course, he took it.

TWENTY: *The End of It*

It's August, 1990, now, nearly eight months since my father's suicide.

A gray metal folding chair squeaks; hard plastic against linoleum. I've been in this bare-walled basement meeting room at St. Luke's Hospital in Cedar Rapids for a good hour and a half.

It's not my choice; Mom wanted it. Weeks ago, I heard about a suicide survivor's group and suggested it might help.

"Eddie, will you go with me?"

There are a dozen people—parents, spouses, lovers, a couple adult children—seated in a not-quite-round circle. The moderator, Bonnie, has been talking about the anger that many survivors feel.

"It's normal to be mad, even outraged," she says.

Mom hasn't said a word the entire night. I've held her hand for the better part of an hour. It's the most sustained body contact we've had since I was a kid.

We haven't talked about my father for months now. Tom Terrific has turned into *persona non grata*. Earlier in the summer, Mom moved into a small two-story a couple blocks from Knollwood. She didn't ask for my advice on whether to buy. I guessed her apartment on the other side of town wasn't big enough.

I mow the small lawn at her house. Occasionally, I solve minor repair problems. My mother has reconnected with old family friends, and on the surface, she appears reasonably happy. The money helps. She's gone through a good chunk effortlessly—shoes, knickknacks, clothes, a trip to Vegas with a friend. It's her money, yet I know I'd handle it differently.

Bonnie moves from sad face to sad face. "Would anyone like to add anything?" She's close to wrapping up.

I raise my hand before I've got a complete thought formed in my head.

"It's too bad my father didn't get the help he needed," I say. I hesitate and then finish. "That's partly what makes it so hard. You think that if only he had talked to a therapist or a doctor, he might have felt better."

I really believe this; that if he had seen a therapist, maybe he'd still be around. Sure, my parents might be divorced and Mom might very well be living near me anyway. At least Dad would be alive. Maybe he would have been able to get sober; maybe not. Regardless, I wouldn't be chained to my mother in a room with a bunch of hopelessly depressed people.

Bonnie nods. "Yes, that's one of the ironies," she says. "Many times, talking to a professional, above anything else, helps prevent suicide. If only people understood that."

I say to myself, *Yeah, if only.*

Four years later, Mom's on a hospital bed in the middle of her living room: lung cancer, now metastasized into her brain.

Aunt Margaret, my father's younger sister who had been put in a Newark orphanage as a kid, moved in two months ago. She's a saint. My other aunt, Rita, has been here for a couple weeks. Lydia walks over every day with Emily and Lily to do what she can.

My mother still smokes when she's conscious. That's less frequent, now. Hospice has been a lifesaver, and the morphine pills a godsend.

Mom's always been a whiner and complainer—that heart-on-the-sleeve thing. Near miraculously, this stopped when she was diagnosed. Through fourteen months of radiation treatment, hair loss, debilitating headaches, nausea, and the other crap that goes with terminal cancer, she hasn't said a word about how bad she's had it.

I'm amazed.

We know the end is near. I'm here every evening for at least a couple hours. Sometimes I bring a deposition transcript to review or a letter to dictate. Tomorrow night, I'll sleep over, just in case.

In the background, news commentators drone on over the O.J.

Simpson drama. The murders happened a few days ago, more death owing to a defective blueprint.

Today, Mom's had a good couple hours. She's awake and lucid; she hasn't been this with-it in weeks.

Sitting upright, a smoldering cigarette at her side, Mom cracks a joke and all of us laugh. My aunts go off into the kitchen to make dinner, and suddenly it's just me and Mom. I feel the need to catch her now, since who knows when, and if, she'll be awake again with me there.

I cup her hand with both of mine. I flash a smile, the innocent kind that's devoid of jaundice or resentment, just like when I was a kid back at Kendall Drive. Mom smiles in return. I think she knows what's coming.

"Mommy," I say, slowly, stumbling, and then righting. "I'm so sorry."

I feel her grip tighten, just as the first tear—mine—forms.

The words flow. "I'm sorry for everything, for how it didn't work out. For all the shit with Dad, and everything else. It just sucked. But I've always loved you, Mommy. Always."

I need a tissue or paper towel or something. Instead, I take off my glasses and wipe my eyes with a finger. I don't want to walk away, not at this moment.

Mom looks at me, beaming and savoring.

"I love you too, Son," she says finally. "You've made me very proud."

The words go right to my core. I start to bawl. Mom reaches up and I bury my head into her. I want to turn back the clock.

"I'm so sorry, Mommy," I say.

Nothing else seems appropriate.

"It's okay," she whispers. "It's okay."

———————

A week and a half later, we're at All Saints Church for the funeral. My mother's church is circular, built to resemble the Crown of the Blessed Virgin Mary. There are stained glass windows every twenty feet or so, high above the pews. I've spent a couple days thinking of what I'd say about my mother, the first woman in my life, the fearful victim and lost soul. I want to honor her, as a good child should.

I eulogize how my mother had it rough as a child—rougher than me, for sure. I talk about how she survived various adversities, some of which didn't need labeling. I describe how she loved her friends and stuck by them, sometimes to her detriment.

As I close, I look up. I point at the stained glass windows, portals of gold, blue, crimson, and other colors. I spot one with Kelly green, my mother's favorite color.

"That window reminds me of Mom's booming laugh," I say.

Off to the side, there's a window heavy with blue.

"And that one there," I motion, "makes me remember the serenity my mother found even in the midst of great pain."

I point out a last window. "That red is for my mother's strength which burned red hot as she battled cancer."

I go on. "The color red has another meaning too. It's a reminder of how my mother taught me one last thing—how to die with dignity and grace, without complaining. I'd never know how to do that if she hadn't shown me."

I'm silent for a few seconds as I try to keep it together.

"We'll miss you, Mom," I say.

I get back to the pew and Lydia grabs my hand. "Good job," she whispers as she squeezes.

Yes, I think. *Good job.*

TWENTY-ONE: *Complete*

I was on my bicycle, a long-ago wedding gift from Lydia, when I decided to have surgery.

For months, I had asked myself, *What's next?* The question always bounced against fear—of anesthesia, pain, hospitals, risk, death. There was another holdback, too: *Will I regret it?*

It was one thing to fantasize about clean lines on my body and quite another to actually go through major surgery to obtain them. Would reality trump fantasy? I had voluntarily amputated Lydia, only to end up in the Black Hole.

Would amputating my penis and scrotum glob produce the same result? What then?

Once more, the lawyer made her case.

Point One: the gut tugs had long ago disappeared. I had been living as a woman for months, in a life that was mine. It felt so natural. *That's why you're a better person, Ellen. It's because you're genuine now.*

Point Two: even with the pain of missing Lydia, I never regretted leaving her. Yes, there was an open wound in my heart, but that didn't mean I had made a mistake. Loving myself more than I loved Lydia wasn't a mistake. Finding peace in my brain wasn't a mistake. *Something has pushed me this far. Trust yourself. Trust me.*

Point Three: as my Buddhist teacher Zuiko had instructed, I needed to step off a hundred-foot pole. I could never be whole as long as my body contained the residue of a gender-in-error. *Being whole, living true to one's self, trumps everything else.*

Point Four, my closing argument finale: *Don't be afraid like he was. Fear forced him into that bathtub. Fear killed him.*

I stopped on a gravel trail along a curve in the late afternoon sun and called Mark to report the verdict.

"Hey, Bro, I need to tell you something," I said. "I'm going to do it. Bottom surgery, sex reassignment surgery, you know, get a vagina. I can't live without it."

Mark didn't miss a beat. "That's great, Sis. I'm happy for you."

"And that isn't all. I'm going for the full boat: bottom surgery plus facial feminization plus breasts. I don't want to chance that I won't pass as a woman."

"Oh boy," Mark said. "You're going to be one hurting puppy with all those surgeries. Are you sure?"

"Yes," I answered. "I'm sure. In fact, I'm quite positive."

Wilmette, Illinois, a Chicago suburb, at 6:17 a.m. on June 22, 2010, a Tuesday.

I stood in front of a mirror. Lines—some red, some black—criss-crossed my face from ear to ear. My facial feminization surgeon, a man named Zukowski, but whom everyone called "Dr. Z," had just left the room to scrub up.

"Let me take a picture," Mark said. He held up his cell phone. I heard a click, and then Mark showed me.

"That's the last picture of who had been Ed Krug," I blurted nervously. I tried not to think about the surgery that would start in minutes.

"I'll save it for you."

The operation lasted nine hours. Dr. Z did just about everything possible: a nose job, my eyes, cheek and chin implants, hairline advancement, a face lift, and even shaving of my Adam's apple. I recovered at a hotel for a week, where Mark spoon-fed me pain pills ground up in chocolate pudding. By the time the wrappings came off, my face had swollen to twice its normal size.

"Ellen, that's the second-worst case of swelling I've ever seen," Dr. Z exclaimed.

Despite the swelling, I saw two younger-looking eyes and a definitely feminine nose. It took weeks of daily facial massaging to get rid of the swelling.

I had attempted to prepare Emily and Lily for how my face would change. They would lose the man's face they'd grown up with. It could be traumatic.

"It's okay with me that you have the surgery," Emily said a month before it was to happen. I didn't believe her, but I didn't press it.

Lily fretted more openly.

"It will be hard to see your new appearance," she said. We were standing in line at Target. "I'm sure I'll get over it, but it will take time, Dad."

Once again, my personal wants clashed with my children's needs. Once more, I wondered about the line between selfishness and self-preservation.

Emily and Lily adjusted to my feminized face. The saving grace: my voice. The surgery did nothing to change it.

For laughs, I told strangers I was Kathleen Turner's way ugly cousin or Lauren Bacall's long-lost relative.

I saw Lydia two months after the surgery. "You look great," she announced; she then leaned in for a closer look.

"I'm jealous," she said. "I'd like to get my eyes that nice."

I made appointments to interview two sex reassignment surgeons: Marci Bowers, in Trinidad, Colorado, and Toby Meltzer in Scottsdale, Arizona. To save money, I would make one big loop by car.

I called Thap to let him know that I'd stop in Boulder on my way to Trinidad.

Suddenly, he had an idea.

"Why don't I come with you to talk to the doctors?"

I nearly dropped the phone. It was one thing to be friends for life and each other's personal attorney. It was an entirely different friendship galaxy to accompany your guy-turned-girl-best-buddy to interview doctors about a sex change operation.

I thought, *Road trip!*

Thap and I had taken long-distance car trips as teenagers and twenty-somethings with not much to lose. They invariably involved beer and a ten-year-old beater. With Heinekens hidden in our laps, we made raunchy comments about girls we encountered, followed by side-of-the-road piss stops.

Then I remembered that we no longer drank and drove. What's more, the whole purpose of the trip was to *get me to be a woman,* so raunchy jokes were out of the question. Also, I detested "pissing," and there was no way I'd "go pee" anywhere but in a spotless women's restroom.

I replied, "I'd love for you to come with me."

Long before this, I had traded in my BMW for a Honda—the end result of reflecting on excesses in my life. Driving the Honda, I left Minneapolis early on a Friday and made it to Boulder by noon the next day. Part of the route—along I-80 through Iowa and Nebraska, and south into Colorado—retraced much of the freedom journey I took in 2004, just before I left Lydia for my own life.

Now I was on another freedom journey, one to liberate me from my male anatomy.

Thap and I left Boulder bound for Trinidad. My appointment with Marci Bowers wasn't until two o'clock the following day. We had no itinerary and no idea where we'd stay that night.

I had learned long before this that with Thap, there's no real planning. His modus operandi was to start at one spot with the stated goal of arriving at another spot. How you got to the second spot was left entirely up to chance. It had been that way when we were eighteen, and it hadn't changed thirty-five years later.

I was at the wheel. As usual, Thap tried to drive from the passenger's seat.

"Watch out for that car ahead of us, Ed, ah, Ellie," he commanded. I cruised at 75 mph, a good hundred feet from a blue Chrysler.

"I've got it under control," I answered.

"Damn, you always tailgate people; I don't know how you do it," he said. "I'm a nervous wreck and I haven't been in the car twenty minutes."

I ignored the comment.

"So," I said, "what's going on in your world? Bring me up to date."

"Oh, I don't know. A lot of things. Work, Bebo, the kids. You name it. And now my best friend is a woman." A wink accompanied the last comment.

With that kind of acceptance, I could put up with his nags about my driving.

We stopped at a downtown canal and promenade in Pueblo, Colorado on a stifling hot afternoon. I wore a tank top, skirt, and sandals. For all anyone knew, Thap and I were a couple, maybe a husband and wife, out for an afternoon stroll.

Later, I pulled into a Holiday Inn. I went ahead while Thap got things out of the car. He walked in just as the desk clerk asked if I was a Priority Club member.

I turned to Thap. "Are you a member of the Priority Club?"

"I'm not, but my wife is," he answered.

At first I didn't get it, but the desk clerk sure did. Her eyes sharpened and face reddened.

I figured it out and laughed. "Oh, don't go there," I said. "We're just friends."

We soon had plastic key cards for a room with two beds.

Thap wanted his afternoon nap. I went to the hotel bar to journal. The bar was filled with loud-talking, darkly tanned, beer-drinking men in dirty jeans and cowboy boots. A NASCAR race lit flat screens. The bartender was a slight woman, mid-twenties, who brightened when she saw me.

I ordered a beer and pulled out my journal. Three paragraphs later, I glanced up to see one of the men eyeing me. He smiled.

If he had made me as a female imposter, it would be anything but a smile.

I stayed expressionless and kept writing. I didn't want to cue that it might be fine to approach me. I knew what bad things could result if that guy or any other man in the bar realized I had a penis under my skirt. It could be far worse than what happened to Elizabeth at another hotel bar in Ohio.

Besides, I had found it best to simply ignore men. Isn't that what most women usually do anyway?

Forty-five minutes later, I finished journaling and got up to leave.

"Hope we weren't too noisy for your writing," the man said as I walked past him. I grinned and swished out the door.

The next day, Thap and I were in Trinidad. Thap's legal practice included advice to sheriffs' departments on various state regulations. The local sheriff's department was his client, and Thap used our visit as a reason to lunch with department contacts.

Lunch was Mexican in a nearly empty downtown restaurant. We met Louisa, a quiet and slightly heavy civilian employee, and Ricardo, a talkative balding deputy sheriff.

Thap led the conversation. I kept quiet because these were his clients. I also didn't want my voice tipping them off. That strategy worked until I got bored and asked about life in Trinidad.

Ricardo responded by talking about the local economy—bad—and a controversial property dispute at the local courthouse where spectators thought it appropriate to bring rifles for self-protection.

Then he veered into left field.

"You know, here in Trinidad, we have a doctor who performs sex change operations. We're known as the sex change capital of the world," Ricardo said. His civic pride was heartfelt.

I breathed lightly.

Ricardo looked at Thap, a good sign. I figured he was still clueless.

He continued. "Certain businesses in town cater to the transsexuals. It's quite an economic boost for us."

His eye contact stayed with Thap. I thought, *I'm pulling it off.* Yes, maybe Ricardo thought as I had hoped: that I was a throaty, low-voiced woman.

"Oh, is that so?" Thap answered. His pitch shifted on "so," which added a touch of wonderment, as if the word "transsexual" was something completely foreign to him.

"Yup, although now I've heard that maybe Dr. Bowers, the surgeon who operates, may be moving to San Francisco. That would be a big loss for our town."

This was news to me. The receptionist at Dr. Bowers' office hadn't said a word about Dr. Bowers possibly relocating when I set up the appointment.

The conversation shifted just as the server brought our food. A few minutes later, I saw sweat on Thap's forehead. He turned fire-engine red and stopped chewing.

Thap had a family history of heart problems. I instantly thought, *Heart attack!*

Before I could yell, *Get a defibrillator!*, Thap shoved more food into his mouth. He stayed upright.

It was merely spicy food at work.

Ricardo kept talking. I listened to stories of escaped convicts and shootouts in the middle of the night. Comfortable now, I peppered him with questions.

As the eating ended, Ricardo's tone changed. Maybe I had vocalized one too many words, or perhaps it was a missed inflection. Or it could have been an inadvertent throat clearing, a horrible sound that no healthy woman makes. Regardless, Ricardo went back to Trinidad's transgender cottage industry.

"It's interesting," he said. "When the transsexuals come to town, they like to shop."

I sensed something was coming. Then, there it was.

Ricardo grinned as he moved from Thap to me. "And we have some wonderful clothing stores *you* might like."

The jig was up.

Oh man, I said to myself. *This is getting so old.*

I stayed mum and smiled. I didn't want to give Ricardo the satisfaction of confirming he had figured me out.

Soon, Thap and I sat in the waiting room of Marci Bowers' office. The entire office was a double-wide trailer-like space perched on a desert hilltop next to the only hospital in the county. Everything looked a bit ragged: worn carpeting, paper-thin walls, and public health posters. Despite this, Marci Bowers had become the best-known sex reassignment surgeon in the country, with many news and network organizations profiling her.

You'd never know that the tall, attractive blonde who entered the examination room was also transgender. Dr. Bowers passed perfectly, voice included.

Envy flowed through me.

She was accompanied by two other female doctors, eastern Europeans visiting to study sex change surgical procedures. They were awfully young, but then again, I was awfully old.

I explained that I was interviewing surgeons. Before I got to my first question, Thap jumped in.

"We just heard a rumor that you're moving to San Francisco. Is it true?"

Dr. Bowers shifted in her chair. I could tell she was surprised by the question.

"I'm ninety percent certain I'm moving my practice to the Bay area, yes," she replied. She didn't elaborate why.

I asked how a move to San Francisco would affect her wait-list, which was almost a year long.

"I suspect it will increase the wait," she answered. "My pricing will stay the same for at least a year, but the wait-list will lengthen."

This wasn't good news. I couldn't envision waiting a year or more for surgery. I'd be fifty-five by then. As far as I was concerned, a year was *forever.*

Thap fired more questions. We learned that Dr. Bowers had performed more than 700 reassignment surgeries; the surgery took approximately three and a half hours; it was followed by four nights in the hospital and another couple nights locally in either a hotel or a for-fee "guest house" that Dr. Bowers owned.

I asked, "Can you give me a brief description of what's actually involved?"

Dr. Bowers straightened and launched into a detailed explanation of how a penis and scrotum glob are transformed into a vulva with all its intricate parts—vagina, urethra, clitoris, and labia. The procedure involved shortening the male urethra while preserving the glans of the penis and major related nerve. This, in turn, becomes a clitoris. The scrotum is turned inside out, and serves as the lining for the new vagina.

I was fascinated but wondered if this was too much information for Thap. I glanced his way. He didn't appear even the least bit uncomfortable, and unlike at lunch, there wasn't a single bead of sweat on his forehead.

I figured he was still in the program.

What had become an interrogation by two lawyers continued.

Everyone who undergoes male-to-female sex reassignment surgery must decide whether to have a "one stage" or "two stage" procedure. The difference is the extent to which skin is placed over the new clitoris to create realistic-looking labia.

I knew this from a website where the handiwork of various reassignment surgeons was displayed—one-stage and two-stage results. On a night when I had nothing better to do, I clicked through seventy or eighty post-surgical pictures of brand-new vulvas. Under each photo was the name of the doctor—some U.S. surgeons, some Canadian or Thai—who performed the work.

It was a sort of crotch-shot beauty contest.

Dr. Bowers only performed the one-stage procedure. She explained, "I've had very few complaints that the end product isn't realistic enough."

There was the question of whether an artificial clitoris would actually produce an orgasm.

"It can take up to a year for you to become orgasmic," Dr. Bowers answered. "If you're orgasmic now, it would be rare not to achieve orgasm eventually."

Of course, I wanted orgasms; who wouldn't? Still, I found it hard to believe that someone—I don't care how talented a surgeon—could take a penis and make it into a functioning clitoris. With the same emotional release I had as a male? I wanted to say, "How the hell can you do that?"

I grinned instead.

Dr. Bowers looked at her watch. There were other appointments. Thap and I thanked her for her time.

On the way out of the hospital parking lot, I asked Thap what he thought.

"Oh, I liked her. She had a sense of humor and it sounded like she knows her stuff," he said. He added, "I would never have known she had been male. She has the voice down pretty well."

I was impressed too. However, her move to San Francisco was a real issue. Now that I had decided on surgery, waiting was the last thing I wanted.

We took the sex change road trip south on I-25 toward Scottsdale. Along the way, Lily called about an old employer's phone number she needed for a part-time job application. She was also distraught; she felt lonely in Minneapolis. I tried to calm her and promised that things would work out.

"Call Mom for the phone number," I said as I ended the call.

I looked over and saw Thap smirking.

"What?"

"It's good to see that I'm not the only one who gives orders."

I begged to differ.

"But, Ellie," Thap interrupted, "I also see how you talk to your children. You're way more patient than me. It's a good thing."

It was nice to hear. Parenting is never easy. Throw in one parent who plans to change genders, and it becomes even more of a crapshoot.

Thirty-six hours later, we were at Toby Meltzer's office. The waiting area included a *waterfall*. Compared to Trinidad, we weren't just in a different state; we had entered an entirely different universe. Each of the women on staff was beautiful, as if perfect proportions and tanned skin were actual job requirements.

Dr. Meltzer's nurse, Lori, wore a billowy golden sundress and sandals. She escorted us to an examining room that looked as if it had been furnished by Room & Board.

Thap couldn't take his eyes off Lori. "She's gorgeous," he whispered—three times.

As someone who had absolutely no chance of achieving anything close to Lori's beauty, I didn't particularly appreciate Thap's fawning.

"Shut up," I said.

Dr. Meltzer entered the room. I guessed he was in his early fifties. He was no taller than 5'6", and he wore a gray three-piece pinstriped suit with brown shoes. He spoke softly and was friendly, which immediately made me comfortable.

His specialty was the "two stage" procedure that Marci Bowers didn't do. He explained that swelling from the surgery makes it difficult to create the skin flaps needed for realistic-looking labia. Thus, he recommended that patients return for a labiaplasty three months after the initial surgery. Approximately sixty percent of his patients opted for this. He had performed over 2,300 male-to-female surgeries, and nearly ninety percent of his patients were orgasmic.

"We track that kind of stuff; it's very important," he said.

Once again, Thap had questions: what was Dr. Meltzer's complication rate? ("less than one percent"); was my age an issue? (it wasn't; Dr. Meltzer had operated on patients in their seventies); and what kind of patient follow-up occurred? (his staff made patient wellness calls for a year).

An office form specified that I needed two ready-for-surgery letters from mental health providers. One signatory had to be either a psychiatrist or PhD-level professional. Before this, I had believed that a letter from a master's-level therapist, like Roberta Livingston, together with a letter from my gynecologist, Deb Thorp, would be good enough. I already had those letters.

I hadn't ever been treated by a PhD or psychiatrist. I thought it a completely unnecessary hoop that could cost me $1,000.

Dr. Meltzer wouldn't make an exception.

"The Harry Benjamin Standards require it," he said. He sat on a padded chair worthy of my living room. "I don't want to run the risk of someone changing their mind and then suing me. This is a one-way process that no one can reverse."

"But I've been in therapy for nearly two decades and can give you letters from three or four therapists," I argued.

He shook his head. "Transgender people are among the smartest patients I've had. They know the right buzz words. I can't chance it."

I began to protest again, but Thap interrupted. "Move on, Ellen, he's answered your question," he ordered.

Oh crap.

We talked about electrolysis; the scrotum needs to be clean of hair follicles since it is used to line the new vagina. I was aware of this, and despite the pain, I had been undergoing electrolysis down there as well.

Dr. Meltzer suggested, "Why don't I take a look under the hood to see where things stand?"

I turned to Thap. "You can wait outside for this part." Thap was happy to oblige.

As Dr. Meltzer donned blue gloves, I pointed at the door. "He used to be the football team quarterback. I was his offensive line guard," I explained. "We've been best friends for forty years."

Dr. Meltzer seemed confused. "Aren't the two of you romantically involved? I thought by his questions and his being here, you were a couple."

I laughed. "Oh no," I said. "He's way too bossy."

"Are you ready for me to take a look?"

I nodded.

Dr. Meltzer lifted my gown and peered closely. "Things look good," he said. I made a mental note to thank my electrologist.

As I sat half naked, Dr. Meltzer explained how he'd build a "vaginal vault."

"I want to give you five and a half to six inches of depth," he said. "The average penis penetration is only four inches, so you'll have plenty of buffer." He measured an imaginary penis using both index fingers, just like a fisherman would describe the big fish he landed over the weekend.

Buffer. It reminded me of football padding instead of space to accommodate a penis.

A half hour later, Thap and I compared notes in a parking lot under a blazing Scottsdale sun. I was nervous. I thought Thap didn't like Dr. Meltzer. I did.

Actually, Thap was impressed. "He's my pick," Thap said without a hint of doubt.

What a relief.

It made all the difference to know that Thap and I had the same impression. It was the last decision I needed before I could get on with my life.

"Besides," Thap added, "you'll get to see Nurse Lori again. She's so gorgeous."

You're such a man, I thought.

I jumped through Dr. Meltzer's extra hoop and found a PhD to write the second letter that would clear me for surgery. I took the first surgical opening available — September 22, 2010.

I telephoned Thap to let him know.

"Why didn't you call me first?" he said, not pleased. "I'm committed to a hunting trip that week with other guys. I can't get out of it."

Drat.

Trying to coordinate the schedules of Thap and Dr. Meltzer would easily put me into 2011. I couldn't wait that long.

I decided to go it alone.

"You'll just have to wait until your hunting trip is over to find out if I died during surgery," I kidded.

I would trade my penis for a vagina three months after my facial feminization surgery. It would be a one-two punch to my body, but I could handle it. I had been exercising four or five times a week for years and had good stamina.

Mid-September soon arrived. At Dr. Meltzer's office the day before surgery, I received instructions for a cleansing, similar to what's needed for a colonoscopy. I also received a terry cloth pouch containing a half dozen "dilators"—clear plastic dildos of varying girths that ranged from petite to super-size.

"For after your surgery," the nurse explained. I'd have to dilate several times a day for months in order to maintain "depth." After that, it would need to be weekly for the rest of my life.

Dr. Meltzer entered the room. Since I wanted breast implants along with sex reassignment surgery, I needed to pick the type of implant (silicone or saline) and size.

Dr. Meltzer discouraged saline. "Your frame is too small," he explained. "They'll stick out the side of your rib cage."

As for size, I didn't want anything too big. "A full-sized B cup will be enough for me," I said. The entire process was equivalent to ordering Chinese takeout.

That night, I called Emily and Lily to say I loved them, just in case.

"Daddy, I love you too. I'll call you tomorrow," Emily answered.

I caught Lily at work—she had landed a sandwich shop job. She was busy, but made the time to talk. "You'll no longer be transgender, Dad. You'll be a woman, and that's awesome," she exclaimed.

The entry from my journal that night: "Will write again when I'm on the other side. Take care, Ellen. Be free."

I slept fairly well, all things considered.

I was up at three the next morning; I had to be at the hospital by five. The house on Durango had been on the market for seven months without a single offer. Just as I had predicted, an offer came in the night before my surgery; my real estate agent had faxed it to the hotel in Scottsdale.

I read the offer in the backseat of a dirty yellow taxi, via passing streetlights.

My phone beeped. It was a text message from Lydia. "Happy Vagina Day, XO."

Suddenly, I felt like I wasn't alone after all.

I asked the hospital intake person if she'd fax my acceptance to the real estate agent in Iowa. "No problem, dear," she replied.

I used a single-person restroom. Pausing at the mirror, I looked at my penis and scrotum glob one last time. Compared to the rest of me— long hair, female cheeks and chin, a woman's hips, a body devoid of hair—it seemed completely out of place.

"Thanks for everything," I said aloud. *"Now it's time for you to go."*

I heard my name. My pulse jumped a hundredfold. Within minutes, I was on a gurney in the pre-op area. Nurses in green scrubs scurried between a half dozen bays separated by thin sheets.

The anesthesiologist was named—the honest-to-god-truth—Dr. Best. He had bicycled to work; as a fellow bicyclist, I thought it was a good omen. He promised to bring me out of the anesthesia, "Like waking up from a nice sleep."

Dr. Meltzer followed. He too had bicycled in, and he was sweaty.

"Don't worry, I'll clean up before you get in there," he assured.

He asked, "How are you doing?"

"I'm scared to death," I confessed, "but ready."

Then I was alone.

I closed my eyes and tried to meditate. It didn't work. There was too much activity in the larger room: beeping machines, loud patients, intercom announcements, the hubbub of modern medicine.

I looked at the ceiling, and saw *it*. In a sea of bland white ceiling panels, directly above me was a special panel. It was colored crystal blue and filled with wonderful white puffy clouds.

How brilliant!

I felt an instant calmness. I left that scary space and found myself on the back deck at Knollwood with Emily and Lily, one on each shoulder, catching clouds on that summer day. I heard their giggles and watched them point out familiar objects in a beautiful sky. The calmness turned to serenity, and with it, the hard-earned confirmation that above anything else, the surgery I was about to have was exactly what I needed.

Six hours later, I opened my eyes in the same surgical bay under the same puffy clouds. I heard Dr. Best's voice: "Ellen, wake up. We're done."

True to his word, there was no grogginess or heavy anesthetic residue.

301

"Thank you," I whispered with a dry throat. "I wanted to be here for this moment."

Before I knew it, Dr. Meltzer was at my bedside, still dressed in green scrubs and a funny surgeon's cap. By then, I had raised my head to look down at the area between my legs. There was an ice pack in place, but it didn't matter.

My clean lines were real now.

A word shot into my head: *Complete.*

I grabbed Dr. Meltzer's hand just as I started to cry. "Thank you for making me complete," I said.

My gentle surgeon smiled back. "You're welcome, Ellen."

It was okay that no family or friend was present. Just as Sam the Hammer had promised, I had the one person whom I needed more than anyone else.

I had me.

I had Ellen.

After

Sex reassignment surgery changed my body and my life, as hoped.

Physically, it took six weeks for the bruising to recede. I put up with intense dilation and other aftercare issues. Considering the magnitude of the surgery, everything went exceedingly well.

Dr. Meltzer knew his stuff.

Two months after the surgery, I stood in my bathroom and looked in the mirror. Reflected back were a woman's face and body, complete with curves and delightful clean lines.

How absolutely wonderful!

There are no words that capture what it actually means to finally be whole as a human being. *Arrival* comes closest: what started with a gut tug when I was a witness to Christine's clean lines pulled me along on a journey of self-discovery. I now know that the tug was my inner, true essence, poking at me from the inside. Never at ease, always impatient, and certainly resilient, she didn't give up or falter on her long march, until she arrived home, breathing as me, as Ellen.

I was lucky that she was so persistent.

For the first time in my life, I understood what "tranquility" meant. It was a balance, an awareness, and a willingness to simply be.

In the end, I gave myself the best gift possible.

Me.

As I adjusted to a new body, I found that I had to adapt to a new place in society, too—a woman's place. It was something I couldn't have possibly understood without actually living it.

Maybe because some women are hailed in American culture—Hillary Clinton, Diane Sawyer, Meryl Streep—I had expected womanhood to be easier than life as a man.

Reality smashed that naiveté.

It started with something simple, like buying meat at the grocery store. When I was a man, I would ask the butcher (almost always a man) for an "eight-ounce ribeye," without specifying any particular piece in the meat display. Invariably, I'd get a nice cut with good marbling.

As Ellen, the same request produced something with too much fat and too little beef. This didn't happen just once. Eventually, I learned to point out the exact steak I wanted.

I started to wonder. *Do men look out for each other even when it comes to cuts of meat?*

My unexpected womanhood lessons continued. It didn't matter where—it could be a courtroom or condominium meeting or non-profit board discussion—when Ed Krug spoke, people listened. Sometimes I saw enthusiastic head nods and note taking.

Often someone followed up with, "Good point," or "I appreciate your perspective." It seemed so automatic, as if that's how things were supposed to work. Another descriptor, although I didn't understand it then: *power.*

Now when Ellen Krug spoke, everyone, women included, went stiff. Suddenly, the conference room was filled with doodlers and smartphone checkers.

Self-doubt crept in. Was this about me being a woman? Or was it because I was transgender, with my voice as the giveaway?

With attention and patience that I couldn't ever hope to muster while living as a man, I kept my mouth shut and watched men and women interact. Soon, my brand-new perspective rang true: men treated women with less regard than they did other men.

Time and again, it was the woman who took notes at meetings. Frequently, people turned to the man in the room for his opinion. Men were more likely to look at other men as they made their points.

Even titles—"Executive Director"—had masculine connotations, regardless of whether a woman actually held the position.

This new perspective even extended to the Minneapolis bike trails. I wondered, *Why is it that men always lead on two-person bicycles?*

I soon understood that the phrase "glass ceiling" existed for a reason.

I also watched how women treated each other. Many times, they deferred to men rather than women.

The good news: This wasn't about me being transgender.

The bad: It was all about being female.

I was back to the same old question: *What have I gotten myself into?*

When I was male, someone could have told me, "This is what it'll be like," every day for a year, and I still wouldn't have completely understood.

There's something about testosterone that puts psychological blinders on men. Most men have no clue they're even wearing blinders. Before women can achieve power parity in our society—something that would radically transform the contemporary political, cultural, and religious landscapes—men will first need to lose their blinders.

In *Half the Sky*, Nicholas Kristof and Sheryl WuDunn document the oppression of women worldwide. The discrimination and harm, sometimes outright murder, occur simply because many cultures consider females less valuable than males.

I read the book while convalescing in Scottsdale, not something I'd necessarily recommend so soon after male-to-female reassignment surgery. Still, it confirmed that everything would be different now.

This included my personal safety. I bought my downtown Minneapolis condo because it was within walking distance of restaurants, movie theaters, and grocery stores. The building was in a mixed-use area of small factories, warehouses, and apartments. Before transitioning to female, I thought nothing of walking alone through this area at midnight.

That changed when I became Ellen.

Now I was super aware of any man in my vicinity at any time of the day. My pace quickened if a man was behind me, especially at night. I held my purse tight, and many times asked myself, *Why did you pick this outfit to wear?*

Lily and I took a police-sponsored personal safety course and learned female survival rules—don't make eye contact, don't let anyone invade your personal space, and use your car or apartment key as a dagger to an assailant's throat.

Afterwards, I told Lily, "If you're in a situation where you have to use a key, do it with every ounce of strength you've got. You won't get a second chance."

Lily nodded. My tone scared her. I intended that.

My other advice: "Don't ever let a man get between you and a door. Always give yourself an out."

As a father, I would of course be concerned about my daughters' safety. As a woman, I was now acutely aware of how men could harm both them and me.

I developed another understanding, thanks to Kristof and WuDunn, of how some men view women as possessions. This point was reinforced one Saturday afternoon on a walk home from Lunds grocery store. As I approached a parking lot, I saw a man and woman, both college-aged, who appeared to be arguing. The woman yanked away from the man and made a beeline to the sidewalk. She briskly walked in the same direction I was headed. The man followed the woman and quickly closed in.

I picked up my pace because I suspected the man might make trouble. The woman stopped for a red light with arms folded. The man repeatedly reached for the woman. Each time he did so, she brushed his hand from her shoulder.

I got within fifteen feet of them. Both hands were weighed down by grocery bags. That didn't stop me from yelling, "Leave her alone," with a not-so-feminine pitch.

The man's head snapped around; his focus shifted to me, a crazy bag lady.

He barked, "This is none of your business, *Sir!*"

His look stopped me cold; it was the old rule that Thap had taught me—you don't fool with a man wanting a woman. Even though my feet were unexpectedly frozen, my mouth still worked. I forgot every speech therapy rule about breathiness and pitch. Everything came out in my old male voice.

I yelled again. "I said, 'Leave her alone.' If she doesn't want to be touched, stop touching her."

"She's my girlfriend!" the man screamed back. "Stop bothering us!"

The woman turned toward me with a horrified look. I assumed she didn't expect someone to speak up for her. Much to my surprise, she grabbed the man's hand and off they went down the street. The man looked back with a victory glare.

It took a block and a half for my heart to even approach a regular beat. I couldn't believe what I had just done.

Was this some newfound sense of sisterhood?

Ed Krug would have veered off before getting to that couple; he'd never stick his nose into some man's business that involved a woman.

But Ellen Krug would?

You go, girl.

I wasn't about to be a wallflower in the New Woman's Club. A key club tenet required that I not stand idly by as a man took advantage of a woman.

Besides, I now understood that all of us, especially women, were interconnected.

What kind of trouble will you be getting yourself into, woman?

There was so much to learn. What I did know: I had to own my new gender. I was grateful to have the chance, even if the rules I had known most of my life were now scrambled.

I got off the plane at Newark and picked up a rental. The ultimate destination was Rita's in Connecticut, but first I needed to do something.

I drove seventy miles northwest, on forested blacktops that I hadn't traveled for thirty years. Each landmark along the way—that curve in the road, a scenic reservoir, the old A&W restaurant—sparked wonderful memories. Two hours later, I parked outside Uncle Ed's old place in The Country.

In an instant, memories clashed with heart-wrenching reality. Peeled battleship-gray paint, broken windows, overgrown bushes, and a huge sign, "Keep Out Property of Acme Financing," greeted me.

The carnival lights, along with some of the mimosas, were apparently long gone.

I lost and recovered a sandal as I got out of the car. I looked down and saw that the flight and drive had totally wrinkled my green linen skirt.

I carried a disposable Kodak. I knew that I'd never be there ever again.

Missing panes on the garage door revealed a dusty, banged-up

Lincoln. Torn boxes and old magazines littered the space.

Dust or not, I couldn't stop myself from breathing deep, reaching for old smells and memory flashes. There was a hint of familiar mustiness; it was enough for me to remember.

I stepped back and snapped a couple pictures.

I went around the garage, along a cracked sidewalk, and then to a patio next to the house. I crouched and looked for initials—"EJK"—and a year—"1966." Blank. I brushed at dirt and crumpled leaves. Blank again.

It was as if someone had taken an eraser to concrete.

There was a chain-link fence in the backyard with a padlock. An impulse—*jump the fence*—went through me, but rationality took hold. I leaned hard and peered around a corner to find a jungle of weeds and brown brush. The dirt pile on which I had learned a crucial life lesson was now a ground depression.

The Kodak clicked again.

I walked back to the car with a part of my soul missing. "He'd be heartbroken," I said to myself.

At the lake, the beach was devoid of blanket or bather, the water absent of boat or swimming raft.

The graves of Uncle Ed, Nan, and Poppy were ten miles away. The wind had picked up by the time I got there.

As small flags flapped around me, I stood in front of a red granite headstone, *Graney-Blow*.

The breeze forced me to grab my skirt.

"I know you're surprised to see me like this," I said. "It's who I've always been."

The first tear started down my cheek.

"I tried my hardest, Uncle Ed. I did my best to keep my promise to Lydia, to marry her forever, but I couldn't. It became too difficult. In the end, I needed to love me more than her."

I wiped tears with my free hand.

"I've broken so many hearts, I know. I suppose this breaks your hearts too. I'm sorry."

The wind ebbed.

"Even if I've disappointed you," I said, "please know that I loved all three of you. I know you loved me too. I hope that you still do, even now."

I put my hands in prayer, with fingers extended. I closed my eyes and bowed in genuine reverence.

"I needed to be me," I whispered. "Please try to understand."

I took one last look at the granite headstone and headed for the car.

I had a last session with Sam.

She greeted me with a recent cut to her strawberry blonde hair. I carried a gift bag and card, which I set on the floor behind my purse and settled in the stuffed chair.

"I'm doing well," I said. "I'm the healthiest in my head that I've ever been. I never knew it could be like this. Peace. Tranquility. I'm willing to live in the gray without knowing how things will turn out."

"Yes," she replied, "it isn't easy to find clarity. That's one of the things I like about you, Ellen; you work hard and now it's paid off."

The words made me beam.

"I'm just very lucky to be able to figure out things," I said. "Now I get the chance to start over, to have a second life. It's a real gift. I hope I don't squander it."

"Oh, you won't," she answered. "I think you understand the meaning of what you've been through. I look forward to hearing what else you find on your journey."

"You know, Sam," I said, "even with all of the loss—Lydia, my home, my law firm, dear friends—I don't regret it, not for one second. For sure, there's a huge hole in my heart, but I don't look back and say I should have stayed a boy."

"Of course not. That's how you know it was the right thing."

I reported on the most recent: Lily's college activities, Emily's perseverance in trying to understand, and Lydia's continued warming.

Soon, we were at the session's end. I pulled out the gift bag and card. "For you."

In the card, I thanked Sam for everything. The gift bag contained an Indian fetish, a steel sculpture that had sat on my office credenza for a decade. The sculpture consisted of a man's body with an eagle's head.

On the man's chest was a cutout in the shape of a heart. A lightning bolt ran through the heart.

"I got this fetish on one of my trips west a long time ago," I explained. "I looked at it a hundred times a day. The lightning bolt reminded me of being torn between Ed and Ellen, of how I fought with myself."

I paused. There was a script in my head.

"So, I'm giving you this as thanks for helping me get to the other side. You got me from the pain and turmoil of a man, to wonderful peace as a woman."

Sam held the fetish with both hands and smiled. "Thank you, Ellen, this means a lot to me," she said. She dabbed her eyes.

So did I.

The fetish moved to Sam's lap as she leaned forward slightly.

"Now, let me share something with you," she said, turning serious once again. "Something that will tell you what this gift really means."

I had no idea what was coming.

"When you started with me nearly three years ago, I didn't know if I could be your therapist," she said. "You were so aggressive, so in my face, telling me what to do. In a word, you were far too *masculine*. It was so bad that I had to see my own therapist for help. He wouldn't let me quit, and told me to stick it out, that I had to work with you."

With those last few words, she resumed smiling.

"So, that's what I did. I stuck it out with you, Ellen. And I'm so happy that I did. In the process, I learned some things about myself. This sculpture will make me think of your bravery, but I'll also think of me, and how having courage can pay off. Working with you has made me more willing to take chances and earn other payoffs."

Her words pushed me back in my chair. I would never have imagined.

As I got up to leave, I felt the real impact of Sam's words: except for her taking a chance on me, I might not have gotten to Ellen.

Oh my god.

We hugged one last time and held for a few seconds longer, the end of something truly special.

I grabbed the door handle.

"Stay in touch."

"I will, Sam. I promise."

I closed the office door behind me and heard it click shut. All I felt was freedom.

I walked into the Hennepin County Bar Association office in Minneapolis. "I'd like to be on your Diversity Committee," I said, figuring that I had some personal experience that might be of use.

Six months later, I was the co-chair of the Diversity Committee. The other chair, a married white guy in his late fifties named Paul, was a liberal's liberal. "Everyone deserves a place at the table," he told me early on.

Over drinks one work session turned happy hour, I told Paul about my former life. We had gone months without even talking about me being transgender.

"You wouldn't have liked me as a man," I said. "I would never have volunteered to be involved in promoting diversity. Even worse, I was a difficult person. Many people, lawyers and friends, thought I was a dick much of the time."

Paul grimaced. "A difficult person? I would never have guessed," he said. "That's not the Ellie Krug I'm familiar with. You're one of the kindest people I know."

His words warmed me. I thought, *You've truly arrived.*

In early 2011, Lydia called.

"I'm moving to Georgia," she announced. Stephen had taken a new position and she would quit her job to go with him.

We had been divorced for almost four years. The house on Knollwood Drive was gone—Lydia had sold it two years before, something she felt was necessary, but which broke everyone's hearts nonetheless. Now, Lydia was leaving the state. The idea that Lydia wouldn't be available for a cosmo or that the girls of Knollwood (even without the actual house) couldn't gather like old times, tore at me.

"I'll be down to help you move," I said as I tried to contain the emotion.

A month later, I pulled up to Lydia's condo in Cedar Rapids. We packed our cars with bins containing childhood artifacts—Emily and Lily's books, dolls, and cherished mementos—and headed to a storage shed.

Lydia couldn't take everything to Georgia, so in short order my car contained boxes and assorted other things: a lamp shade, pillows, and empty flower pots.

I had enough room for one last item: the pastel dappled sunlight picture that had been with Lydia since the divorce. It was time for me to take custody.

I found a black magic marker and asked Lydia to inscribe the back of the picture while I loaded some last items. When I returned from the garage, I purposely avoided looking so I could save the inscription for later. Lydia helped put the picture in the car, face up.

Back inside Lydia's quiet condo, I surprised her with two ruby red mosaic-tiled coffee table coasters. One coaster was for her and the other for Stephen. I wrote a note that the coasters should always remain together, just as I knew that Lydia and Stephen would be together forever.

I needed to go. I grabbed Lydia and we easily wrapped arms around each other. A second later, I was bawling.

"I don't want you to leave," I whispered. "I'll miss you so much."

Lydia grabbed tighter. "Shush. It'll be all right. Everything will be okay. I'll miss you too," she said.

There were tears in her voice.

For a moment, I was back in the Corolla on that bone-cold night when Lydia first met Tom Terrific, and where I found Bo, the love of my life, my soul mate.

I pulled Lydia tight one last time and released.

In a flash, I was out the door. I left Lydia in the hall waving goodbye.

On the way to Minneapolis, I called Thap.

"How did it go, Ellie?"

"It wasn't easy," I said, feeling as if I had been wrung dry.

"Be thankful for what you had," he answered. "Most people never even come close."

Five hours and 280 miles later, I unpacked the car. I cautiously hoisted the dappled sunlight picture onto the middle of my dresser and propped it against the wall. I smiled at my two young daughters coloring in chalk surrounded by sun spots.

The location was perfect for the picture.

I pulled it back to read Lydia's inscription.

"Ellen—good memories of our girls and our life together. Love, Lydia."

I replanted the picture and stood back.

Lydia's words settled in. I felt grace and gratitude and remembered what Sam had said: glimpses of sunlight may be all that we get.

Everything was as it had to be.

Acknowledgments

When I started this memoir in early 2009, I only knew how to write as a lawyer, something that's not very conducive to personal storytelling. My subsequent learning curve and this memoir were possible only through the help of many people.

I thank Laura Flynn, Sally Heuer, Maggie Hood, Patti Frazee, and Jan Miller for their wonderful insights and gentle pushing. Steve Lenius, my book architect, was particularly helpful in shaping the final work. I am grateful to the members of the Thursday Writing Group, to wit, Mary Barrow, Judy Berglund, Elizabeth Brenner, Lucinda Cummings, Pete Magee, Ann Nerland, Leif Olav, and Krista Westendorp. Thanks also to The Loft instructors, Nancy Raeburn and Mary Jean Port.

A number of readers provided crucial commentary on the final product. My thanks to Barbara Andrews, Allison Ballentine, Mary Bednarowski, Delia Bujold, Jillian Chmiel, Lyn Culbert, Vickie Davis-Kohler, Paul Floyd, Joe Jennison, Peg Kavaney, Sheilah Kavaney, Patricia Kiland, Michael Mooney, Paul Quast, Bonnie Radunz, and Judy Wing.

Karen Hoyt of Marion, Iowa, created the dappled sunlight picture that appears on the cover and which is prominent in my story.

Joe Clark and Beth Ann Strong provided ideas and designs that were incorporated into the memoir formatting.

Thanks to Lawrence Callahan for the cover photography and to Kara Wischnack and Jen Mullenix for styling.

Finally, this memoir and my life as Ellen Krug wouldn't have been possible without the unwavering support of Mark Krug, Dennis Tharp, Alexandria Carey, and my daughters, Emily and Lily.

Reader Prompts

- What are the main themes from Ellen's story? Do they apply only to transgender people or do they have broader application to the wider community of straight (heterosexual) people? If so, in what ways?
- Ed struggled with believing he could choose between loving Lydia and an inner need to be Ellen. Do you agree that it is more important to love one's self than it is to love another person, such as a spouse (or soul mate) or child? Why or why not? Is it ever absolutely necessary that a person "self-sacrifice" for another?
- Inherent in *Getting to Ellen* is the idea that gender identities are shaped by societal norms. What role does society at large play in a person's choice about identity? At what point in life or at what age does a person get the right to choose who they are?
- How significant was Tom Terrific to Ellen's journey? Would Ed have transitioned to Ellen sooner if she wouldn't have had to deal with her father's alcoholism and subsequent suicide?
- How did alcoholism impact Ed/Ellen's life? What are the residual effects of "alcoholic quicksand"?
- What are society's attitudes toward suicide? Does it still retain the stigma that Ellen alludes to in the memoir? If so, why? What message does *Getting to Ellen* have for suicide survivors?
- Why did some key people in Ed's life remain supportive as she transitioned to Ellen, and why did some people not? What is it about gender change that makes people so uncomfortable?
- Assume a loved one announced that he/she was transgender and needed to transition to the other gender. How would you react? How would other family members or friends react? Why?

- Why did Ed succeed in transitioning to Ellen? What personal quali-ties or characteristics made that possible?

- How difficult was it for Emily and Lily to accept Ellen? Identify the losses they suffered. What accounts for their resiliency in preserving their relationships with Ellen?

- What role does fear play in this story? Or loss? Or regret? How did Ellen deal with these various emotions? Is it possible to make a key life decision that results in great loss but not regret?

- *Getting to Ellen* begins with boys bribing a girl to remove clothing and reveal something very private. At the end of the memoir, Ellen confronts a man harassing a woman. What important issues about male-female power dynamics does this memoir raise?

- Has reading *Getting to Ellen* shaped your understanding of trans-gender people? If so, in what ways?

- The memoir raises questions about the difference between "self-preservation" and "selfishness." What are your definitions of these phrases? In the end, was Ed/Ellen selfish?

- What role did therapy play in Ed's transition to Ellen? What does the memoir say about the value of therapy and different therapist personalities?

- How did Ed's conversion from Catholicism to Buddhism impact the transition to Ellen? What was it about Buddhist principles that she found so important?

- Finally, what does *Getting to Ellen* say about the importance of key relationships? Would Ed have transitioned to Ellen without Thap and Mark in her life? What made them so understanding?

About the Author

Ellen (Ellie) Krug's business card reads: "writer, lawyer, human."

She is a graduate of Coe College and Boston College Law School. She is one of the few attorneys in the United States to try separate jury trials in separate genders.

Ellen is a freelance writer for several publications and frequent lecturer on the life lessons learned during her gender journey. She presently serves as the executive director of a nonprofit organization.

She is the parent of two adult children.

Getting to Ellen is her first book.

Made in the USA
Charleston, SC
07 February 2013